Learning Drupal 6 Module Development

A practical tutorial for creating your first Drupal 6 modules with PHP

Matt Butcher

PUBLISHING

BIRMINGHAM - MUMBAI

Learning Drupal 6 Module Development

First published: May 2008

Production Reference: 1020508

Published by Packt Publishing Ltd.
32 Lincoln Road
Olton
Birmingham, B27 6PA, UK.

ISBN 978-1-847194-44-2

www.packtpub.com

Cover Image by Cadym Guryevich (dgurevich@holbi.co.uk)

Credits

Author

Matt Butcher

Reviewers

Jason Flatt

John Forsythe

Edward Peters

David Norman

Sherif

Senior Acquisition Editor

Douglas Paterson

Development Editor

Swapna V. Verlekar

Technical Editor

Akshara Aware

Editorial Team Leader

Mithil Kulkarni

Project Manager

Abhijeet Deobhakta

Project Coordinator

Patricia Weir

Indexer

Monica Ajmera

Proofreader

Chris Smith

Production Coordinator

Aparna Bhagat

Cover Work

Aparna Bhagat

About the Author

Matt Butcher is the principal consultant for Aleph-Null, Inc.
(`http://aleph-null.tv`), where he specializes in content management systems,
Linux system integration, and Open Source technologies. He has been an active
participant in open-source technologies for over a decade. Along with *Learning
Drupal 6*, Matt has also written *Mastering OpenLDAP, Managing and Customizing
OpenCms 6*, and *Building Websites with OpenCms*, all of which are published by
Packt. When not pushing bits, Matt likes to explore Colorado with his wife and
three daughters.

The Drupal community has not only been a boundless source of
information, but also a positive environment. This community is to
be commended for creating a successful habitat for growing a
top-quality application. Writing this book has involved a veritable
army of editors, technical reviewers, and proofreaders. This book
has benefited tremendously from their hard work. I would like
to thank Douglas Patterson not only for being my editor, but for
getting me involved with Drupal in the first place. Thanks to Patricia
Weir and Swapna V.Verlekar, who have worked tirelessly on the
book. I owe a huge debt of gratitude to John Forsythe and Jason
Flatt, whose meticulous reading and copious suggestions have had
a profound influence on the final state of this book. I'd also like to
thank: Edward Peters, David Norman, and Sherif for their invaluable
suggestions. Thanks also to the many individuals at Drupalcon 2008
who provided input and who took the time to chat with me about
Drupal. Finally, thanks to Angie, Katherine, Claire, and Annabelle
for putting up with a few late nights and some occasional whining.

About the Reviewers

Jason Flatt has been involved with the Drupal community since 2005. He has been involved in the computer industry professionally since 1992 and at the hobby level since 1978. He was heavily involved in the open-source Linux distribution Source Mage GNU/Linux from 2001 through 2005, where he got his introduction to Drupal in looking for a replacement CMS for its website.

Since 1995, Jason has been an owner or part owner in four different computer consulting companies. He currently owns his own computer consulting company and is in the process of developing a Drupal consulting and web application development company.

He has developed and maintains contributed modules on drupal.org. Jason's Drupal user account (oadaeh) can be found at `http://drupal.org/user/4649`.

> I would like to thank my wife, Corrine, for giving me the time, freedom, and encouragement to pursue Drupal-related tasks, including reviewing this book.

John Forsythe is a programmer and web developer who's been building websites since 1997. In 2006, he left a full time job in tech support to concentrate on Drupal development. He currently runs a number of popular Drupal sites, including DrupalModules.com, a community-powered module rating and review service, and Blamcast.net, a web development blog.

John's Drupal account can be found at `http://drupal.org/user/101901`.

> I would like to thank my parents for their continued support and encouragement.

Edward Peters has worked all his adult life with Initiatives of Change (IofC), an international trust-building network (`www.iofc.org`). Since 2002 he has managed IofC's global Internet operation, servicing the needs of activists in many countries and languages. He is currently overseeing the move of the organization's proprietary CMS into Drupal. He also does freelance web development work for a number of small clients (`www.edwardpeters.co.uk`).

Table of Contents

Preface

Drupal is a highly successful open-source Content Management System (CMS). It is well-respected for its robustness, its flexible and immaculate code, and its seemingly infinite capacity for extension and customization.

Drupal 6, released early in 2008, represents a significant evolution in this already mature CMS. In this book, we build extensions for Drupal 6, focusing on the important APIs and libraries. We also highlight the new features introduced in version 6, making this book appropriate not only for those new to Drupal, but also those who are transitioning from version 5.

This book provides a practical, hands-on approach to developing Drupal modules. We also take a developer-centered look at themes and installation profiles—two other facets of Drupal that the developer should be familiar with. Each chapter focuses on the creation of a custom extension. Using this approach we develop a handful of modules, a theme, and an installation profile. However, more importantly, we get a practical perspective on how to make the most of Drupal.

By the end of the book, you will have a solid understanding of how to build modules for Drupal. With the knowledge of foundational APIs and libraries, you will be able to develop production-quality code that fully exploits the power and potential of Drupal 6.

What This Book Covers

This book focuses on developing modules for Drupal 6. Each chapter introduces new concepts, libraries and APIs, while building on material from previous chapters.

Chapter 1 is a developer's introduction to Drupal. We take a look at Drupal's **architecture**, focusing on **modules** and **themes**. After covering some of the important concepts and taking a high-level look at foundational APIs and libraries, we finish up with a look at some useful **development tools**.

Chapter 2 gets us working on our first module. In this chapter, we develop a Drupal module that takes data from an **XML feed** and displays it as a block on our Drupal site. In this chapter, you will learn about the basics of module development, including what files need to be created and where they go. **Hooks**, a major component of Drupal development, are also introduced here.

Chapter 3 switches gears from modules to **themes**. Learning the theming system is integral to being able to produce high-quality modules. In this chapter, we create a theme using **CSS**, **HTML**, and **PHPTemplates**. We also take a look at the theme system architecture, along with some of the APIs.

Chapter 4 builds on the introduction to theming. In this chapter, we develop a new module that deals with a custom **content type**, a quote. This module uses the theming subsystem to prepare quotes for display. Our focus here is using the theme system to enrich modules. The **theme API** covered in this chapter is used throughout the rest of the book.

Chapter 5 focuses on Drupal's **JavaScript libraries**. Starting with the module we built in Chapter 4, we use the **jQuery** library and a couple of Drupal hooks to implement an **AJAX (Asynchronous JavaScript and XML)** service. This chapter also introduces the **Database API** and the **menu system**.

Chapter 6 is focused on building an administration module. This module provides an interface for administrators to send email messages to users. However, the **Mail API** is not the only thing we will look at. The tremendously important **Forms API** is also introduced here. We also get our first look at Drupal's **access control** features.

Chapter 7 takes a closer look at Drupal nodes. In this chapter, we use the **Schema API**, the **Database API**, and the **node system** to build a content type that represents a biography. Module installation files are introduced, and the Forms API and access control mechanisms are revisited.

Chapter 8 discusses **filters**, **actions**, and **hooks** — three of the more advanced features of Drupal. We create a module for emailing a newsletter to our users. We implement filters to prepare content for the email message. Actions and triggers are used to automatically send our newsletter when it is ready. Also, to allow other modules to interact with this one, we define our own custom hook that other modules can implement.

Chapter 9 changes tracks, focusing on **installation profiles**. In this chapter, we build an installation profile that can install a custom version of Drupal preloaded with the modules and themes of our choice. Working with the installer, we get a glimpse into Drupal's inner workings. Along with learning how to write code in this minimalistic pre-installation environment, we also look at **registering themes** and **defining triggers** automatically.

Who Is This Book For?

This book is written for PHP developers who want to add custom features to Drupal. You will need to know the basics of PHP and MySQL programming, but no experience of programming Drupal is required, although you will be expected to be familiar with the basic operation of Drupal.

Conventions

In this book, you will find a number of styles of text that distinguish between different kinds of information. Here are some examples of these styles, and an explanation of their meaning.

Code words in text are shown as follows: "One thing that should stand out is the use of a `require_once` directive at the very beginning of the file."

A block of code will be set as follows:

```
function _philquotes_get_quote() {
  $sql = "SELECT nid FROM {node} ".
       "WHERE status=1 AND type='quote' ORDER BY RAND() LIMIT 1";
  $res = db_query($sql);
  $item = db_fetch_object($res);
  // Do something with the $item.
}
```

When we wish to draw your attention to a particular part of a code block, the relevant lines or items will be made bold:

```
function philquotes_block($op = 'list', $delta = 0, $edit = array()) {
  switch ($op) {
    case 'list':
      $blocks[0]['info'] = t('Philosophical Quotes');
      return $blocks;
    case 'view':
      $item = _philquotes_get_quote();
      if(!empty($item)) {
```

New terms and **important words** are introduced in a bold-type font. Words that you see on the screen, in menus or dialog boxes for example, appear in our text like this: "Clicking the **Add content type** tab will load the form used to create our new content type."

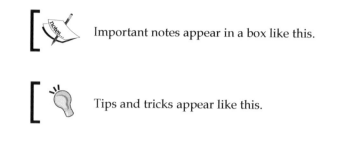

Important notes appear in a box like this.

Tips and tricks appear like this.

Reader Feedback

Feedback from our readers is always welcome. Let us know what you think about this book, what you liked or may have disliked. Reader feedback is important for us to develop titles that you really get the most out of.

To send us general feedback, simply drop an email to feedback@packtpub.com, making sure to mention the book title in the subject of your message.

If there is a book that you need and would like to see us publish, please send us a note in the **SUGGEST A TITLE** form on www.packtpub.com or email suggest@packtpub.com.

If there is a topic that you have expertise in and you are interested in either writing or contributing to a book, see our author guide on www.packtpub.com/authors.

Customer Support

Now that you are the proud owner of a Packt book, we have a number of things to help you to get the most from your purchase.

Downloading the Example Code for the Book

Visit http://www.packtpub.com/files/code/4442_Code.zip to directly download the example code.

The downloadable files contain instructions on how to use them.

Errata

Although we have taken every care to ensure the accuracy of our contents, mistakes do happen. If you find a mistake in one of our books—maybe a mistake in text or code—we would be grateful if you would report this to us. By doing this you can save other readers from frustration, and help to improve subsequent versions of this book. If you find any errata, report them by visiting http://www.packtpub.com/support, selecting your book, clicking on the **let us know** link, and entering the details of your errata. Once your errata are verified, your submission will be accepted and the errata added to the list of existing errata. The existing errata can be viewed by selecting your title from http://www.packtpub.com/support.

Questions

You can contact us at questions@packtpub.com if you are having a problem with some aspect of the book, and we will do our best to address it.

1
Introduction to Drupal Modules

Drupal (pronounced *Droo-puhl*) is a web-based **Content Management System (CMS)**. Like many other CMS frameworks, Drupal provides a modular interface, so that developers can customize and extend the CMS system. However, one thing that distinguishes Drupal from other web CMS platforms is the power and flexibility of its modular system.

This module system is the main focus of the book. In this chapter, we will take an introductory look at Drupal modules, and how they fit within the Drupal framework. Specifically, we will look at the following:

- The Drupal structure
- An introduction to modules and themes
- A developer's overview of important Drupal concepts and APIs such as nodes, menus, and forms
- Using tools for module development

Drupal's Architecture

In one sentence, Drupal is a web-based content management system written in PHP that uses a relational database (usually MySQL) for storage.

PHP, which stands for PHP Hypertext Processor, is a high-level language designed for developing web applications. PHP offers a flexibility that supports both procedural and **object-oriented (OO)** approaches to software development.

The Drupal core is meticulously written in procedural-style PHP. Code follows strict conventions and every file and function is documented in the source code. APIs are often minimalistic, kept brief and functional. These factors make Drupal's source code easier to read in many regards than run-of-the-mill PHP code. However, the minimalism of the code can be deceptive too; the simple tools and modules are combined to produce the surprisingly complex features of this robust content management system.

> **Why isn't Drupal object-oriented?**
>
> This question is asked often. The answer has several facets, one of which is simply that when the project began, PHP still wasn't up to snuff on the OO side. However, looking beyond the absence of constructors and classes, it turns out that Drupal employs many of the OO principles: encapsulation, inheritance, polymorphism, etc. The OO programmer will quickly feel at home with Drupal's architecture.

A simplified stack diagram of Drupal looks something like the following:

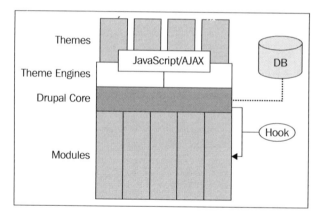

At the center of Drupal is a core set of files consisting of bootstrapping code and important oft-used libraries. The **Drupal Core Libraries** act as the glue layer to bind Drupal's modules. They provide services such as database connectivity and management (illustrated by the dashed line to the database above), as well as the highly customizable hook framework about which we will talk throughout this book. Other standard features such as mail and image library abstractions, internationalization, and Unicode support are also included as Drupal Core Libraries.

> Many of the required system modules are referred to as Drupal Core Modules. In the above diagram, I would include these along with the rest of the modules, as they are modules in all proper respects.

But as important as these files are, there is a reason why the Drupal Core Libraries section in the above diagram is comparatively small. While these libraries provide a potent feature set, the real power in Drupal comes from its modular architecture.

Module Architecture

What exactly is a module and what is its purpose?

The second question is easier to answer: Drupal's module mechanism is designed to provide a uniform method of extending Drupal's capabilities. The purpose of a module is to extend Drupal's capabilities. This answer brings us much closer to answering the first question. A module is a bundle of PHP code and supporting files that use Drupal's APIs and architecture to integrate new functional components into the Drupal framework.

The purpose of this book, then, is to explain how to write these bundles of code. The above definition means we will need to get familiar with the Drupal framework and its APIs. That is precisely what we will be doing as we progress through the book. Let's start here by taking a glance at the module architecture.

The files that make up modules are grouped into specific locations under Drupal's directory structure. That is, in the Drupal installation on a server's file system, Drupal modules must reside in a few specific locations (we will look at these in the next chapter).

When Drupal needs information about its modules, it will look in these predetermined locations. Each module is contained in its own directory, and has at least two files—one describing the module's content and one or more files containing code and other supporting material. (We will create both these files when we build our first module in the next chapter.)

Before a module can be used, it must be enabled by a Drupal administrator. However, once a module is enabled, then it is loaded as required, and Drupal passes requests to the module as necessary.

Core Modules

Some modules are so important that removing them would disable features essential for Drupal's operation. Likewise, there are some modules that provide features needed by a wide variety of systems. These two batches of modules, both of which are maintained by the Drupal development team, are collectively referred to as the **Drupal Core Modules**. These modules are included by default in the Drupal distribution, and enjoy active maintenance and development by the Drupal community.

Besides their prominent role in Drupal's operation, there is little to architecturally distinguish the Drupal Core Modules from any other module. They follow the same guidelines and use the same APIs. There is nothing particularly arcane about these modules.

From Drupal's administration section, you can look at the list of core modules in **Administer| Site building | Modules**. The most important modules are the five that are required: Block, Filter, Node, System, and User. These cannot be uninstalled or disabled. Others, such as Menu, Locale, and Taxonomy provide basic services that are needed even in basic installations.

| ▾ Core - required | | | |
Enabled	Name	Version	Description
☑	**Block**	6.0-rc3	Controls the boxes that are displayed around the main content. (Code Review)
☑	**Filter**	6.0-rc3	Handles the filtering of content in preparation for display. (Code Review)
☑	**Node**	6.0-rc3	Allows content to be submitted to the site and displayed on pages. (Code Review)
☑	**System**	6.0-rc3	Handles general site configuration for administrators. (Code Review)
☑	**User**	6.0-rc3	Manages the user registration and login system. (Code Review)

One of the diamonds in Drupal's architectural crown is the ease with which various modules can interact. Using the hook architecture, the services that modules provide can be woven together to create robust features without copious amounts of code.

In the course of this book, we will often make use of APIs and facilities provided by Drupal Core Modules. However, don't expect any chapters to walk through existing Drupal code. We make use of these modules, but we won't dwell closely on the implementation details of specific core modules. In this book, we will focus on writing our own modules.

That said, the core modules do provide an excellent reference for how Drupal code should be written. You may find it beneficial to read through some of that code in conjunction with this book.

Hooks

How does Drupal know when to invoke a module to handle a particular request?

This is done through Drupal's **hook mechanism**, which we will examine carefully in this book. To start out, here is a brief explanation of how hooks work.

When Drupal handles a request from a user, it proceeds through a series of steps. For example, the Drupal core first bootstraps the application, defining critical variables and oft-used functions. Next, it loads critical libraries, themes, and modules. Next, it continues processing the request, mapping the requested URI to the correct handling code, and so on. Later, it applies a theme to the data, formatting information for output. Finally, it returns this output to the user's browser.

At predefined moments in this step-by-step process, Drupal executes hooks. What does this mean? In short, it means that Drupal examines some or all of the currently enabled modules, looking for functions that follow specific, predefined patterns. Some have linked this process to the "callback" method often used in event handling models. It is similar to this, but more dynamic.

For example, while it is creating the content for a page view, Drupal might scan modules for functions named `<modulename>_block()` and `<modulename>_view()` (where `<modulename>` is replaced by the name of each module that it checks). Modules that contain such functions are said to implement the `hook_block()` and `hook_view()` hooks.

When Drupal finds such functions, it executes them, and uses the data these functions return to build a response to send to the user. Drupal then continues its step-by-step processing of the request, perhaps executing many other hooks as it goes.

Once all the steps have been completed and a response sent to the user, Drupal cleans itself up and exits.

Hooks for Object-Oriented Programmers

Those familiar with object-oriented (OO) programming may find it helpful to think of a hook as a mechanism similar to interface methods (or abstract methods) in OO languages. Hooks are functions that Drupal will look for, and in certain cases, expect in your module. Like interface methods, a hook's function signature must match Drupal's expected signature. Unlike interfaces, however, the module developer can choose (to a certain degree) which hooks to implement, and which to ignore. Drupal does not require that every defined hook be implemented.

Modules can define their own hooks, which other modules can then use. In this way, the hook mechanism can be extended to provide complex customized behavior.

When a module provides a function that matches a hook's signature, we say that that module *implements* that hook. For example, imagine that Drupal has a hook called `hook_example()`. If we were to define a module called `mymodule` that contained a function called `mymodule_example()`, we would be implementing `hook_example()`.

We will write our first hook implementation in the next chapter.

Themes

Processing power isn't everything, especially for a web-based CMS system. A commercial-grade CMS must make it possible for site designers to give the site the look and feel they desire. Drupal provides a robust theme system for just this purpose.

The Drupal theme system is surprisingly complex. Just as with modules, the system is designed to allow extension and improvement and the hook mechanism is employed to allow this sort of extension.

While the code under the hood boasts a large (and complex) API, the top layer is surprisingly uncomplicated, and revolves around the idea of a theme.

A **theme** is a bundle of resources, including PHP templates, CSS, JavaScript, and images, that provides layout and style information for some or all of the Drupal content.

At its simplest, a theme may be composed of only a handful of files—a stylesheet, an information file, and a couple of images. In fact, using existing Drupal styles, one can create a custom theme in no time.

But themes can grow to meet the needs of the implementer. Custom templates, usually written in the PHP template language, can specify the details of the HTML structure. Special PHP files can be written to override theme engine behaviors. Complex configurations of JavaScript and CSS files are supported as well. Even modules can be used to interact with the theming system.

In short, a theme can be as simple or complex as the implementer desires.

Chapter 3 is devoted to themes, and in that chapter we will first create a simple theme, and then build up to a moderately complex theme.

Themes and modules are critical components in the Drupal architecture, and obviously the main focus of this book. However, before moving on, let's look at Drupal from another angle. Let's briefly examine how Drupal handles content.

Crucial Drupal Concepts

This book is geared toward developers, and to keep the book manageable, some introductory material must be glossed or skipped.

For a thorough introduction to Drupal 6, I recommend David Mercer's book *Building Powerful and Robust Websites with Drupal 6*, also published by Packt Publishing.

Throughout the book, it is assumed that the reader has a moderate amount of Drupal experience, and is comfortable administering a Drupal site.

However, there are some particular facets of Drupal that deserve an introduction. We will look at some of the aspects in this book. Others are common Drupal terms that take on additional shades of meaning when examined from a developer's perspective.

In this section, we will focus on Drupal concepts that will be crucial in this book. We will start out with one of the biggest topics: nodes.

Nodes

Drupal is a content management framework. When we think of content in this context, we typically think about text objects like news articles or blog entries.

This concept of a generic text-based piece of content is captured in Drupal with the term **Node**. A node, in Drupal parlance, is a generic object for representing textual content.

While nodes are designed to be text-based, some of the contributed multimedia modules extend the node system to handle content that is not text-centric, such as images or audio files.

Nodes are stored in the database and retrieved as needed. Among other things, all nodes have:

- A unique **Node ID (nid)**
- At least one **Version ID (vid)** used to track revisions
- Creation and modification dates, as well as identifying information for the user who worked on the node
- Metadata such as publishing state (status), language of the node (and translations), and so on

In addition to these, most nodes also have a **title** and a **body** (contents). (Administrators and developers may choose to turn off a title or body, though the database always has a place for these.)

Nodes are used to back many different kinds of text content in Drupal. To understand this, let's look briefly at the process of creating new content.

By default, creating new content in Drupal is done by clicking on the **Create content** link in the main navigation. On this page, the user is prompted to select the content type for their new page:

Home

Create content

Page
        If you want to add a static page, like a contact page or an about page, use
        a page.
Quotes
        Quotations and witticisms.
Story
        Stories are articles in their simplest form: they have a title, a teaser and a
        body, but can be extended by other modules. The teaser is part of the body
        personal blog or for news articles.

The above screenshot shows three different available content types.

The **Story** and **Page** content types are included by default. The **Quotes** content type is one we will create in this book.

 In Chapter 4, we will create the Quotes content type. In Chapter 7, we will extend the node object to create an even more elaborate content type representing a biography.

In fact, all the three content types are text-based and each of them is implemented using nodes. For practical purposes, the node is the heart of Drupal's content management system.

In this book we will deal with nodes many times, and we will take a close look at the node API.

Comments Are Not Nodes

While most article-like content is based on the node, one major text component stands out as an exception—the comment. A comment is usually implemented as a user-level feedback mechanism attached to stories, pages, blog entries, and similar articles. When you create a new page, for example, you have the opportunity to allow or disallow user comments. If comments are enabled in read/write mode, users will be able to comment on articles.

Following is an example comment-posting screen:

Reply to comment

Antigone and Philosophy

Antigone, part of Sophocles' Oedipus Trilogy, plays an important role in philosophical writing on aesthetics, as well as on moral and ethical philosophy.

» **Add new comment**

Reply

Your name:
matt

Subject:

Comment: *

‣ Input format

Preview

Comments serve a different role than nodes. For example, a comment is always linked to a node.

While comments will not play a big role in this book, they illustrate a point: Drupal is a very flexible architecture, and can accommodate extensions (like comments) that do not fit "the pattern" of typical text content and do not make use of the node API.

 Since comments are, in many ways, very node-like, there is discussion among Drupal developers of transitioning comments into the node framework in Drupal 7.

While it is possible to implement a new form of content by creating a library that does not make use of nodes, it is often more efficient to build on the existing (well-tested, robust) node API.

Users

Another important type of object in Drupal is the **user**. User records are maintained using this object type. Just as with comments and nodes, user data is stored in the database, and drawn out during processing.

Information about a user is used for purposes such as authentication, determining preferences and permissions, and logging.

In the course of this book, we will make use of the user APIs to perform permissions checks, get contact information, and discover user preferences.

Access and Security

Permissions are closely linked to the user object. Drupal provides a role-based mechanism for granting permissions to collections of users. In a nutshell, a user belongs to a **role**, and **permissions** are granted to (or revoked from) a role.

Thus, when checking access to a resource, Drupal loads a user object, finds the user's roles, and then finds the roles' permissions.

Does this sound like a lot of work? Well, it's not work the module developer must do. Drupal provides functions for performing permissions checks. Most of the time, module code does not need to directly discover a user's role before determining permissions. The users API does that work for us.

Blocks and Page Rendering

The term **block** is equally important. While a node is used to store and present articles and "larger" pieces of content, a block is used to present smaller bits of content. For example, navigational menus, daily quotes, polls, and search boxes are often presented using blocks.

A block is not a type of content. Actually, it is a unit of abstraction (a placeholder) used primarily to display other content. Administrators can use the **Blocks editor** to determine where blocks are displayed on a themed page:

The highlighted sections in the above screenshot show where blocks can be displayed.

From the developer's perspective, blocks are an important part of module creation. In fact, our very first module (which we will create in the next chapter) will display a block.

Defining a block in a module is a matter of selecting content to display, and then passing it on to the correct formatting tools.

In Chapters 3 and 4, we will look into themes, where we will format block content.

Menus

Closely related to blocks are menus. Drupal has a sophisticated menu system whose main purpose is the construction of navigation. For example, the above screenshot shows the main menu, with such items as **Code review**, **My account**, **Create content**, and so on. This menu is dynamically generated by the Drupal menu system.

But the Drupal menu system is a more sophisticated device than this simple description. It also functions as the primary tool for mapping URLs to specific handling routines. Using the menu API, developers can correlate paths with specially defined functions.

In chapter 5, we will use the menu system to create a **JSON (JavaScript Over the Network)** service, and in chapter 6 we will examine the more traditional way of mapping a path to a module.

Forms

The primary method of submitting content over the Web is through HTML forms. While the ubiquity of forms makes life easy for the web user, the dearth of good forms processing tools usually makes form development a joyless chore for programmers.

However, forms processing is one area in which Drupal excels. The **Forms API (FAPI)** provides a programming interface that takes the pain out of form development (or at least significantly reduces the pain).

Using the FAPI, developers can provide a single form definition and let Drupal build and display the form, collect the results, and even validate and escape form data. Drupal even provides forms caching and advanced **AHAH (Asynchronous HTML And HTTP)** features.

As Drupal development has progressed, the Forms API has got better and better, and the Drupal 6 version exhibits many improvements.

Chapter 6 is the first to explicitly cover the forms API, and it is used again in Chapter 7.

Database and Schema APIs

Beneath many of these higher-level frameworks and APIs is the layer responsible for managing and manipulating the database. Drupal provides a low-level database API to simplify the process of writing SQL queries.

This API provides some degree of security for database queries, and also makes it easier to write SQL that is portable across different databases.

Also the new **Schema API**, introduced in Drupal 6, makes it possible to define how a database should be structured without writing the actual SQL. Since different databases use different constructs for defining tables, this API simplifies the project of writing portable modules.

These APIs are discussed primarily in Chapter 7.

There are other aspects of Drupal that we will touch upon in this book, including taxonomies (sometimes called categories), filters, and actions. But there is no in-depth discussion of these here. To learn more, consult the Drupal handbooks: `http://drupal.org/handbooks`.

[⟨note icon⟩ Chapters 8 and 9 will make use of filters and actions inside modules.]

Developers' Tools

So far, we've looked at some of the preliminary concepts involved in Drupal development. To finish off this chapter, we will switch focus to development tools.

There are a few Drupal-specific tools that you might find helpful when creating your own modules. These tools are themselves provided by two modules, which can both can be obtained from the Drupal site.

Developer Module

The **Devel Module** provides several tools that are extremely useful for Drupal development, including cache management, SQL debugging tools, investigation tools, a module reinstaller, an API reference tool, and many more.

You can find out more about this module at the official website:
`http://drupal.org/project/devel`.

The main part of this module (the Devel module) provides these tools as items in a block. So after installing the module, you will need to go to **Administer | Site building | Modules** and enable the module, and then go to **Administer | Site building | Blocks** to tell Drupal where to display the new content.

This module also includes tools for building themes, a macro generator to simulate form data entry, and a tool to generate testing data. As the module continues to improve, new features will be added as well.

Any serious module developer will want to install the Devel module. In the writing of this book, it has proven an invaluable tool for reinstalling modules, clearing caches, and debugging difficult code.

Coder Module

As we shall see in this book, Drupal developers adhere to strict conventions in their code. The **Coder Module** is a tool designed to help you, the developer, locate and fix code that does not adhere to these conventions.

In addition to making sure code follows conventions, it also does some basic security auditing regarding how text is handled. This can be useful for spotting mistakes before they become security risks.

The Coder Module is also hosted on the official Drupal site: `http://drupal.org/project/coder`.

While it does not improve productivity in the same way that the Devel module does, Coder can help you generate clean and "Drupalish" code. Its strict syntax checking also occasionally turns up bugs.

"Drupalish"

Drupal developers are fond of using the word *Drupalish* to refer to practices, styles, and approaches that mesh well with the Drupal philosophy. For example, Drupalish code adheres to coding guidelines and makes use of data structures common in Drupal (like nested associative arrays).

In addition to these modules, there is a wealth of information on the Drupal website about how to configure your favorite development environment (including Emacs, VI, FireBug, and Eclipse PDT) for Drupal development: `http://drupal.org/node/147789`.

A Word on Our Demonstration Site

Since this book focuses on development, we won't walk through the standard process of downloading, installing, and configuring Drupal. If you need to review any of this information, the Drupal website at `http://drupal.org` has a complete installation handbook. We will begin assuming that Drupal is already installed and configured.

In this book, we will develop modules for a fictional website called **Philosopher Bios**. This website provides news and biographical sketches of famous philosophers. Most of the modules we develop in this book will be reflective of the kind of functionality such a site would need.

While this is the theme of the website, the modules we create will be broadly applicable to other sites, and are reflective (I hope) of the sorts of real-world applications that we commonly develop for Drupal.

I've tried to come up with unique modules (not re-inventing the wheel). However, with such a popular and mature platform, it seems inevitable that I have repeated *something* someone has already done. The primary goal of the modules presented in this book, though, is to provide instructive and practical examples of Drupal modules.

Summary

This chapter is an introduction to Drupal's architecture. Taking a developer's perspective, we examined the basic structure of Drupal. After that, we looked at some of the concepts and systems that will be important in this book.

Now that this preliminary chapter is done, we are going to shift focus. No more theory-laden chapters and high-level explanations. From here on, our focus will be practical.

In the next chapter, we will build our first module—and no, it's not going to be a garden-variety "Hello, World" module. We will use a remote XML-based API to fetch content and display it as a Drupal block. So strap yourself in, and let's get coding.

2
Creating Our First Module

In the last chapter, we looked at the basics of Drupal module development. Now we will dive in and create our first module. Our first module will make use of an existing web service to pull in some XML data, format it, and display it as a block in the site's layout.

We will cover the following topics in this chapter:

- Creating the `.info` and `.module` files
- Creating a new module
- Using basic hooks
- Installing and configuring the module
- Using important Drupal functions

Starting Out

Our first module is going to fetch XML data from Goodreads (`http://www.goodreads.com`), a free social networking site for avid readers. There, users track the books they are reading and have read, rate books and write reviews, and share their reading lists with friends.

Reading lists at Goodreads are stored in **bookshelves**. These bookshelves are accessible over a web-based XML/RSS API. We will use that API to display a reading list on the Philosopher Bios website we introduced in Chapter 1.

To integrate the Goodreads information in Drupal, we will create a small module. Since this is our first module, we will get into greater details, since they will be commonplace in the later chapters.

A Place for the Module

In Drupal, every module is contained in its own directory. This simplifies organization; all of the module's files are located in one place.

To keep naming consistent throughout the module (a standard in Drupal), we will name our directory with the module name. Later, we will install this module in Drupal, but for development, the module directory can be wherever it is most convenient.

Once we have created a directory named `goodreads`, we can start creating files for our module. The first file we need to create is the `.info` (dot-info) file.

Creating a .info File

Before we start coding our new module, we need to create a simple text file that will hold some basic information about our module. Various Drupal components use the information in this file for module management.

The `.info` file is written as a PHP INI file, which is a simple configuration file format.

> If you are interested in the details of INI file processing, you can visit `http://php.net/manual/en/function.parse-ini-file.php` for a description of this format and how it can be parsed in PHP.

Our `.info` file will only be five lines long, which is probably about average.

The `.info` file must follow the standard naming conventions for modules. It must be named `<modulename>.info`, where `<modulename>` is the same as the directory name. Our file, then, will be called `goodreads.info`.

Following are the contents of `goodreads.info`:

```
;$Id$
name = "Goodreads Bookshelf"
description = "Displays items from a Goodreads Bookshelf"
core = 6.x
php = 5.1
```

This file isn't particularly daunting. The first line of the file is, at first glance, the most cryptic. However, its function is mundane: it is a placeholder for Drupal's CVS server.

Drupal, along with its modules, is maintained on a central **CVS (Concurrent Version System)** server. CVS is a version control system. It tracks revisions to code over time. One of its features is its ability to dynamically insert version information into a file. However, it needs to know where to insert the information. The placeholder for this is the special string Id. But since this string isn't actually a directive in the .info file, it is commented out with the PHP INI comment character, ; (semi-colon).

> You can insert comments anywhere in your .info file by beginning a line with the ; character.

The next four directives each provide module information to Drupal.

The name directive provides a human-readable display name for the module. In the last chapter, we briefly discussed the Drupal module installation and configuration interface. The names of the modules we saw there were extracted from the name directive in their corresponding .info files. Here's an example:

▼ Core - optional			
Enabled	**Name**	**Version**	**Description**
☐	**Aggregator**	6.0-rc3	Aggregates syndicated content (RSS, RDF, and Atom feeds). (Code Review)
☐	**Blog**	6.0-rc3	Enables keeping easily and regularly updated user web pages or blogs. (Code Review)

In this above screenshot, the names **Aggregator** and **Blog** are taken from the values of the name directives in these modules' .info files.

While making the module's proper name short and concise is good (as we did when naming the module directory goodreads above), the display name should be helpful to the user. That usually means that it should be a little longer, and a little more descriptive.

However, there is no need to jam all of the module information into the name directive. The description directive is a good place for providing a sentence or two describing the module's function and capabilities.

The third directive is the core directive.

> The core and php directives are new in Drupal 6.

This directive specifies what version of Drupal is required for this module to function properly. Our value, 6.x, indicates that this module will run on Drupal 6 (including its minor revisions). In many cases, the Drupal packager will be able to automatically set this (correctly). But Drupal developers are suggesting that this directive be set manually for those who work from CVS.

Finally, the php directive makes it possible to specify a minimum version number requirement for PHP. PHP 5, for example, has many features that are missing in PHP 4 (and the modules in this book make use of such features). For that reason, we explicitly note that our modules require at least PHP version 5.1.

That's all there is to our first module .info file. In later chapters, we will see some other possible directives. But what we have here is sufficient for our Goodreads module.

Now, we are ready to write some PHP code.

A Basic .module File

As mentioned in the first chapter, there are two files that every module must have (though many modules have more). The first, the .info file, we examined above. The second file is the .module (dot-module) file, which is a PHP script file. This file typically implements a handful of hook functions that Drupal will call at pre-determined times during a request.

[For an introduction to hooks and hook implementations, see the previous chapter.]

Here, we will create a .module file that will display a small formatted section of information. Later in this chapter, we will configure Drupal to display this information to site visitors.

Our Goal: A Block Hook

For our very first module, we will implement the hook_block() function. In Drupal parlance, a block is a chunk of auxiliary information that is displayed on a page alongside the main page content. Sounds confusing? An example might help.

Think of your favorite news website. On a typical article page, the text of the article is displayed in the middle of the page. But on the left and right sides of the page and perhaps at the top and bottom as well, there are other bits of information: a site menu, a list of links to related articles, links to comments or forums about this article, etc. In Drupal, these extra pieces are treated as blocks.

The `hook_block()` function isn't just for displaying block contents, though. In fact, this function is responsible for displaying the block and providing all the administration and auxiliary functions related to this block. Don't worry... we'll start out simply and build up from there.

Starting the .module

As was mentioned in the last chapter, Drupal follows rigorous coding and documentation standards (`http://drupal.org/coding-standards`). In this book, we will do our best to follow these standards. So as we start out our module, the first thing we are going to do is provide some API documentation.

Just as with the `.info` file, the `.module` file should be named after the module. Following is the beginning of our `goodreads.module` file:

```php
<?php
// $Id$
/**
 * @file
 * Module for fetching data from Goodreads.com.
 * This module provides block content retrieved from a
 * Goodreads.com bookshelf.
 * @see http://www.goodreads.com
 */
```

The `.module` file is just a standard PHP file. So the first line is the opening of the PHP processing instruction: `<?php`. Throughout this book you may notice something. While all of our PHP libraries begin with the `<?php` opening, none of them end with the closing `?>` characters.

This is intentional, in fact, it is not just intentional, but conventional for Drupal. As much as it might offend your well-formed markup language sensibilities, it is good coding practice to omit the closing characters for a library.

Why? Because it avoids printing whitespace characters in the script's output, and that can be very important in some cases. For example, if whitespace characters are output before HTTP headers are sent, the client will see ugly error messages at the top of the page.

After the PHP tag is the keyword for the version control system:

```
// $Id$
```

When the module is checked into the Drupal CVS, information about the current revision is placed here.

The third part of this example is the API documentation. API documentation is contained in a special comment block, which begins /** and ends with a */. Everything between these is treated as documentation. Special extraction programs like Doxygen can pull out this information and create user-friendly programming information.

> The Drupal API reference is generated from the API comments located in Drupal's source code. The program, Doxygen, (http://www.stack.nl/~dimitri/doxygen/) is used to generate the API documents from the comments in the code.

The majority of the content in these documentation blocks (docblocks, for short) is simply text. But there are a few additions to the text.

First, there are special identifiers that provide the documentation generating program with additional information. These are typically prefixed with an @ sign.

```
/**
 * @file
 * Module for fetching data from Goodreads.com.
 * This module provides block content retrieved from a
 * Goodreads.com bookshelf.
 * @see http://www.goodreads.com
 */
```

In the above example, there are two such identifiers. The @file identifier tells the documentation processor that this comment describes the entire file, not a particular function or variable inside the file. The first comment in every Drupal PHP file should, by convention, be a file-level comment.

The other identifier in the above example is the @see keyword. This instructs the documentation processor to attempt to link this file to some other piece of information. In this case, that piece of information is a URL. Functions, constants, and variables can also be referents of a @see identifier. In these cases, the documentation processor will link this docblock to the API information for that function, constant, or variable.

As we work through the modules in this book, we will add such documentation blocks to our code, and in the process we will encounter other features of docblocks.

With these formalities out of the way, we're ready to start coding our module.

The hook_block() Implementation

Our module will display information inside a Drupal block. To do this, we need to implement the hook_block() function.

Remember, what we are doing here is providing a function that Drupal will call. When Drupal calls a hook_block() function, Drupal passes it as many as three parameters:

- $op
- $delta
- $edit

The $op parameter will contain information about the type of operation Drupal expects the module to perform. This single hook implementation is expected to be able to perform a variety of different operations. Is the module to output basic information about itself? Or display the block? Or provide some administration information? The value of $op will determine this.

$op can have the following four possible values:

- list: This is passed when the module should provide information about itself. For example, when the list of modules is displayed in the module administration screen, the $op parameter is set to list.

- view: This value is passed in $op when Drupal expects the block hook to provide content for displaying to the user.

- configure: This value is passed when Drupal expects an administration form used to configure the block. We will look at this later.

- save: This value is passed when configuration information from the form data generated by configure needs to be saved.

The $delta parameter is set during a particular operation. When $op is set to the string view, which is the operation for displaying the block, then the $delta will also be set. $delta contains extra information about what content should be displayed. We will not use it in our first example, but we will use it later in the book. Take a look at Chapter 4 for another example of a hook_block() implementation.

Using deltas, you can define a single hook_block() function that can display several different blocks. For example, we might define two deltas—one that displays our Goodreads bookshelf, and the other that displays information about our Goodreads account. Which one is displayed will depend on which $delta value is passed into the goodreads_block() function. Other modules in this book will make use of deltas.

Finally, the $edit parameter is used during configuration (when the save operation is called). Since we are not implementing that operation in our first module, we will not use this parameter.

Drupal is meticulously documented, and the API documents are available online at http://api.drupal.org. More information about hook_block() parameters is available at this URL: http://api.drupal.org/api/function/hook_block/6.

All hook methods should follow the module naming convention: <module name>_<hook name>. So our goodreads block hook will be named goodreads_block().

```
/**
 * Implementation of hook_block()
 */
function goodreads_block($op='list', $delta=0, $edit=array()) {
  switch ($op) {
    case 'list':
      $blocks[0]['info'] = t('Goodreads Bookshelf');
      return $blocks;
    case 'view':
      $blocks['subject'] = t('On the Bookshelf');
      $blocks['content'] = t('Temporary content');
      return $blocks;
  }
}
```

Following Drupal conventions, we precede the function with a documentation block. For hooks, it is customary for the documentation therein to indicate which hook it is implementing.

Next is our function signature: function goodreads_block($op='list', $delta=0, $edit=array()). The $op, $delta, and $edit parameters are all explained above. Each parameter is initialized to a default value. Here, we follow the customary defaults, but you can define them otherwise if you prefer.

As I mentioned earlier the $op parameter might be set to one of several different values.

What we do in this function is largely determined by which of those four values is set in the $op flag. For that reason, the first thing we do in this function is use a switch statement to find out which operation to execute.

Each case in the switch statement handles one of the different operations. For now, we don't have any administration configuration to perform, so there are no cases to handle either configure or save operations. We just need to handle the list and view operations. Let's look at each.

```
case 'list':
  $blocks[0]['info'] = t('Goodreads Bookshelf');
  return $blocks;
```

When Drupal calls this hook with $op set to 'list', then this module will return a two-dimensional array that looks as follows:

```
array(
  [0]=> (
    'info' => 'Goodreads Bookshelf'
  ))
```

Each element in this array is a **block descriptor**, which provides information about what this block implementation does. There should be one entry here for every $delta value that this function recognizes. Our block will only return one value (we don't make use of deltas), so there is only one entry in the block descriptor array.

A block descriptor can contain several different fields in the associative array. One is required: the 'info' field that we have set above. But we could also provide information on caching, default weighting and placement, and so on.

 For detailed information on this and other aspects of the hook_block() hook, see the API documentation: http://api.drupal.org/api/function/hook_block/6

Drupal uses the 'info' field to display an item in the module management list, which we will see in the *Installing a Module* section of this chapter.

The t() Function

In this example, there is one more thing worthy of mention. We use the function `t()`. This is the **translation function**. It is used to provide multi-language support and also provide a standard method of string substitution. When `t()` is called, Drupal will check to see if the user's preferred language is other than the default (US English). If the user prefers another language, and that language is supported, then Drupal will attempt to translate the string into the user's preferred language.

> For multi-language support, you will need to enable the **Content translation** module.

Whenever we present hard-coded text to a user, we will use the `t()` function to make sure that multi-language support is maintained.

In simple cases, the `t()` function takes just a string containing a message. In this case, the entire string will be translated. But sometimes, extra data needs to be passed into the string function. For example, we may want to add a URL into a string dynamically:

```
'Trying to access !url.'
```

In this case, we want `t()` to translate the string, but to substitute a URL in place of the `!url` placeholder. To do this, we would call `t()` with the following parameters:

```
t('Trying to access !url.', array('!url'=>'http://example.com'));
```

In this example, `t()` has two arguments: the string to translate, and an associative array where the key is the placeholder name and the value is the value to be substituted. Running the above when the locale is set to English will result in a string as follows:

```
Trying to access http://example.com.
```

There are three different kinds of placeholder. We have seen one above.

- `!`: Placeholders that begin with the exclamation point (`!`) are substituted into the string exactly as is.

Sometimes it is desirable to do some escaping of the variables before substituting them into the string. The other two placeholder markers indicate that extra escaping is necessary.

- `@`: Placeholders that begin with an `@` sign will be escaped using the `check_plain()` function. This will, for example, convert HTML tags to escaped entities. `t('Italics tag: @tag', array('@tag', '<i>'))` will produce the string `'Italics tag: &lt;i&gt;'`.

- %: Placeholders that begin with the percent sign (%) are not only escaped, like those that start with the @, but are also themed. (We will look at theming in the next chapter.) Usually, the result of this theming is that the output value is placed in italics. So t('Replacing %value.', array('%value=>'test') will result in something like 'Replacing <em>test</em>'. The <em></em> tags are added by the translation function.

> **Don't trust user-entered data**
>
> It is always better to err on the side of caution. Do not trust data from external sources (like users or remote sites). When it comes to the t() function, this means you should generally not use placeholders beginning with ! if the source of the string to be substituted is outside of your control. (For example, it is inadvisable to do this: t('Hello !user', array('!user' => $_GET['username']). Using @user or %user is safer.

We will use the t() function throughout this book. For now, though, let's continue looking at the hook_block() function we have created.

A view Operation

Now let's turn to the view case. This second case in our switch statement looks as follows:

```
case 'view':
  $blocks['subject'] = t('On the Bookshelf');
  $blocks['content'] = t('Temporary content');
  return $blocks;
```

The view operation should return one block of content for displaying to the end user. This block of content must have two parts stored as name/value pairs in an associative array: a subject and a content item.

The subject is the title of the block, and the content is main content of the block. The value of the subject entry will be used as a title for the block, while the content will be placed into the block's content.

Again, we used the translation function, t(), to translate the title and content of this block.

While it is not terribly exciting yet, our module is ready to test. The next thing to do is install it.

Installing a Module

We have a working module. Now we need to install it. This is typically done in three steps:

1. Copying the module to the correct location

2. Enabling the module

3. Configuring Drupal to display the module's content

 Some of the contributed modules for Drupal require additional setup steps. Such steps are documented by the module's authors. In Chapter 4, we will create a module that requires a few additional steps before the module is useful.

We will walk through each of these three steps.

Step 1: Copying the Module

Modules in Drupal are stored in one of the three places under Drupal's root directory:

- `modules/`: This is the directory for core modules. Only modules supplied as part of the Drupal distribution should be stored here. None of our modules will ever be located here.

- `sites/all/modules/`: This is the directory for modules that should be available to all of the sites hosted on this Drupal installation. Usually, this is where you want to put your module.

- `sites/<site name>/modules`: Drupal can host multiple sites. Each site has a directory inside the `sites/` folder. For example, the default site is located in `sites/default/`. If you want to install site-specific modules on an instance of Drupal that runs multiple sites, the modules should go into the `sites/<site name>/modules/` directory, where `<site name>` should be replaced by the correct site name.

In this book, we will be storing our modules under the `sites/all/modules/` directory.

However, this directory is not created by default, so we will need to create it by hand.

On my Linux server, Drupal is installed in /var/www/drupal/. (Yours may be somewhere else.) All of the file system paths will be relative to this directory. We will add the appropriate subdirectory inside the sites/all/ directory:

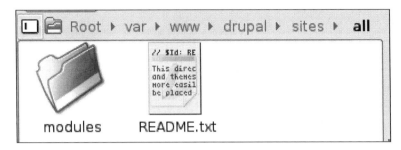

In this example, we change into the appropriate directory, create the new modules/ directory.

 By default, the permissions on the directory should be set to allow the web-server user (such as www-data) access to the files in the module. However, on some systems you may have to set these yourselves.

On Windows, the same can be done through Windows explorer, and the same goes for Mac and Finder. Simply locate your Drupal installation directory, navigate down to sites\all, and create a new folder named modules.

Next, we need to copy our module into this directory.

 UNIX and Linux users: Don't move it; link it!

If you are actively developing a module, sometimes it is more convenient to create a symbolic link to the module directory instead of moving or copying the directory:

ln -s /home/mbutcher/modules/goodreads
/var/www/drupal/sites/all/modules/goodreads

Now we have our module in a location where Drupal expects to find modules.

Copying the module to the correct location is all we need to do for Drupal to recognize the module, but new modules are disabled by default. We will need to log in to the web interface and enable the module.

Step 2: Enabling the Module

A module is enabled through the Drupal Administration interface. Once logged into Drupal, navigate to **Administer | Site Building | Modules** in the left-hand navigation.

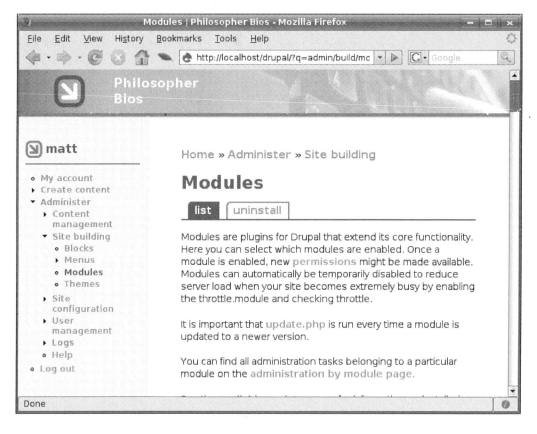

This page lists all the modules, beginning with the core modules (those installed by default). At the very bottom of this page is the list of third-party modules. Our module will appear in that list.

To activate the module, simply check the box under the **Enabled** heading, and then click the **Save configuration** button.

> Where did Drupal get the information about our module? For most of this part, this information came from our `goodreads.info` file.

Next, we need to configure the module to display on our site.

Step 3: Displaying the Module's Content

The module we have created is a block module. Typically, blocks are displayed in specifically defined locations on the screen. What we want to do now is tell Drupal where to display our block content.

Just as with enabling the module, this is done through the administration interface. Go to **Administer | Site Building | Blocks** to configure block placement.

This tools allows us to configure the details of how blocks appear on the site. In fact, the site uses the templates that a site visitor would see. You can see how the site looks as you configure it.

At the bottom of this page is the block configuration tool—lists of modules along with page placement parameters. We will configure our goodreads module to appear in the **right sidebar**.

If all goes well, then our goodreads module should display in the right sidebar. Make sure to press the **Save Blocks** button at the bottom. Otherwise the block's new location will not be saved.

 To generate the preceding screen, the block placement screen calls the hook_block() functions for each of the block modules, setting $op to list.

When the block's new location is saved, it will be displayed in the right-hand column on all of our pages.

What is the content in this module? What we see in the above screenshot are the fields returned when Drupal's module manager calls the hook_block() function of our module with something equivalent to this:

```
goodreads_block('view');
```

This will return the $blocks array, whose contents look like this:

```
array(
    'subject' => 'On the Bookshelf',
    'content' => 'Temporary content'
)
```

The subject value is used as the block's title, and the content item is used as the block's content.

Our module is installed. But it is doing very little. Next, we will add some sophistication to our module.

Using Goodreads Data

So far, we have created a basic module that uses hook_block() to add block content and installed this basic module. As it stands, however, this module does no more than simply displaying a few lines of static text.

In this section, we are going to extend the module's functionality. We will add a few new functions that retrieve and format data from Goodreads.

Goodreads makes data available in an XML format based on RSS 2.0. The XML content is retrieved over **HTTP (HyperText Transport Protocol)**, the protocol that web browsers use to retrieve web pages. To enable this module to get Goodreads content, we will have to write some code to retrieve data over HTTP and then parse the retrieved XML.

Our first change will be to make a few modifications to goodreads_block().

Modifying the Block Hook

We could cram all of our new code into the existing goodreads_block() hook; however, this would make the function cumbersome to read and difficult to maintain. Rather than adding significant code here, we will just call another function that will perform another part of the work.

```
/**
 * Implementation of hook_block
 */
function goodreads_block($op='list' , $delta=0, $edit=array()) {
  switch ($op) {
    case 'list':
      $blocks[0]['info'] = t('Goodreads Bookshelf');
      return $blocks;
    case 'view':
      $url = 'http://www.goodreads.com/review/list_rss/'
            .'398385'
            .'?shelf='
            .'history-of-philosophy';
      $blocks['subject'] = t('On the Bookshelf');
      $blocks['content'] = _goodreads_fetch_bookshelf($url);
      return $blocks;
  }
}
```

The preceding code should look familiar. This is our hook implementation as seen earlier in the chapter. However, we have made a few modifications, indicated by the highlighted lines.

First, we have added a variable, $url, whose value is the URL of the Goodreads XML feed we will be using (`http://www.goodreads.com/review/list_rss/398385?shelf=history-of-philosophy`). In a completely finished module, we would want this to be a configurable parameter, but for now we will leave it hard-coded.

The second change has to do with where the module is getting its content. Previously, the function was setting the content to `t('Temporary content')`. Now it is calling another function: `_goodreads_fetch_bookshelf($url)`.

The leading underscore here indicates that this function is a private function of our module—it is a function not intended to be called by any piece of code outside of the module. Demarcating a function as private by using the initial underscore is another Drupal convention that you should employ in your own code.

Let's take a look at the `_goodreads_fetch_bookshelf()` function.

Retrieving XML Content over HTTP

The job of the `_goodreads_fetch_bookshelf()` function is to retrieve the XML content using an HTTP connection to the Goodreads site. Once it has done that, it will hand over the job of formatting to another function.

Here's a first look at the function in its entirety:

```
/**
 * Retrieve information from the Goodreads bookshelp XML API.
 *
 * This makes an HTTP connection to the given URL, and
 * retrieves XML data, which it then attempts to format
 * for display.
 *
 * @param $url
 * URL to the goodreads bookshelf.
 * @param $num_items
 * Number of items to include in results.
 * @return
 * String containing the bookshelf.
 */
function _goodreads_fetch_bookshelf($url, $num_items=3) {
  $http_result = drupal_http_request($url);
```

```
    if ($http_result->code == 200) {
      $doc = simplexml_load_string($http_result->data);
      if ($doc === false) {
        $msg = "Error parsing bookshelf XML for %url: %msg.";
        $vars = array('%url'=>$url, '%msg'=>$e->getMessage());
        watchdog('goodreads', $msg, $vars, WATCHDOG_WARNING);
        return t("Getting the bookshelf resulted in an error.");
      }

      return _goodreads_block_content($doc, $num_items);

      // Otherwise we don't have any data
    }
    else {
      $msg = 'No content from %url.';
      $vars = array('%url' => $url);
      watchdog('goodreads', $msg, $vars, WATCHDOG_WARNING);
      return t("The bookshelf is not accessible.");
    }
  }
}
```

Let's take a closer look.

Following the Drupal coding conventions, the first thing in the above code is an API description:

```
/**
 * Retrieve information from the Goodreads bookshelp XML API.
 *
 * This makes an HTTP connection to the given URL, and retrieves
 * XML data, which it then attempts to format for display.
 *
 * @param $url
 * URL to the goodreads bookshelf.
 * @param $num_items
 * Number of items to include in results.
 * @return
 * String containing the bookshelf.
 */
```

This represents the typical function documentation block. It begins with a one-sentence overview of the function. This first sentence is usually followed by a few more sentences clarifying what the function does.

Near the end of the docblock, special keywords (preceded by the @ sign) are used to document the parameters and possible return values for this function.

- @param: The @param keyword is used to document a parameter and it follows the following format: @param <variable name> <description>. The description should indicate what data type is expected in this parameter.

- @return: This keyword documents what type of return value one can expect from this function. It follows the format: @return <description>.

This sort of documentation should be used for any module function that is not an implementation of a hook.

Now we will look at the method itself, starting with the first few lines.

```
function _goodreads_fetch_bookshelf($url, $num_items=3) {
    $http_result = drupal_http_request($url);
```

This function expects as many as two parameters. The required $url parameter should contain the URL of the remote site, and the optional $num_items parameter should indicate the maximum number of items to be returned from the feed.

> While we don't make use of the $num_items parameter when we call _goodreads_fetch_bookshelf() this would also be a good thing to add to the module's configurable parameters.

The first thing the function does is use the Drupal built-in drupal_http_request() function found in the includes/common.php library. This function makes an HTTP connection to a remote site using the supplied URL and then performs an HTTP GET request.

The drupal_http_request() function returns an object that contains the response code (from the server or the socket library), the HTTP headers, and the data returned by the remote server.

> Drupal is occasionally criticized for not using the object-oriented features of PHP. In fact, it does—but less overtly than many other projects. Constructors are rarely used, but objects are employed throughout the framework. Here, for example, an object is returned by a core Drupal function.

When the drupal_http_request() function has executed, the $http_result object will contain the returned information. The first thing we need to find out is whether the HTTP request was successful—whether it connected and retrieved the data we expect it to get.

We can get this information from the response code, which will be set to a negative number if there was a networking error, and set to one of the HTTP response codes if the connection was successful.

We know that if the server responds with the 200 (OK) code, it means that we have received some data.

[
In a more robust application, we might also check for redirect messages (301, 302, 303, and 307) and other similar conditions. With a little more code, we could configure the module to follow redirects.
]

Our simple module will simply treat any other response code as indicating an error:

```
if ($http_result->code == 200) {
  // ...Process response code goes here...
  // Otherwise we don't have any data
} else {
  $msg = 'No content from %url.';
  $vars = array( '%url' => $url );
  watchdog('goodreads', $msg, $vars, WATCHDOG_WARNING);
  return t("The bookshelf is not accessible.");
}
```

First let's look at what happens if the response code is something other than 200:

```
} else {
  $msg = 'No content from %url.';
  $vars = array( '%url' => $url );
  watchdog('goodreads', $msg, $vars, WATCHDOG_WARNING);
  return t("The bookshelf is not accessible.");
}
```

We want to do two things when a request fails: we want to *log an error*, and then *notify the user* (in a friendly way) that we could not get the content. Let's take a glance at Drupal's logging mechanism.

The watchdog() Function

Another important core Drupal function is the watchdog() function. It provides a logging mechanism for Drupal.

[
Customize your logging

Drupal provides a hook (hook_watchdog()) that can be implemented to customize what logging actions are taken when a message is logged using watchdog(). By default, Drupal logs to a designated database table. You can view this log in the administration section by going to **Administer | Logs**.
]

The watchdog() function gathers all the necessary logging information and fires off the appropriate logging event.

The first parameter of the watchdog() function is the logging category. Typically, modules should use the module name (goodreads in this case) as the logging category. In this way, finding module-specific errors will be easier.

The second and third watchdog parameters are the text of the message ($msg above) and an associative array of data ($vars) that should be substituted into the $msg. These substitutions are done following the same translation rules used by the t() function. Just like with the t() function's substitution array, placeholders should begin with !, @, or %, depending on the level of escaping you need.

So in the preceding example, the contents of the $url variable will be substituted into $msg in place of the %url marker.

Finally, the last parameter in the watchdog() function is a constant that indicates the log message's priority, that is, how important it is.

There are eight different constants that can be passed to this function:

- WATCHDOG_EMERG: The system is now in an unusable state.
- WATCHDOG_ALERT: Something must be done immediately.
- WATCHDOG_CRITICAL: The application is in a critical state.
- WATCHDOG_ERROR: An error occurred.
- WATCHDOG_WARNING: Something unexpected (and negative) happened, but didn't cause any serious problems.
- WATCHDOG_NOTICE: Something significant (but not bad) happened.
- WATCHDOG_INFO: Information can be logged.
- WATCHDOG_DEBUG: Debugging information can be logged.

Depending on the logging configuration, not all these messages will show up in the log.

The WATCHDOG_ERROR and WATCHDOG_WARNING levels are usually the most useful for module developers to record errors. Most modules do not contain code significant enough to cause general problems with Drupal, and the upper three log levels (alert, critical, and emergency) should probably not be used unless Drupal itself is in a bad state.

There is an optional fifth parameter to watchdog(), usually called $link, which allows you to pass in an associated URL. Logging back ends may use that to generate links embedded within logging messages.

The last thing we want to do in the case of an error is return an error message that can be displayed on the site. This is simply done by returning a (possibly translated) string:

```
return t("The bookshelf is not accessible.");
```

We've handled the case where retrieving the data failed. Now let's turn our attention to the case where the HTTP request was successful.

Processing the HTTP Results

When the result code of our request is 200, we know the web transaction was successful. The content may or may not be what we expect, but we have good reason to believe that no error occurred while retrieving the XML document.

So, in this case, we continue processing the information:

```
if ($http_result->code == 200) {
    // ... Processing response here...
    $doc = simplexml_load_string($http_result->data);
    if ($doc === false) {
      $msg = "Error parsing bookshelf XML for %url: %msg.";
      $vars = array('%url'=>$url, '%msg'=>$e->getMessage());
      watchdog('goodreads', $msg, $vars, WATCHDOG_WARNING);
      return t("Getting the bookshelf resulted in an error.");
    }
    return _goodreads_block_content($doc, $num_items);
    // Otherwise we don't have any data
} else { // ... Error handling that we just looked at.
```

In the above example, we use the PHP 5 **SimpleXML** library. SimpleXML provides a set of convenient and easy-to-use tools for handling XML content. This library is not present in the now-deprecated PHP 4 language version.

For compatibility with outdated versions of PHP, Drupal code often uses the **Expat** parser, a venerable old event-based XML parser supported since PHP 4 was introduced. Drupal even includes a wrapper function for creating an Expat parser instance. However, writing the event handlers is time consuming and repetitive. SimpleXML gives us an easier interface and requires much less coding.

For an example of using the Expat event-based method for handling XML documents, see the built-in **Aggregator module**. For detailed documentation on using Expat, see the official PHP documentation: http://php.net/manual /en/ref.xml.php.

We will parse the XML using `simplexml_load_string()`. If parsing is successful, the function returns a SimpleXML object. However, if parsing fails, it will return `false`.

In our code, we check for a `false`. If one is found, we log an error and return a friendly error message. But if the Goodreads XML document was parsed properly, this function will call another function in our module, `_goodreads_block_content()`. This function will build some content from the XML data.

Formatting the Block's Contents

Now we are going to look at one more function—a function that extracts data from the SimpleXML object we have created and formats it for display.

The function we will look at here is basic and doesn't take advantage of the Drupal theming engine. Usually, formatting data for display is handled using the theming engine. Themes are the topic of our next chapter.

Here is our `_goodreads_block_content()` function:

```
/**
 * Generate the contents of a block from a SimpleXML object.
 * Given a SimpleXML object and the maximum number of
 * entries to be displayed, generate some content.
 *
 * @param $doc
 * SimpleXML object containing Goodreads XML.
 * @param $num_items
 * Number of items to format for display.
 * @return
 * Formatted string.
 */
function _goodreads_block_content($doc, $num_items=3) {
  $items = $doc->channel->item;
  $count_items = count($items);
  $len = ($count_items < $num_items) ? $count_items : $num_items;

  $template = '<div class="goodreads-item">'
          .'<img src="%s"/><br/>%s<br/>by %s</div>';
  // Default image: 'no cover'
  $default_img = 'http://www.goodreads.com/images/nocover-60x80.jpg';
  $default_link = 'http://www.goodreads.com';

  $out = '';
  foreach ($items as $item) {
```

```
    $author = check_plain($item->author_name);
    $title = strip_tags($item->title);
    $link = check_url(trim($item->link));
    $img = check_url(trim($item->book_image_url));

    if (empty($author)) $author = '';
    if (empty($title)) $title = '';
    if (empty($link)) !== 0) $link = $default_link;
    if (empty($img)) $img = $default_img;

    $book_link = l($title, $link);
    $out .= sprintf($template, $img, $book_link, $author);
  }
  $out .= '<br/><div class="goodreads-more">'
        . l('Goodreads.com', 'http://www.goodreads.com')
        .'</div>';
  return $out;
}
```

As with the last function, this one does not implement a Drupal hook. In fact, as the leading underscore (_) character should indicate, this is a private function, intended to be called only by other functions within this module.

Again the function begins with a documentation block explaining its purpose, parameters, and return value. From there, we begin the function:

```
function _goodreads_block_content($doc, $num_items=3) {
   $items = $doc->channel->item;
```

The first thing the function does is get a list of `<item/>` elements from the XML data. To understand what is going on here, let's look at the XML (abbreviated for our example) returned from Goodreads:

```
<?xml version="1.0"?>
<rss version="2.0">
  <channel>
    <title>Matthew's bookshelf: history-of-philosophy</title>
    <copyright>
      <![CDATA[
      Copyright (C) 2006 Goodreads Inc. All rights reserved.]]>
    </copyright>
    <link>http://www.goodreads.com/review/list_rss/398385</link>
    <item>
      <title>
          <![CDATA[Thought's Ego in Augustine and Descartes]]>
      </title>
      <link>http://www.goodreads.com/review/show/6895959?
                        utm_source=rss&amp;utm_medium=api</link>
      <book_image_url>
        <![CDATA[
```

```
                        http://www.goodreads.com/images/books/96/285/964285-s-
                                       1179856470.jpg
            ]]>
        </book_image_url>
        <author_name><![CDATA[Gareth B. Matthews]]></author_name>
    </item>
    <item>
        <title>
        <![CDATA[Augustine: On the Trinity Books 8-15 (Cambridge Texts
                              in the History of Philosophy)]]>
        </title>
        <link>http://www.goodreads.com/review/show/6895931?
                         utm_source=rss&amp;utm_medium=api</link>
        <book_image_url>
        <![CDATA[
           http://www.goodreads.com/images/books/35/855/352855-s-
                                  1174007852.jpg
           ]]>
        </book_image_url>
        <author_name><![CDATA[Gareth B. Matthews]]></author_name>
    </item>
    <item>
        <title>
        <![CDATA[A Treatise Concerning the Principles of Human
                     Knowledge (Oxford Philosophical Texts)]]>
        </title>
        <link>http://www.goodreads.com/review/show/6894329?
                         utm_source=rss&amp;utm_medium=api</link>
        <book_image_url>
        <![CDATA[
           http://www.goodreads.com/images/books/10/138/1029138-s-
                                  1180349380.jpg
           ]]>
        </book_image_url>
        <author_name><![CDATA[George Berkeley]]></author_name>
    </item>
  </channel>
</rss>
```

The above XML follows the familiar structure of an RSS document. The `<channel/>` contains, first, a list of fields that describes the bookshelf we have retrieved, and then a handful of `<item/>` elements, each of which describes a book from the bookshelf.

We are interested in the contents of `<item/>` elements, so we start off by grabbing the list of items:

```
$items = $doc->channel->item;
```

The SimpleXML `$doc` object contains attributes that point to each of its child elements. The `<rss/>` element (which is represented as `$doc`) has only one child: `<channel/>`. In turn, `<channel/>` has several child elements: `<title/>`, `<copyright/>`, `<link/>`, and several `<item/>` elements. These are represented as `$doc->title`, `$doc->copyright`, and so on.

What happens when there are several elements with the same name like `<item/>`?

They are stored as an array. So in our code above, the variable `$items` will point to an array of `<item/>` elements.

Next, we determine how many items will be displayed, specify a basic template we will later use to create the HTML for our block, and set a few default values:

```
$count_items = count($items);
$len = ($count_items < $num_items) ? $count_items : $num_items;

$template = '<div class="goodreads-item">'
            .'<img src="%s"/><br/>%s<br/>by %s</div>';
// Default image: 'no cover'
$default_img = 'http://www.goodreads.com/images/nocover-60x80.jpg';
$default_link = 'http://www.goodreads.com';
```

In the first line, we make sure that we don't use any more than `$num_items`. Next, we assign the `$template` variable an `sprintf()` style template. We will use this to format our entries in just a moment.

Finally, we set default values for a logo image (`$default_img`) and a link back to Goodreads (`$default_link`).

Once this is done, we are ready to loop through the array of `$items` and generate some HTML:

```
$out = '';
foreach ($items as $item) {
  $author = check_plain($item->author_name);
  $title = strip_tags($item->title);
  $link = check_url(trim($item->link));
  $img = check_url(trim($item->book_image_url));
  if (empty($author)) $author = 'Unknown';
  if (empty($title)) $title = 'Untitled';
  if (empty($link)) $link = $default_link;
  if (empty($img)) $img = $default_img;
  $book_link = l($title, $link);
  $out .= sprintf( $template, $img, $book_link, $author);
}
```

Using a `foreach` loop, we go through each `$item` in the `$items` list. Each of these items should look something like the following:

```
<item>
  <title>
     <![CDATA[Book Title]]>
  </title>
  <link>http://www.goodreads.com/something/</link>
  <book_image_url>
    <![CDATA[
    http://www.goodreads.com/images/something.jpg
    ]]>
  </book_image_url>
  <author_name><![CDATA[Author Name]]></author_name>
</item>
```

We want to extract the title, link, author name, and an image of the book. We get these from the `$item` object:

```
$author = check_plain($item->author_name);
$title = strip_tags($item->title);
$link = check_url(trim($item->link));
$img = check_url(trim($item->book_image_url));
```

While we trust Goodreads, we do want to sanitize the data it sends us as an added layer of security. Above, we check the values of `$author` and `$title` with the functions `check_plain()` and `strip_tags()`.

The `strip_tags()` function is built into PHP. It simply reads a string and strips out anything that looks like an HTML or XML tag. This provides a basic layer of security, since it would remove the tags that might inject a script, applet, or ActiveX object into our page. But this check does still allow HTML entities like `&amp;` or `&raquote;`.

Drupal contains several string encoding functions that provide different services than `strip_tags()`. Above, we use `check_plain()` to perform some escaping on `$item->author_name`. Unlike `strip_tags()`, `check_plain()` does not remove anything. Instead, it encodes HTML tags into entities (like the @ modifier in `t()` function substitutions). So `check_plain('<em>Example</em>')` would return the string `&lt;em&gt;Example&lt;/em&gt;`.

 The `check_plain()` function plays a very important role in Drupal security. It provides one way of avoiding cross-site scripting attacks (XSS), as well as insertion of malicious HTML.

There is a disadvantage to using `check_plain()`, though. If `check_plain()` encounters an HTML entity, like `&lt;`, it will encode it again. Thus, `&lt;` would become `&amp;lt;`. The initial ampersand (`&`) is encoded into `&amp;`.

With the `$item->link` and `$item->book_image_url` objects, though, we have to do two things. First, we must `trim()` the results to remove leading or trailing white spaces. This is important because Drupal's `l()` function, which we will see in just a moment, will not process URLs correctly if they start with white spaces.

We also use Drupal's `check_url()` function to verify that the URL is legitimate. `check_url()` does a series of checks intended to catch malicious URLs. For example, it will prevent the `javascript:` protocol from being used in a URL. This we do as a safety precaution.

Next, we check each of the newly assigned variables. We want to make sure that if a variable is `null` or empty, it gets a default value.

```
if (empty($author)) $author = 'Unknown';
if (empty($title)) $title = 'Untitled';
if (empty($link)) $link = $default_link;
if (empty($img)) $img = $default_img;
```

The last thing we do in this `foreach` loop is format the entry as HTML for display:

```
$book_link = l($title, $link);
$out .= sprintf( $template, $img, $book_link, $author);
```

First, we create a link to the book review page at Goodreads. This is done with Drupal's `l()` function (that's a single lowercase L). `l()` is another important Drupal function. This function creates a hyperlink. In the above code, it takes the book title (`$title`), and a URL (`$link`), and creates an HTML tag that looks like this:

```
<a
href="http://www.goodreads.com/review/show/6894329?utm_
source=rss&amp;amp;utm_medium=api">
  A Treatise Concerning the Principles of Human Knowledge (Oxford
  Philosophical Texts)
</a>
```

That string is stored in `$book_link`. We then do the HTML formatting using a call to the PHP `sprintf()` function:

```
$out .= sprintf( $template, $img, $book_link, $author);
```

The `sprintf()` function takes a template (`$template`) as its first argument. We defined `$template` outside of the `foreach` loop. It is a string that looks as follows:

```
<div class="goodreads-item"><img src="%s"/><br/>%s<br/>by %s</div>
```

`sprintf()` will read through this string. Each time it encounters a placeholder, like `%s`, it will substitute in the value of an argument.

There are three string placeholders (`%s`) in the string. `sprintf()` will sequentially replace them with the string values of the three other parameters passed into `sprintf()`: `$img`, `$book_link`, and `$author`.

So `sprintf()` would return a string that looked something like the following:

```
<div class="goodreads-item">
<img src="http://www.goodreads.com/something.jpg"/>
<br/><a href="http://www.goodreads.com/somepath">
Thought&#039;s Ego in Augustine and Descartes
</a><br/>by Gareth B. Matthews</div>
```

That string is then added to `$output`. By the time the `foreach` loop completes, `$output` should contain a fragment of HTML for each of the entries in `$items`.

> The PHP `sprintf()` and `printf()` functions are very powerful, and can make PHP code easier to write, maintain, and read. View the PHP documentation for more information: `http://php.net/manual/en/function.sprintf.php`.

Once we are done with the `foreach` loop, we only have a little left to do. We need to add a link back to Goodreads to our `$out` HTML, and then we can return the output:

```
    $out .= '<br/><div class="goodreads-more">'
            . l('Goodreads.com', 'http://www.goodreads.com')
            .'</div>';
    return $out;
}
```

The block hook (`goodreads_block()`) will take the formatted HTML returned by `_goodreads_block_content()` and store it in the `contents` of the block. Drupal will display the results in the right-hand column, as we configured in the previous section:

The first three items in our Goodreads history of philosophy bookshelf are now displayed as blocks in Drupal.

There is much that could be done to improve this module. We could add caching support, so that each request did not result in a new retrieval of the Goodreads XML. We could create additional security measures to check the XML content. We could add an administration interface that would allow us to set the bookshelf URL instead of hard coding the value in. We could also use the theming system to create the HTML and style it instead of hard coding HTML tags into our code.

In fact, in the next chapter, we will take a closer look at the theming system and see how this particular improvement could be made.

However, to complete our module, we need a finishing touch. We need to add some help text.

Finishing Touches: hook_help()

We now have a functioning module. However, there is one last thing that a good Drupal module should have. Modules should implement the `hook_help()` function to provide help text for module users.

Our module is not very complex. Our help hook won't be, either:

```
/**
 * Implementation of hook_help()
 */
function goodreads_help($path, $arg) {

  if ($path == 'admin/help#goodreads') {
    $txt = 'The Goodreads module uses the !goodreads_url XML '
      .'API to retrieve a list of books and display it as block '
      .'content.';
    $link = l('Goodreads.com', 'http://www.goodreads.com');
    $replace = array(
      '!goodreads_url' => $link
    );
    return '<p>'. t($txt, $replace) .'</p>';
  }
}
```

The `hook_help()` function gets two parameters: `$path`, which contains a URI fragment indicating what help page was called, and `$arg`, which might contain extra information.

In a complex instance of `hook_help()`, you might use a switch statement on the `$path`, returning different help text for each possible path. For our module, only one path is likely to be passed in: the path to general help in the administration section. This path follows the convention `admin/help#<module name>`, where `<module name>` should be replaced with the name of the module (e.g. `goodreads`).

The function is straightforward: The help text is stored in the `$txt` variable. If our module required any additional setup or was linked to additional help, we would want to indicate this here. But in our case, all we really need is a basic description of what the module does.

We also want to insert a link back to Goodreads.com. To do this, we create the placeholder (`!goodreads_url`) in the `$txt` content, and then create the link (`$link`) by calling the `l()` function.

Since we are going to pass the `$txt` string and the link into the translation function, and let that function replace the placeholder with the link, we need to put `$link` inside an array—the `$replace` array.

Finally the help text is returned after being passed through the `t()` translation function.

This help text will now be accessible on the **Administer | Help** page:

Home » Administer » Help

Goodreads Bookshelf

The Goodreads module uses the Goodreads.com XML API to retrieve a list of books and display it as block content.

That is all there is to creating help text.

It is good coding practice to include help text with your module. And the more complex a module is, the better the help text should be. In future chapters, we will start every module by implementing `hook_help()`. Often, though, we will keep text in the help function brief for the sake of keeping the book concise and readable.

In your own modules you may want to create more verbose help text. This is helpful to users who don't have access to the code (or to a book explaining how the module works in detail).

Summary

In this chapter we created our first module. We created our first `.info` and `.module` files. We implemented our first two hooks, `hook_block()` and `hook_help()`. We installed our module, and then went on to extend the module to access an outside XML source for content.

We also looked at several important Drupal functions, with `t()`, `l()`, `watchdog()`, and `check_plain()` being the most important functions of the bunch.

In the coming chapters, we will build on the concepts covered in this chapter. Next, we will turn to the theming system to learn how to cleanly separate layout and styling information from the rest of the code.

3
The Theme System

In this chapter, we will look at the Drupal theme system. Strictly speaking, the theme system is not a module. However, modules interact with the theme system, which is made up of tools, templates, and libraries for configuring the look and feel of just about all aspects of Drupal.

By the end of this chapter, you should be able to create a theme based on the PHPTemplate engine. In later chapters, we will draw upon topics covered in this chapter to make our modules more theme-aware.

In this chapter, we will cover the following:

- Understanding the basic architecture of the theme system
- Using theme inheritance to create derivative themes
- Customizing the site's appearance with CSS (Cascading Style Sheets)
- Creating custom PHPTemplate files
- Overriding theme hooks to create custom theming

The Theme System's Architecture

The theme system was briefly introduced in the first chapter. In this chapter, we will start out with a more detailed overview of the theme system's architecture.

With each major release of Drupal, the theme system has enjoyed significant revision, and version 6 of Drupal is no exception. The new release of Drupal has introduced theme hook registration, theme `.info` files, and other features. We will make use of these new features in this chapter.

The goal of most theming systems—and Drupal's is no exception—is to separate the design elements from the processing logic. Doing so achieves two important (and related) goals:

- A new look and feel can be created without the need to re-write any of the processing code. This makes the theme creator's life easier—one need not possess detailed knowledge of Drupal's internals to change the way the site looks.

- Program logic is easier to maintain. When code isn't cluttered with layout elements (like HTML tags and CSS properties), the code can be cleaner and more readable. This, in turn, makes it easier to make changes to the code base.

To achieve this separation of the user-interface layer from the underlying processing logic, Drupal employs a complex theme system, which makes use of the module architecture we discussed in the previous chapters.

There are three main elements of the theming system that we will cover here: themes, theme engines, and hooks. These work in cooperation with the Drupal core system, and also with individual modules (which make use of hooks to interact with the template system).

The basic architecture, as we look at the theme system, is illustrated in the following figure.

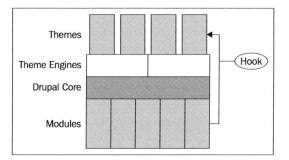

Themes provide the look and feel for the user interface. Typically, they require an underlying theme engine as an interface between the Drupal core and the theme templates. Hooks, considered in the context of the theme system, provide a convenient method for modules and the theme system to interact.

> Not all themes use a theme engine. For example, the Chameleon theme, included in Drupal 6 by default, bypasses the theme engine layer. Instead, it implements the appropriate theme hooks in a PHP file (`drupal/themes/chameleon/chameleon.theme`). These hooks simply return chunks of HTML. Additional styling is done with CSS.

Theme Templates

Of the three main elements of the theming system, the themes are the easiest to understand.

Themes are usually composed of a collection of templates, plus a handful of supporting files like images, CSS files, and occasionally JavaScript files as well. Here, we will focus on templates using the PHPTemplate engine. We will use CSS when we create a theme later in the chapter.

A **template** provides layout information for particular pieces of data—elements like blocks or nodes. So when a typical Drupal page is rendered, several templates are involved (one for the overall page layout, one for node content, one for block content, and so on). Often, templates format data as HTML, though there is no specific requirement that HTML be the target output language.

Most Drupal templates are written in the **PHPTemplate** "template language", which is actually just a specially formatted PHP file with access to a limited number of Drupal variables.

 Themes based on the PHPTemplate engine are the focus of this chapter. There are other routes for creating Drupal themes, but the PHPTemplate engine, which is a built-in component of Drupal, is flexible and powerful. That is why most themes use this engine.

Following is an example template from Drupal's Garland theme, one of the templates included by default in Drupal 6. This template is stored in themes/garland/block.tpl.php:

```php
<?php
// $Id: block.tpl.php,v 1.3 2007/08/07 08:39:36 goba Exp $
?>
<div id="block-<?php print $block->module .'-'. $block->delta; ?>"
  class="clear-block block block-<?php print $block->module ?>">

<?php if (!empty($block->subject)): ?>
  <h2><?php print $block->subject ?></h2>
<?php endif;?>

  <div class="content"><?php print $block->content ?></div>
</div>
```

The above code is the block template in its entirety. What exactly does this template do? It themes blocks. This template is used every time block content is rendered using the Garland theme.

Usually, blocks are embedded inside a complete page. Thus, the HTML returned from this block would be inserted into a larger HTML document. But when is this template used?

In the last chapter, we created a module that returned block content. We implemented `hook_block()` to create a block that displayed a bookshelf from Goodreads. When Drupal renders that block (that is, when it calls `goodreads_block('view')`), it passes the object returned from the block into the theme system as the variable `$block`.

The theme system, based on user configuration, determines which template engine and template files or functions should be used to render the content.

In this case, the theme system hands the block data (`$block`) over to the template that we have just seen, named `block.tpl.php`.

As you saw in this snippet, the attributes of the `$block` object are used to populate the template. This information is not only used for displaying textual content, but also for creating identifiers, such as HTML `id` and `class` attributes used by JavaScript and CSS to manipulate the block on the client side. (We will look at CSS later in this chapter and JavaScript in Chapter 5.)

The structure of the template should be familiar to any PHP developer. It is composed of HTML elements with PHP code fragments inserted where needed.

For the moment, let's take a quick look at the portion of the template that displays the subject and content of a block.

```php
<?php if (!empty($block->subject)): ?>
  <h2><?php print $block->subject ?></h2>
<?php endif;?>
  <div class="content"><?php print $block->content ?></div>
```

In the above snippet, lines 1 to 3 determine whether a subject exists. If it does exist, it is displayed. The last line displays the content.

This is a good example of a typical template work. There is very little programming logic. The little logic that is there is usually limited to checking for the existence of content, or perhaps looping through some content. All other data manipulation is done before the template is called.

To get a good idea of how this template works in action, let's consider a simple module named `goodadvice` with a block hook that looks as follows:

```php
/**
 * Implementation of hook_block
 */
function goodadvice_block($op='list' , $delta=0, $edit=array()) {
```

```
switch ($op) {
  case 'list':
    $blocks[0]['info'] = t('A Little Advice...');
    return $blocks;
  case 'view':
    $advice = "I'd rather have a bottle in front of me ".
      "than a frontal lobotomy.";

    $blocks['subject'] = t('A Little Advice...');
    $blocks['content'] = t($advice);
    return $blocks;
  }
}
```

The highlighted portion in the above snippet shows the case that would be executed when a block is requested for viewing.

If the above block hook is executed with $op set to 'view', it will return an array that looks as follows:

```
array(
  'subject' => 'A little Advice...'
  'content' => 'I'd rather have a bottle in front of me than a frontal
labotomy.'
);
```

When the results are rendered through the block template we saw earlier, the result will look as follows:

```
<div id="block-goodadvice-0"
  class="clear-block block block-goodadvice">

  <h2>A Little Advice...</h2>
  <div class="content">I'd rather have a bottle in front of me than
  a frontal lobotomy.</div>
</div>
```

Accessed from a browser, where all of the Garland theme's stylesheets are applied, it looks like this:

As you can see, some of the block data was used to generate an ID (`block-goodadvice-0`) and a class name (`block-goodadvice`). Then, the `$block->subject` and `$block->content` information was used to render the title and text of the block.

Templates like the one we just examined make up the core of most themes. But themes are also composed of stylesheets, images, and other auxiliary files. We will look at creating a custom theme, complete with templates, in the second part of this chapter, *Creating a Custom Theme*. But before we go there, we need to look at the engine that drives template rendering.

Theme Engines

In the above section, we looked at a template written as a `PHPTemplate`. This is one particular template "language." There are other template languages as well, such as the well-known PHP Smarty template language (`http://smarty.php.net/`) and the Xtemplate language used by default in older Drupal 4 versions. Is it possible to use one of these template languages instead of the default PHPTemplate?

The short answer is yes. New template languages can be supported by creating a custom chunk of code that implements the appropriate hooks and handles passing information from Drupal modules into the appropriate template or templates. This chunk of code is not, as we might expect, implemented as a module. Instead, it is implemented as a **theme engine**.

A theme engine is a special set of files (resembling, in some ways, a module) that handles rendering of data, usually with templates. Themes are written for particular theme engines. For example, one theme may use the PHPTemplate engine, while another uses the Smarty template engine. But due to the nature of the theme code and template files, it is difficult (and not good practice) to use multiple theme engines for one theme.

Custom theme engines can be built and packaged, though installing them is a manual procedure that must be done at the command line. We won't cover building a custom theme engine in this book. If you are interested in developing an engine, the Smarty theme engine (`http://drupal.org/project/smarty`) is a good starting point for learning to create one.

> **Other template engines**
>
> A list of alternative template engines is maintained on the Drupal website. At the time of this writing, there are only three: Xtemplate, Smarty, and Plain PHP: `http://drupal.org/node/176129`.

In this book, we will use only of the PHPTemplate engine for the following reasons:

- It is the default theme engine, and the only one packaged with Drupal 6.

- Since templates are written in plain old PHP, there is no learning curve to pick up the template language.

- It is deeply integrated with Drupal, and we can accomplish more with less effort than it would take to implement similar features with other template engines.

Along with these, the PHPTemplate engine has no external dependencies and no configuration external to Drupal.

Theme Hooks

The last major piece of Drupal's theme system is the theme-specific hook support. In the last two chapters we've already discussed hooks at some length. Hooks are used as a sort of callback mechanism used to facilitate inter-module interaction with a high degree of flexibility.

The theme system, too, makes use of hooks for this purpose. It does so in some interesting ways:

- Themes and theme engines implement hooks for various purposes such as registering, handling a particular request for display, and so on.

- Template files do, to a certain extent, behave like hooks. Just as Drupal searches for hook functions, it may, depending on the configuration, search for template files that follow certain naming conventions, and load those instead of executing a hook.

- Modules may implement theming hooks either to make certain data available for formatting by the theme system, or to perform some amount of theming themselves. For example, the `syslog` module included with Drupal 6 makes use of some theming hooks in order to format log file output.

We will make use of some theme hooks later in this chapter. Also, as we work on our templates in the next section, we will see several theme hooks in action.

 Most other chapters in this book make use of theme hooks, too. In coming chapters, you will see such hooks used to add default theming to new content and even to theme non-HTML content like email messages (Chapter 8).

At this point, we've covered the basic architecture of the theme system. We spent a little more time on themes themselves—especially templates. This introduction will serve as the bedrock for our coming work.

Next, we will create our first theme.

Creating a Custom Theme

In this section, we will investigate a few strategies for creating custom themes. We will create a custom theme, initially changing only CSS stylesheets, and then move on to a more sophisticated theme, making use of custom templates. Finally, we will create some PHP code that works more closely with the theme system itself. We will even implement a theme hook to provide a higher degree of customization for our theme.

Organization of Themes

In Drupal 6, themes are organized simiilarly to modules. Inside the main Drupal directory is a `themes/` folder, which in turn has a number of subfolders, each named after the theme it provides:

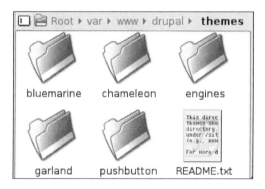

These are the main "top level" themes that come with Drupal 6: Bluemarine, Chameleon, Garland, and Pushbutton. Later in the book, we will talk about sub-themes, (or derivative themes,) which are not visible here at the top level. By convention, they exist in subfolders within the "top level" theme that they rely upon.

> Theme engines are stored in the `drupal/themes/engines` directory. By default, the only folder inside of `drupal/themes/engines` is `phptemplate/`.

Inside each theme directory are the files necessary for the theme to function. Each theme must have a theme `.info` file. Those that use the PHPTemplate engine have template files whose names end with the `.tpl.php` extension.

Stylesheets (particularly `style.css`), images, and other files will also be stored inside the theme directory. If there are a lot of these supporting files, the theme developers may have chosen to further organize the theme folder into subfolders.

Finally, some themes make use of a `template.php` file, which the PHPTemplate engine automatically loads if present. This file can be used to provide additional theming in the form of PHP functions.

Sub-themes (Derivative Themes)

Drupal 6 offers a new feature that developers call **theme inheritance**, a concept borrowed from Object-Oriented Programming. Roughly speaking, the idea is that a new theme can be created that draws upon the resources of another (parent) theme. This new derivative theme can make use of files, images, stylesheets, and other resources of the parent. But it can also strategically "override" or augment the parent theme.

Overriding occurs when a derivative theme supplies a new behavior or configuration that is designed to *replace* a behavior or configuration in the parent. For example, if a parent stylesheet specifies that the borders on all block elements are blue, a child might *override* this, declaring that all block elements be surrounded by a green border instead. Overriding need not be restricted to CSS statements, though; PHPTemplates, entire stylesheets, JavaScript files, and images can all be overridden.

But sub-themes can do more than override existing elements. They can add new resources — new images, styles, or scripts — without overtly changing the parent.

 Theme inheritance is one of many instances of the Drupal developers taking the principles behind object-oriented programming and successfully adapting them to Drupal's architecture.

In the theme examples seen here, we only deal with one layer of derivative themes. However, multiple levels of inheritance are supported. A parent theme can have a sub-theme, which in turn may have another sub-theme. Nesting themes this way, though, may lead to maintenance headaches, and should be done only when it is clearly the best choice.

Creating sub-themes themes has some obvious benefits. It is faster than creating a new theme from scratch. Less code is duplicated. Sets of similar (but different) themes can be created quickly and easily. In short, derivative themes ease the burden of the theme developer.

But there is a significant gotcha to be wary of. A sub-theme depends on its parent. But what happens when a parent theme is changed? A changed stylesheet, template, or JavaScript file in a parent module might lead to unpredictable behavior in derivative themes. One should particularly be aware of this possibility when basing a sub-theme on a parent theme that is maintained by someone else.

Now that we have a bit of theory under our belts, let's take a look at the themes provided with the Drupal core.

How Each Theme Functions

You can log into Drupal and check out the **Administer | Site building | Themes** page and check out the screenshots to find out how each theme *looks*. But we are more interested in how they *function*. Here's a brief overview of the architecture of each module. Derivative Marvin and Minelli themes are listed here as second-level bullets beneath the top-level themes they use.

- **Bluemarine**: The Bluemarine theme is a very simple example of a PHPTemplate-based theme. It uses HTML tables and CSS for layout, and it makes very little use of images.

- **Chameleon**: The Chameleon theme was mentioned earlier because it does not make use of any theme engine. Instead, the `chameleon.theme` file (found in `drupal/themes/chameleon`) contains PHP code that implements half a dozen different theming hooks.

    - The derivative **Marvin** theme makes use of chameleon. Marvin is located in `drupal/themes/chameleon/marvin`.

- **Garland**: Garland is the default Drupal 6 theme. It is powerful, but also complex. It makes use of the PHPTemplate engine. Along with the usual features, it includes support for configuring custom color schemes (see **Administer | Site building | Themes** and click the **configure** link next to the Garland theme). Along with the normal PHP templates, Garland has some specialized theming functions in the `drupal/themes/garland/template.php` file.

    - **Minelli**: The Minelli theme is a derivative theme based on Garland. Since it borrows all of the PHP-coded functionality from its parent, it has the same features as Garland (such as the color chooser).

- **Pushbutton**: Like Bluemarine and Garland, Pushbutton uses the PHPTemplate engine. While it makes heavy usage of images, it is not much more complex than the Bluemarine theme.

This brief overview should provide food for thought. Here are six very different themes. One does not use templates at all. Two are sub-themes. One, Garland, makes use of a sophisticated directory structure, theme-specific PHP functions, and other advanced features. Another, Bluemarine, is a minimal PHPTemplate module with only one image, a couple of stylesheets, and a handful of template files. Together, these modules illustrate the flexibility of the Drupal theme system.

We will base our themes on the Bluemarine theme. Its simplicity makes it the optimal starting point for exploration. Leveraging theme inheritance, we will create a custom derivative theme.

Creating a Theme

Rather than creating a full-fledged theme, we will make a sub-theme based on Bluemarine. This makes it easy for us to strategically modify a few files without the need to create a full set of templates.

As mentioned above, a derivative theme draws on the functionality of an existing theme. We can be very selective about which files we create. For example, we could just make a few stylesheet modifications, or just change around a few images. In fact, we could do all of this without touching a single PHP file.

In this first part, we will create a new sub-theme and manipulate the `style.css` stylesheet. We will also add a new background image.

Creating the Theme Directory

The first step in creating a theme is to create the directory to house the new theme. Where do we put this directory?

Earlier, we saw the convention of placing the derivative theme inside the parent theme's directory.

However, in the previous chapter, we discussed the conventions for modules: custom modules belong in `drupal/sites/all/modules`. This would indicate that we should store themes in `drupal/sites/all/themes`.

So which is the case?

Most of the time, themes should follow an organizational convention similar to that used for modules. There are two reasons why it is best to keep themes under the `drupal/sites/all/themes` directory (or, for site-specific configuration, under `drupal/sites/<sitename>/themes`):

- This method maintains a degree of separation between the official Drupal code and the custom code, making it easier to maintain.
- While Drupal upgrades might change the core themes (including, perhaps, recreating or removing directories), if custom themes are outside the core themes directory, they will not be touched during upgrades.

There is one notable exception, though. In the case where the same theme author or authors make use of theme inheritance to create multiple themes, it may be best to maintain them in the sort of directory structure employed by Drupal core themes.

In our case, we are extending a theme that we did not create. Clearly, we would do best to put our module in the `drupal/sites/all` area.

When Drupal is first installed, there will be no `themes/` directory there. *The directory may need to be created*, and in rare cases, the permissions on the directory may need to be set so that they are readable by the user the web server runs as (by default, this should be the case already).

We are going to create a new theme called Descartes (`descartes`), named after the famous early modern philosopher. We will put it in the `drupal/sites/all/themes` folder.

All our theme files go in this new directory.

A .info File

The next thing our new Descartes theme needs is a `.info` file. This file provides Drupal with information about the theme. Some of that information is simply used for display, while other directives provide Drupal with information necessary for serving and executing the theme code.

Just as with a module's `.info` file, this file should be named with the machine-readable name of the theme. Thus, our file is named `descartes.info`.

Also like the module's `.info` file, this file is in the PHP configuration format, and it has many of the same directives.

Here is our theme configuration file:

```
; $Id$
name = Descartes
description = Table-based multi-column theme with a Cartesian flavor.
version = 1.0
core = 6.x
base theme = bluemarine
```

There is very little to note in this simple file. The first four fields function in the same capacity for themes as they do for modules.

The `name` field should contain the user-friendly title of the theme, and the `description` should provide a one-line description of the theme. Likewise, `version` should give the version number of the theme.

The most interesting directive, though, is the `base theme` directive. This tells Drupal that this theme makes use of resources from another theme—the `bluemarine` theme. It is this directive that effectively makes this a sub-theme of Bluemarine. The name passed to the `base theme` directive must be the *machine-readable* name.

That's all there is to our first theme `.info` file. There are, of course, many other directives that can be used in a theme's `.info` file. We will look at a few more of these later in the chapter. A complete list is available at: `http://drupal.org/node/137062`.

Now we are ready to create a custom stylesheet.

A CSS Stylesheet

The first step in creating a new stylesheet is answering a question—How divergent is this theme's style going to be from the parent style?

We are basing our Descartes theme on the Bluemarine theme. But how similar will style elements be? Will we keep the same fonts? The same colors? The same paddings, borders, and margins? The degree to which the styles differ will determine how we create our stylesheet.

Let's take a quick glance at our site with the Bluemarine style:

How much will our new style differ from this one?

If our new style is to be radically divergent from the Bluemarine style, then we might want to create a new `style.css` file (or copy over the `style.css` from Bluemarine and begin a major overhaul).

However, the stylistic changes we will make here are minor. We will change the look and feel of the left-hand column, turn the right-hand column on again (it is off by default), and change some of the colors.

Since these changes can be accomplished with just a dozen or so lines of CSS, we will take a different course of action. Instead of copying the entire `style.css` file from Bluemarine, we will create a new stylesheet that overrides some of Bluemarine's settings.

As of now, there is no convention for naming these auxiliary stylesheets, so we will go with the uninspiring name `new.css`. Following are the contents of this CSS file:

```
/*
** Styles to override the styles.css in
** bluemarine.css
** $Id$
*/
```

```
/*
 * Plain white right nav.
 */
#sidebar-right {
  border-left: 1px solid #ea940c;
  background-color: white;
}
/*
 * Add background image.
 */
#sidebar-left {
  background: url(leMonde_sidebar.png) no-repeat top left;
  border-right: 1px solid #ea940c;
}
/*
 * Set the background for the mission.
 */
#mission {
  background-color: #ea940c;
  padding: 5px 15px 5px 15px;
  text-align: center;
}
```

Here we are adding styles to three specific IDs in the HTML: sidebar-right, which identifies the right-hand sidebar; sidebar-left, identifying the left-hand sidebar; and mission, which identifies the box containing the site's mission (**"All philosophy is a footnote to Plato"**).

The right-hand sidebar in the Bluemarine theme is battleship gray by default. We want it to be white with an orange (#ea940c) border on the left side.

On the left-hand side, we want something more ornate: a background image (leMonde_sidebar.png). Before this image can be successfully used, it must be copied into our module directory.

 Make sure you copy any necessary images into the theme directory. Even if you are using images from the parent theme, it is best to copy those images into the derivative theme.

As in our left-hand sidebar, we want an orange border to set this off from the main page content.

CSS and URLs

Theme URLs are resolved relative to the theme directory. For example, the CSS statement `url(leMonde_sidebar.png)` will attempt to find the file `drupal/sites/all/themes/descartes/leMonde.png`.

Finally, we want to fix up the display of the mission statement by reducing the padding, changing the background color, and aligning the text to the center of the box instead of the left-hand side.

With `new.css` created, we have only one more thing to do. We need to direct Drupal to use our new CSS in addition to the `style.css` of the parent. This is done by adding the following lines to our `descartes.info` file:

```
stylesheets[all][] = style.css
stylesheets[all][] = new.css
```

These two lines provide explicit instructions to load the `style.css` and `new.css` stylesheets.

What's the idea with all the square brackets? Square bracket notation was introduced in Drupal 6 as a method for specifying multiple values for a directive in a `.info` file. They function analogously to arrays in PHP.

The stylesheet directives above have two sets of square brackets apiece: `stylesheet[all][]`. The first set, `[all]`, indicates which **media type** of pages the given stylesheet should be used in.

Those familiar with CSS will recognize the term 'media type'. It refers to the output medium that the stylesheet is used for. Common media types are `screen` (for a device with a screen) and `print` (for printed pages). The media type `all` applies to any media type the browser requests.

Using the media type, then, we could set special stylesheets for printer-friendly pages:

```
stylesheets[print][] = printed.css
```

The Garland theme, for example, has printer-specific CSS files.

The second pair of square brackets, `[]`, function like the array assignment syntax for PHP. Just as `$my_array[] = 'foo'` places the string `foo` at the last place in the array, so the directive `stylesheets[all][] = 'new.css'` puts `new.css` at the end of the stylesheets list.

> **Clearing the template cache**
>
> When developing new templates, you may need to clear the template cache before the latest theme changes show up. To do this, use the **Empty cache** item in the **Devel module**'s module development block. See Chapter 1 for more information on the Devel module.
>
> devel
> * Devel settings
> * Empty cache
> * PHPinfo()
> * func theme elements sess
> * Reinstall modules
> * Rebuild menus
> * Variable editor

With these modifications made to the theme's `.info` file, we are ready to take a look at the fruits of our labor.

Since our theme is located in the `drupal/sites/all/themes` directory and has a `.info` file, Drupal should automatically find it. All we need to do is go to **Administer | Site building | Themes** and enable the theme, setting it to default for testing.

You may notice that the screenshot of our Descartes theme shows the Bluemarine theme instead. That's because we haven't yet created our own screenshot image (`screenshot.png` in the theme directory). Drupal is "inheriting" the parent theme's screenshot.

Once the theme is enabled, we can navigate to the home page to see how it looks.

> Do not set the administration theme to a theme in the development or testing phase. Doing so can result in an unfortunate predicament. Errors in the theme files can prevent you from accessing the administration screens. Only stable themes should be used on the administration side of Drupal.

Our new site should look something like the following screenshot:

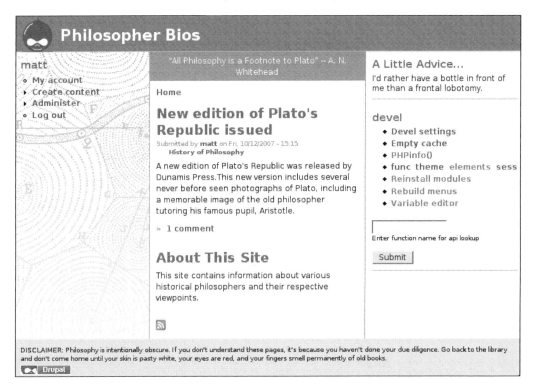

While many of the elements of this design look the same as they did in the Bluemarine theme, our changes should be immediately evident—different left and right sidebars, a background image in the left-hand sidebar, and a lot more orange.

We have just successfully created a working derivative theme. All of this was done with just a handful of files—and no PHP coding. A final glance at the Descartes theme directory shows only four files:

The `logo.png` file was simply copied over from the Bluemarine theme. We created only three new files for this theme.

However, sometimes a little CSS isn't enough to attain the desired look and feel. Sometimes we need to customize the templates themselves. How do we do that?

A PHPTemplate Theme

We could start a new theme from scratch, creating each new theme file as we go, but it is often easier to begin by copying a similar theme and modifying it.

The Bluemarine theme is table-based, following the older practice of laying out an HTML page with tables. We will start with that. But we will change it, making the right-hand navigation "float" so that text can wrap around it.

Template Structure

There are five templates in the Bluemarine theme. These five templates make an appearance in almost all PHPTemplate-based themes, as they represent the pieces that Drupal composes into a page. The templates are:

- `page.tpl.php`: The main template for a page. This template should contain the main elements of an HTML page, including the `<html/>`, `<head/>` and `<body/>` elements. The theme system provides this template access to over 30 variables.

- `node.tpl.php`: This template is responsible for displaying the contents of a node. It is passed several variables, most of which relate directly to the node being processed. For example, `$title`, `$content`, and `$terms` contain (respectively) the node's title, text content, and associated taxonomy tags.

- `block.tpl.php`: As we saw earlier in the chapter, this template is responsible for rendering a single block. The `$block` object passed into this template contains most of the information necessary for generating a block, though there are a few other variables passed in as well.

- `box.tpl.php`: This template paints a simple box. It is used less frequently. It has access to only three variables: `$title`, `$content`, and `$region`.

- `comment.tpl.php`: This template is used to display comments. It is given access to about a dozen variables, which pertain to the comment, the comment poster, and the context of the posting.

When a template is omitted from a theme (and from its parent, if it has one), Drupal uses the default theme function to render the contents. For example, when `box.tpl.php` is missing and a box is drawn, Drupal will use the `theme_box()` method to theme the box data. Such default theme functions are defined in `include/theme.inc`.

The main `page.tpl.php` template is responsible for providing the framework into which Drupal content will be rendered. Most Drupal content items, including blocks, are grouped into **regions**.

The main page template, then, isn't responsible for displaying individual nodes, blocks, comments, and so on. Instead, it is responsible for displaying regions.

A **region** is a partition of the page where content can be displayed. By default, there are five pre-defined regions:

- `header`: This region describes the header area of the template. In our theme, for example, this area is located in the blue box along the top.

- `content`: This describes the main area of the page. For our theme, this is the section in the center of the page.

- `left`: This describes one sidebar. Typically, as the name indicates, this sidebar is located on the left side of the page (though that is, of course, contingent on the theme creator's whims.)

- `right`: This describes the second sidebar, usually located on the right side.

- `footer`: The footer section contains information that should usually appear after the rest of the content. In our theme, footer content would appear in the gray box running along the bottom of the page.

Regions can be tailored to your needs. Existing regions can be omitted, and new regions can be defined. As of version 6 of Drupal, this is all done in the theme's `.info` file using the `region[]` directive. Region configuration is explained further at: `http://drupal.org/node/137062`.

As Drupal processes a request, the content of blocks, nodes, comments, and so on is appended to the appropriate region or regions. These regions are made accessible to the main page template in the form of eponymously named variables: `$content`, `$header`, `$left`, `$right`, and `$footer`.

For example, the main content of a page is stored in the $content variable made accessible to page.tpl.php. Likewise, the title is stored in $title. Hence, the page template could display the main page content with something like this:

```
<h1><?php print $title; ?></h1>
<?php print $content; ?>
```

What about blocks? The precise region that a particular block is assigned to is easily configurable. In the last chapter, we used the **Administer | Site building | Blocks** page to tell Drupal where we wanted our Goodreads module to be displayed. What Drupal did, under the hood, was assign the module to a region (the right region).

The page template is supplied with many other variables, as well. Some contain site information, such as the $site_name, $logo, and $site_slogan variables. Others contain references to CSS ($styles) or JavaScript ($scripts, $closure). Many of them provide template designers access to dynamically-generated pieces of content. For example, the $breadcrumb variable provides access to the breadcrumb navigation:

All of these variables, and there are over 30, are documented in the page.tpl.php template in Bluemarine (and the other core themes).

Armed with this information, we can now edit the template.

A Page Template for Descartes

We have already created a theme, Descartes, and added some custom CSS. Now, we are going to modify just one of the templates provided by the Bluemarine theme. We will change the page template to allow the right sidebar (the right region) to float.

The first thing to do is to copy the Bluemarine page template into our descartes/ theme directory.

```
$ cp drupal/themes/bluemarine/page.tpl.php \
      drupal/sites/all/themes/descartes
```

Now we have a copy of the template that we can tailor to our needs. According to the rules of theme inheritance, this new template now overrides the Bluemarine page.tpl.php file. The theme system will use the Descartes page.tpl.php, now, and will ignore the parent Bluemarine template.

Taking a glance at the template, we can see many of the variables that we have discussed in action. Don't feel obligated to labor over the details of this template. We will be focusing on the highlighted section.

```php
<?php
// $Id: page.tpl.php,v 1.25 2007/09/05 08:42:02 dries Exp $
?><!DOCTYPE html PUBLIC "-//W3C//DTD XHTML 1.0 Strict//EN"
  "http://www.w3.org/TR/xhtml1/DTD/xhtml1-strict.dtd">
<html xmlns="http://www.w3.org/1999/xhtml" lang="<?php print
  $language->language ?>" xml:lang="<?php print $language->language
  ?>">

<head>
  <title><?php print $head_title ?></title>
  <?php print $head ?>
  <?php print $styles ?>
  <?php print $scripts ?>
  <script type="text/javascript"><?php /* Needed to avoid Flash of
          Unstyle Content in IE */ ?> </script>
</head>
<body>
<table border="0" cellpadding="0" cellspacing="0" id="header">
  <tr>
    <td id="logo">
      <?php if ($logo) { ?><a href="<?php print $base_path ?>"
          title="<?php print t('Home') ?>"><img src="<?php print $logo
          ?>" alt="<?php print t('Home') ?>" /></a><?php } ?>
      <?php if ($site_name) { ?><h1 class='site-name'><a href="<?php
          print $base_path ?>" title="<?php print t('Home') ?>"><?php
          print $site_name ?></a></h1><?php } ?>
      <?php if ($site_slogan) { ?><div class='site-slogan'><?php
          print $site_slogan ?></div><?php } ?>
    </td>
    <td id="menu">
      <?php if (isset($secondary_links)) { ?><?php print
          theme('links', $secondary_links, array('class' => 'links',
          'id' => 'subnavlist')) ?><?php } ?>
      <?php if (isset($primary_links)) { ?><?php print theme('links',
          $primary_links, array('class' => 'links', 'id' =>
          'navlist')) ?><?php } ?>
      <?php print $search_box ?>
    </td>
  </tr>
  <tr>
    <td colspan="2"><div><?php print $header ?></div></td>
  </tr>
</table>
```

```
<table border="0" cellpadding="0" cellspacing="0" id="content">
  <tr>
    <?php if ($left) { ?><td id="sidebar-left">
      <?php print $left ?>
    </td><?php } ?>
    <td valign="top">
      <?php if ($mission) { ?><div id="mission"><?php print $mission
?></div><?php } ?>
      <div id="main">
        <?php print $breadcrumb ?>
        <h1 class="title"><?php print $title ?></h1>
        <div class="tabs"><?php print $tabs ?></div>
        <?php print $help ?>
        <?php if ($show_messages) { print $messages; } ?>
        <?php print $content; ?>
        <?php print $feed_icons; ?>
      </div>
    </td>
    <?php if ($right) { ?><td id="sidebar-right">
      <?php print $right ?>
    </td><?php } ?>
  </tr>
</table>
<div id="footer">
  <?php print $footer_message ?>
  <?php print $footer ?>
</div>
<?php print $closure ?>
</body>
</html>
```

The highlighted table in the above code provides the basic layout for the page. It is composed of three cells, all arranged in one row. Each sell corresponds to a region: left, content, and right.

> **CSS and the left and right regions**
>
> Notice that while the left and right regions are stored in the $left and $right variables, the IDs for the corresponding containers are named sidebar-right and sidebar-left. We styled these while developing our CSS-only theme earlier.

Instead of this three-column table layout, we want only two columns: one for the right region, and the other for the content region.

The left region will reside inside a `<div/>` element inside of the content section, and we will modify our `new.css` stylesheet to move that region over to the right.

To do this, we will remove the third `<td/>` element that looks as follows:

```php
<?php if ($right) { ?><td id="sidebar-right">
  <?php print $right ?>
</td><?php } ?>
```

Note that this third column is only displayed if the `$right` variable is defined. We will preserve this characteristic as we move the right region into the second column of the table.

```php
<td valign="top">
  <?php if ($mission) { ?><div id="mission"><?php print $mission
     ?></div><?php } ?>
  <div id="main">
    <?php if ($right) { ?>
      <div id="sidebar-right">
      <?php print $right ?>
      </div>
    <?php } ?>
    <?php print $breadcrumb ?>
    <h1 class="title"><?php print $title ?></h1>
    <div class="tabs"><?php print $tabs ?></div>
    <?php print $help ?>
    <?php if ($show_messages) { print $messages; } ?>
    <?php print $content; ?>
    <?php print $feed_icons; ?>
  </div>
</td>
```

We've added only five lines to implement our change. Now, if the `$right` variable is defined, the template will encapsulate the region's content inside a `<div/>` element with the same ID (`sidebar-right`) that the `<td/>` element uses in the Bluemarine style.

If we look at the site, we can see the result of this small change:

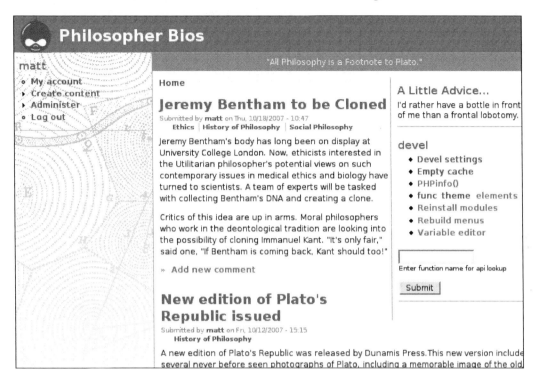

What are the effects of this change? First, the orange mission section on the top now spans two-thirds of the screen, crossing over the right sidebar.

Glancing back at the above code, we can see why: The `<div id="mission"/>` element is above the `<div id="sidebar-right"/>` element.

The second difference is the wrapping of text. In the old template, the right-hand sidebar extended the length of the table. Now it only extends as far as it requires to display all of its content. Material in the center section (which displays the `$content`) can now extend to the right beneath the right-hand region.

 Remember, Drupal caches theme information. To see your changes, you may need to clear the cache using the Devel module.

Should we want to change the HTML code for blocks, boxes, comments, or nodes, we could use a similar strategy. Copy the template or templates from the parent theme, and modify them at will.

Using PHP to Override Theme Behavior

Sometimes there are cases where we want to perform some additional manipulation on data before passing it on to the templates.

Some such manipulation *could be done* inside the PHPTemplate files. After all, they are really just PHP files. However, that violates the principle of separation we have adopted; templates should simply display content, not do any processing.

Additionally, some data comes into the theme in a somewhat unpredictable way. The content of the $right variable in the page.tpl.php template, for example, is an arbitrary string. Operating on each node or block represented in that variable is difficult, as it would require sophisticated (and error-prone) parsing.

Fortunately, there is a better way. We can interoperate with the theming system at a lower level. We can use a template.php file to override theme functions.

The template.php file is a construct supported by the PHPTemplate engine. Not all engines support template.php files. Some themes, like Chameleon, use a similar technique to that of the template.php file, but without using any theme engine at all. Chameleon strategically uses and overrides theme functions to create HTML.

Theme functions, the core of which are defined in drupal/includes/theme. inc, define how themes process information passed into the theme system. These functions are part of the Drupal core (and, in some cases, part of modules), and are executed before control is handed over to the theme engine.

Theme functions are similar to hooks. Just like hooks, they can be overridden. The template.php file provides PHPTemplate-based themes with the ability to override default theme behavior.

Custom Breadcrumbs

Let's look at a simple example. While creating our page.tpl.php template, we looked briefly at the $breadcrumb variable as it is passed into the page template. $breadcrumb, as passed in here, contains a string that looks something like the following code snippet:

```
<div class="breadcrumb">
<a href="/drupal/">Home</a> »
<a href="/drupal/?q=node/add">Create content</a>
</div>
```

This code is generated from the `theme_breadcrumb()` function in `drupal/includes/theme.inc`. The function in its entirety looks as follows:

```
/**
 * Return a themed breadcrumb trail.
 *
 * @param $breadcrumb
 *    An array containing the breadcrumb links.
 * @return a string containing the breadcrumb output.
 */
function theme_breadcrumb($breadcrumb) {
  if (!empty($breadcrumb)) {
    return '<div class="breadcrumb">'. implode(' » ', $breadcrumb)
                                        .'</div>';
  }
}
```

The `theme_breadcrumb()` function gets an array of strings, each one a breadcrumb item wrapped in a link. The function then combines all the items in this array, separated by the double right angle quote (»). The whole thing is then wrapped in a `<div/>` and returned.

This markup is hard-coded into Drupal, and cannot be easily changed from a template.

But what if we don't like separating breadcrumbs with a double right angle quote?

The answer: We can override this theme function with a PHPTemplate function defined in a `template.php` file inside our Descartes theme.

For example, let's look at a method for using an image as a separator.

Here is our `drupal/sites/all/themes/descartes/template.php` file:

```
<?
// $Id$
/**
 * @page
 * Override theme_() functions for the Descartes theme.
 */
// Overrides theme_breadcrumb()
function phptemplate_breadcrumb($breadcrumb) {
  if (empty($breadcrumb)) return;
  $sep = '<div class="breadcrumb-separator">  </div>';
  $breadcrumb_string = '<div class="breadcrumb">'
      . implode($sep, $breadcrumb) .'</div>';
  return $breadcrumb_string;
}
```

This file follows the same coding conventions as Drupal modules. We have one function here—`phptemplate_breadcrumb()`. This function, which acts as part of the PHPTemplate engine, overrides the `theme_breadcrumb()` function we examined earlier.

Whereas the `theme_breadcrumb()` function separated elements with the double right angle quote, this function separates them with this string (the value of `$sep`):

```
<div class="breadcrumb-separator">  </div>
```

A `<div/>` with a new `breadcrumb-separator` class wraps a couple of non-breaking spaces. This function will print output that looks something like the following code:

```
<div class="breadcrumb">
  <a href="/drupal/">Home</a>
  <div class="breadcrumb-separator">  </div>
  <a href="/drupal/?q=node/add">Create content</a>
</div>
```

Now with an extra class declaration in `new.css`, we can add a small background image, which will appear "behind" the two blank spaces. It will give the appearance of a separator:

```
div.breadcrumb-separator {
  display: inline;
  background: url(orange_dot.gif) no-repeat bottom left;
}
```

Viewed through the browser, we now have a breadcrumb trail that looks as follows:

Our `phptemplate_breadcrumb()` theme function is now performing some custom pre-processing on the breadcrumb trail.

But the HTML (and CSS) produced by this method is admittedly a little clunky. Let's look at a more elegant solution, which involves interacting with another theme function.

Interacting with Other Theme Functions

A quick perusal of the contents of `drupal/includes/theme.inc` will give you some indication of what theming functions can do. Here are just a few to give some idea:

- `theme_image()`: Format an image for display.
- `theme_links()`: Format a list of links.
- `theme_progress_bar()`: Display a progress bar.
- `theme_username()`: Format a username for display.
- `theme_table()`: Format data and display it as a table.

> These functions can be called by modules as well as by themes.
>
> The preferred method of calling them in the module context is `theme('<hookname>', $arg1, $arg2, ...)`, where `<hookname>` should be replaced by the string after the first underscore in the theme function.

Rather than calling these theme functions directly, it is better to call them through a mediating function, `theme()`. The `theme()` function takes the theme hook suffix as the first argument, and the theme hook's arguments as additional arguments. In other words, a call to theme should look something like this: `theme('<hookname>', $arg1, $arg2,...)`. Here, `<hookname>` should be replaced by the string after the first underscore in the theme function. For example, invoking `theme('image', 'images/ socrates.png', 'Bust of Socrates')` would result in some version of `theme_ image()` being executed with the arguments `'images/socrates.png'` and `'Bust of Socrates'`.

What do we mean by "some version of `theme_image()`"? The answer to this question explains why it is better to use `theme()` than to call a `theme_<hookname>()` function itself.

As we have seen in the previous example, it is possible to override a theme function. Invoking `theme('images', $a, $b)` causes the theme system to check for a function or template that overrides `theme_image()`. If one is found, that function or template is used instead.

In short, `theme()` makes use of the full theme system, while calling `theme_<hookname>()` function directly may cause your application to ignore the current theme configuration and use only the default.

> **Templates can override theme hooks**
>
> A `theme_<hookname>()` function can also be overridden with a PHPTemplate template file. For example, to override `theme_image()`, we could create a template named `image.tpl.php`. The variables normally available as arguments will be accessible here as variables according to the method signature for `theme_image()`.

With that explanation, we are ready to move on to our revised breadcrumb implementation.

One way to represent our breadcrumb trail is as a list. Lists are easier to style, and we have a nice built-in theme function for taking an array and generating a list: `theme_item_list()`.

The `theme_item_list()` function takes up to four arguments, though only the first is required:

1. Array of list items
2. Title of list (optional, default: `null`)
3. List type, `ul` for unordered, `ol` for ordered
4. An associative array of attributes to add to the list element (the `<ol/>` or `<ul/>` elements)

Of course, we don't want to call `theme_item_list()` directly. Instead, we will access the hook via the `theme()` function.

Re-working our earlier example, we can create a `phptemplate_breadcrumb()` function that looks as follows:

```
// Overrides theme_breadcrumb()
function phptemplate_breadcrumb($breadcrumb) {
  if (empty($breadcrumb)) return;
  $attr = array(
    'class' => 'breadcrumb-items'
  );
  $crumbs = theme('item_list', $breadcrumb, null, 'ul', $attr);
  return '<div class="breadcrumb">' . $crumbs . '</div>';
}
```

This function now makes use of `item_list` to create an unordered list of breadcrumb items with the style class name set to `breadcrumb-items`.

Since we still want existing style information to apply where appropriate, we wrap the new list in a `<div>` with the `breadcrumb` class.

We can now make use of our newly-defined `breadcrumb-items` class in our stylesheet:

```
ul.breadcrumb-items li {
  list-style-image: url(orange_dot.gif);
  float: left;
  margin-right: 1em;
  margin-left: 1em;
}
ul.breadcrumb-items li.first {
  margin-left: 0px;
  list-style: none;
}
```

These first definition instructs the browser to display the list as a single row of links, using the `orange_dot.gif` image (the same one we used before) instead of a bullet.

But we don't want the first item to display a bullet. Nor do we want a blank space on the left. So we create a second definition that applies only to the first item in the list.

The HTML output is now a little more elegant than the previous version:

```
<div class="breadcrumb">
  <div class="item-list">
    <ul class="breadcrumb-items">
      <li class="first"><a href="/drupal/">Home</a></li>
      <li class="last"><a href="/drupal/?q=node/add">Create
        content</a></li>
    </ul>
  </div>
</div>
```

Notice that the `theme_item_list()` function wrapped the returned list in a `<div/>` with the `item-list` class. This makes it easier to apply global styles to all lists rendered through the theme.

What does this look like when rendered by the browser? It should look something like this:

Since the HTML is now based on lists, we can now do any fine tuning of the appearance in pure CSS.

The `template.php` file provides a convenient way to override the default theme behavior. It also provides access to data before the data is handed on to the template. Accessing such data before it is themed is called **preprocessing**. For example, you can make additional variables accessible to the `page.tpl.php` template by overriding the `theme_preprocess_page()` hook. See the API documentation for details: `http://api.drupal.org/api/function/template_preprocess_page/6`.

template.php Gotchas

When using a `template.php` file in PHPTemplate themes, there are a couple of things you might want to watch out for.

First, you can only override a theme function once. While this seems simple, there is one circumstance in which this may be surprising.

While you can declare a `template.php` file in a sub-theme even if there is a `template.php` in the parent, you cannot override functions declared in the parent. If the parent's `template.php` declares `phptemplate_breadcrumb()`, then the sub-theme's `template.php` cannot declare `phptemplate_breadcrumb()`. Doing so will result in a PHP errors for redeclaring a function.

Second, we have seen that theme hooks (`theme_<hookname>()`) can be overridden by PHPTemplate templates and also by functions in the `template.php` file. But what happens if you declare both?

The `phptemplate_<hookname>()` function overrides the theme function that would otherwise load the template. Therefore, if `phptemplate_block()` is defined in `template.php` and there is a template named `block.tpl.php`, the `phptemplate_block()` function will be called to render all blocks, and the `block.tpl.php` file will never be used.

If you need to manipulate some content before it is passed to a template, don't do this by defining `phptemplate_<hookname>()`. Instead, use one of the preprocessor functions, such as `phptemplate_preprocess_block()`, `phptemplate_preprocess_node()`, or `phptemplate_preprocess_page()`.

At this point, we've created a new theme. We've added custom CSS, images, PHPTemplate files, and even some custom theme hooks... what else does it take to complete a theme?

One more thing.

Creating a Screenshot

A complete theme ought to have a screenshot that can be displayed in the theme manager in **Administer | Site building | Themes**.

Once the theme is completed, we can generate a screenshot, scale it to the requisite 150x90 pixel dimensions, and then save it as a PNG image named `screenshot.png`.

All we need to do now is copy `screenshot.png` into our theme directory and Drupal will automatically display it as necessary.

If for some reason you want to name the screenshot something else, you can set the `screenshot` directive in the theme's `.info` file: `screenshot = image.png`.

That's it. We're done creating our new theme.

Of course, this theme is a derivative theme. What does it take to go on and build a top level theme—one with no parent?

From Here to a Full Theme

We have been looking at sub-themes. But technically speaking, it is not that difficult to move from here to a top-level theme. Since theming is not the focus of the book, we will just glance at what it takes to create a full theme.

If the theme is based on PHPTemplates, the process of creating a top-level theme doesn't differ much from what we have done already. You will need to make sure to do a few things. Here is a short checklist:

- Create a theme `.info` file that doesn't set the `base theme` to some other theme. Instead of using the `base theme` directive, you should use the engine directive: `engine = phptemplate`.
- Create all the major templates: `page.tpl.php`, `node.tpl.php`, `block.tpl.php`, and `comment.tpl.php`. Of course, you can create others, as well.
- Add a `logo.png` image. Of course, you can use one of the standard Druplicon images as a starting point (`http://drupal.org/node/9068`).
- Create a `style.css` file, as well as any other CSS files the theme needs. The `style-rtl.css` ("right to left") and `print.css` stylesheets are good to include.
- Add a `screenshots.png` image with a 150x90 screenshot of your theme.

The included Pushbutton and Bluemarine themes are good guides for getting started. In short, though, it is a small step from creating derivative themes to creating top-level themes.

More advanced PHPTemplate themes may also make use of the `template.php` preprocessing page, additional JavaScript files, and other rich features. Garland is an example of a complex theme.

For more information on developing themes, including links to the relevant APIs and auxiliary documents, the official Drupal theme tutorial is the best place to go: `http://drupal.org/node/165706`.

Summary

In this chapter, we created a sub-theme derived from the Bluemarine template included with Drupal 6. After an overview of the theme architecture, we created the Descartes theme. Initially, we made changes using only CSS. Then we added a custom PHPTemplate. To add a little additional functionality, we implemented the `theme_breadcrumb()` function in our `template.php` file. And we wrapped up our theme by adding a screenshot. Finally, we took a look at the steps necessary for moving from a sub-theme on to an independent theme.

But this chapter isn't the last time we will hear about themes. As we continue creating new modules, we will make use of our newly-gained theme knowledge to provide default theming for new content and to interact with the theme system from within a module.

4
Theming Modules

In the last chapter, we took a look at the Drupal theme system, and created our own theme. This chapter will begin where we left off, but with a twist—this time we will create a module with a default theme. To do this, we will develop a new module.

The Philosophy Quotes module that we will create in this chapter will use Drupal's theme system and a simple database query to theme the content of a custom content type.

Here are some of the items we will cover while working on this module:

- Creating a custom content type
- Performing simple database operations
- Registering a module's theme functions with the `hook_theme()` function
- Adding theme hooks to a module
- Adding CSS stylesheets to a module's default theme
- Using theme CSS and template files to override default module theme functions

In the next chapter, we will continue with this module. There, we will augment our Philosophy Quotes module with some JavaScript.

Our Target Module: What We Want

Before we begin developing a module, here's a brief overview of what we want to accomplish.

The module we will write in this chapter is the Philosophy Quotes module (`philquotes` will be our machine-readable name). The goal of this module will be to create a block that displays pithy philosophical quotes.

We will implement the following features:

- Quotes should be stored along with other basic content, making it possible to add, modify, and delete this content in exactly the same way that we create other articles.
- Since our existing themes aren't aware of this quotes module, it must provide some default styling.

We will progress through the creation of this module by first generating a new "quote" content type, and then building a theme-aware module.

Creating a Custom Content Type

As Drupal evolved, it incorporated an increasingly sophisticated method for defining content. Central to this system is the idea of the **content type**. A content type is a definition, stored in Drupal's database, of how a particular class of content should be displayed and what functionality it ought to support.

Out of the box, Drupal has two defined content types: Page and Story. Pages are intended to contain content that is static, like an "About Us" or "Contact Us" page. Stories, on the other hand, are intended to contain more transient content—news items, blog postings, and so on.

Creating new pages or stories is as simple as clicking on the **Create Content** link in the default menu.

Obviously, not all content will be classified as either a page or a story, and many sites will need specialized content types to adequately represent a specific class of content. Descriptions of events, products, component descriptions, and so on might all be better accomplished with specialized content types.

Our module is going to display brief quotes. These quotes shouldn't be treated like either articles or pages. For example, we wouldn't want a new quote to be displayed along with site news in the center column of our front page.

Thus, our quotes module needs a custom content type. This content type will be very simple. It will have two parts: the text of the quote and the origin of the quote.

For example, here's a famous quote:

The life of man [is] solitary, poor, nasty, brutish, and short. — Thomas Hobbes.

The text of this quote is "The life of man [is] solitary, poor, nasty, brutish, and short", and the origin in this example is *Thomas Hobbes*. We could have been more specific and included the title of the work (*Leviathan*) or even the exact page reference, edition, and so on. But all this information, in our simple example, would be treated as the quote's origin.

Given the simplicity of our content type, we can simply use the built-in Drupal content type tool to create the new type.

To generate even more sophisticated content types, we could install the **CCK (Content Creation Kit)** module, and perhaps some of the CCK extension modules. CCK provides a robust set of tools for defining custom fields, data types, and features. (And in the next chapter, we will code our own Drupal content type.)

But here our needs are simple, so we won't need any additional modules or even any custom code to create this new content type.

Using the Administration Interface to Create a Content Type

The process of creating our custom content type is as simple as logging into Drupal and filling out a form.

The content type tool is in **Administer | Content management | Content types**. There are a couple of tabs at the top of the page:

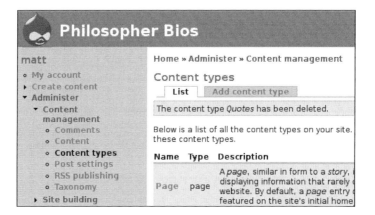

Clicking the **Add content type** tab will load the form used to create our new content type.

Content types

| List | **Add content type** |

To create a new content type, enter the human-readable name, the machine-readable name, and all other relevant fields that are on this page. Once created, users of your site will be able to create posts that are instances of this content type.

Identification

Name: *

Quote

The human-readable name of this content type. This text will be displayed as part of the list on the *create content* page. It is recommended that this name begin with a capital letter and contain only letters, numbers, and **spaces**. This name must be unique.

Type: *

quote

The machine-readable name of this content type. This text will be used for constructing the URL of the *create content* page for this content type. This name must contain only lowercase letters, numbers, and underscores. Underscores will be converted into hyphens when constructing the URL of the *create content* page. This name must be unique.

Description:

Quotations and witticisms.

A brief description of this content type. This text will be displayed as part of the list on the *create content* page.

On this form, we need to complete the **Name** and **Type** fields — the first with a human-friendly name, and the second with a computer-readable name. Description is often helpful.

In addition to these fields, there are a few other form fields under the **Submission form settings** and **Workflow settings** that we need to change.

▼ Submission form settings

Title field label: *

Origin

Body field label:

Text

To omit the body field for this content type, remove any text and leave this field blank.

Minimum number of words:

0 ▾

The minimum number of words for the body field to be considered valid for this content type. This can be useful to rule out submissions that do not meet the site's standards, such as short test posts.

Explanation or submission guidelines:

This text will be displayed at the top of the submission form for this content type. It is useful for helping or instructing your users.

▼ Workflow settings

Default options:

☑ Published

☐ Promoted to front page

☐ Sticky at top of lists

☐ Create new revision

Users with the *administer nodes* permission will be able to override these options.

In the **Submission form settings** section, we will change the labels to match the terminology we have been using. Instead of **Title** and **Body**, our sections will be **Origin** and **Text**.

> Changing labels is a superficial change. While it changes the text that is displayed to users, the underlying data model will still refer to these fields as `title` and `body`. We will see this later in the chapter.

In the **Workflow settings** section, we need to make sure that only **Published** is checked. By default, **Promoted to front page** is selected. That should be disabled unless you want new quotes to show up as content in the main section of the front page.

Once the form is complete, pressing the **Save content type** button will create the new content type.

That's all there is to it. The **Create content** menu should now have the option of creating a new quote:

As we continue, we will create a module that displays content of type `quote` in a block.

Before moving on, we want a few pieces of content. Otherwise, our module would have no data to display.

Here's the list of quotes (as displayed on **Administer | Content management | Content**) that will constitute our pool of quotations for our module.

Title	Type	Author	Status	Operations
W. V. Quine	Quote	matt	published	edit
R. Descartes	Quote	matt	not published	edit
T. Hobbes	Quote	matt	published	edit
P. Feyerabend, Against Method	Quote	matt	published	edit
F. Nietzsche	Quote	matt	published	edit
W. V. Quine	Quote	matt	published	edit
S. Kierkegaard	Quote	matt	published	edit

Content and Nodes

How does Drupal treat content for this custom content type and where is the content that we create stored?

Drupal treats such content—even for custom content types—as **nodes**. A node is a generic data type that represents a piece of content. Drupal assigns each node a **Node ID (NID)**, which is unique within the Drupal installation. Along with the basic information that the node comprises (like title and body), Drupal also tracks information on the status of the node, modifications of the node, related comments, and so on.

Nodes are stored inside the Drupal database. In fact, there are several database tables devoted to maintaining nodes. Later on, we will interact with the database to retrieve our quotes. However, the module we create in this chapter will only make scant direct use of the database layer.

Now that we have a custom content type and a few new content items, we are ready to proceed to module development.

The Foundations of the Module

In the second chapter, we developed a module with the `.info` and `.module` files. These files are common to all modules, and we will begin this module by creating `.info` and `.module` files.

Our module will be named `philquotes`, and (as would be expected) will be located in `drupal/sites/all/modules/philquotes`.

Inside that directory, we will first create a standard module `.info` file: `philquotes.info`.

```
; $Id$
name = "Philosophy Quotes"
description = "Dynamic display of philosophy quotes."
core = 6.x
php = 5.1
```

There should be nothing unfamiliar about the above code. It follows the same format as the module we created in Chapter 2.

Next, we will start our new `philquotes.module` file:

```
<?php
// $Id$
/**
 * @file
 * Module for dynamic display of pithy philosophy quotes.
 */
/**
 * Implementation of hook_help()
 */
function philquotes_help($path, $arg) {

  if ($path == 'admin/help#philquotes') {
    $txt = 'This module displays philosophical quotes in blocks. '.
      'It assumes the existence of a content type named "quote".';
    return '<p>'. t($txt) .'</p>';
  }
}
```

The above code implements `hook_help()` to provide some information about the module. This is also similar to the code we wrote in Chapter 2.

Just as with the module in Chapter 2, our `philquotes` module is mainly intended to provide block content.

Next, we will implement `hook_block()` — the hook that controls what content is displayed in a block. (A description of this hook was also given in Chapter 2.)

Here's our block hook:

```
/**
 * Implementation of hook_block().
 */
function philquotes_block($op = 'list', $delta = 0, $edit = array()) {
  switch ($op) {
```

```
    case 'list':
      $blocks[0]['info'] = t('Philosophical Quotes');
      return $blocks;
    case 'view':
      $item = _philquotes_get_quote();
      if(!empty($item)) {
        $content = theme('philquotes_quote',
          check_plain($item->body),
          check_plain($item->title));

        $blocks['subject'] = t('Pithy Quote');
        $blocks['content'] = $content;
        return $blocks;
      }
  }
}
```

For the most part, this code should also look familiar. In the case where the operation ($op) passed into the hook is list, this should simply return information about the blocks this hook makes available. In our case, there is just one block.

The more important case for us, though, is the highlighted section above. In the case where view is passed in as the operation, the module should be returning some content destined for display to the user. This content is wrapped in the $blocks variable.

As far as this hook_block() implementation is concerned, we will focus on the highlighted portion above.

When a block is generated for viewing, every block item contains two pieces: a subject and some content. The subject of our block will always be Pithy Quote, but the content is generated by a two-step process:

- Getting a quote from the database
- Adding any necessary theming information to that quote

In the above code, this is done by the following two statements:

```
$item = _philquotes_get_quote();
if(!empty($item) {
  $content = theme('philquotes_quote',
    check_plain($item->body),
    check_plain($item->title));
  // ...
}
```

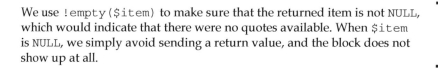

We use !empty($item) to make sure that the returned item is not NULL, which would indicate that there were no quotes available. When $item is NULL, we simply avoid sending a return value, and the block does not show up at all.

The first statement performs the database lookup, and the second handles theming. Let's take a detailed look at each.

A Simple Database Lookup

The philquotes_block() hook calls the _philquotes_get_quote() function to get content for display. The _philquotes_get_quote() function is considered a private (module only) function, since it begins with the underscore character.

The task of this private function will be to return a single quote content item from the database. Quotes are stored as nodes. To add some spice to our module, we'll get a random quote node rather than progressing sequentially through the quotes.

The process of retrieving our content item can be broken down into two steps:

1. We need to get the node ID of the random quote we are going to display.
2. We need to retrieve the node's data, specifically the title (which contains the quote's origin) and the body (which holds the text of the quote).

To accomplish these tasks, we will use the Drupal API on two levels. To get a random node ID, we will have to write some simple (but low-level) SQL. Once we have that, though, we can use a higher-level function to get the node's content.

Getting the Node ID

The first step is to get the Node ID for a quote. To get this, we will interact with the database using Drupal's database API.

The database API provides low-level access to the database using SQL statements. Drupal will handle the details of connection management. It also provides some level of type checking, string escaping, and other protective features.

We will look at more features of the database API in later chapters (especially Chapters 6 and 7). Here, though, we need to construct only a basic query.

Drupal developers have provided a useful overview of the database API. It is available as part of the standard API docs: http://api.drupal. org/api/group/database/6.

The Drupal database has six tables devoted to node maintenance. Right now, we only need to use one directly: the node table. As the generic name implies, this is a high-level table that contains basic information about each node in Drupal.

The node ID is the only field we need returned from the node table. But we don't want just any node from the table to be returned. What constraints must be placed on the returned node?

- We want the node to be published. By default, our quotes are published on creation, but it is possible that one was unpublished, and we don't want to display such a node. The status field in the node table indicates whether a node is published (1) or unpublished (0).
- We want the node to have the content type quote. The type field in the node table contains the name of the node's content type.

Those are the only constraints we need to place. Of course, constraints can be a lot more complicated—we could limit it to only quotes newer than last week, or quotes that are owned by a particular user, and so on. Such restraints would be implemented in SQL.

Now we have all the information we need to construct our SQL. If we were to run the query from a MySQL monitor, it would look as follows:

```
SELECT nid FROM node
WHERE status=1 AND type='quote'
ORDER BY RAND() LIMIT 1
```

This will return one random node ID for a node that is published (status=1) and is of the right content type (type='quote').

To execute a similar query using Drupal's database API, we need to make a minor change.

Wrapping the SQL in PHP code, we create a function that looks as follows:

```
function _philquotes_get_quote() {
  $sql = "SELECT nid FROM {node} ".
      "WHERE status=1 AND type='quote' ORDER BY RAND() LIMIT 1";
  $res = db_query($sql);
  $item = db_fetch_object($res);
  // Do something with the $item.
}
```

The $sql variable contains our quote, but in a slightly altered form. Instead of referring directly to the table name, we have substituted a **table placeholder** denoted by curly braces. Before executing the query, Drupal will substitute the correct name of the table where the {node} placeholder appears.

> Table name placeholders provide administrators the ability to change table names to better fit existing conventions. For example, some ISPs require that all tables have certain pre-determined prefixes. By using table name placeholders, we can avoid the need to make changes to code when table names are changed in the database.

The Drupal `db_query()` function handles the execution of the query. It returns a resource handle (`$res`) that can be used to manipulate the results of the query.

The `db_fetch_object()` function provides access to the rows returned from the database.

Our query was limited to only one result. So rather than looping through the result set, we can simply fetch the first returned item: `$item = db_fetch_object($res);`.

Now we have an object, `$item`, that contains the `$nid` attribute. We can use this attribute to access the contents of the node.

Getting the Node's Content

Armed with the Node ID, we can retrieve a specific piece of content from the database.

To do this, we *could* write another (more complex) SQL statement to get the node contents. Since node content is spread across multiple tables, we would have to make use of a couple of joins to get the desired content. Fortunately, there is a simpler way.

The Drupal node API provides a convenient function that does the heavy lifting for us: `node_load()`. If we pass this function the NID, it will return an object that contains the node's contents.

>
> Nodes are implemented using a Drupal module. The main node API (found in `drupal/modules/node/node.module`) provides dozens of methods for working with nodes.

Using `node_load()`, we can finish off our function as follows:

```
function _philquotes_get_quote() {
  $sql = "SELECT nid FROM {node} ".
         "WHERE status=1 AND type='quote' ORDER BY RAND() LIMIT 1";
  $res = db_query($sql);
  $item = db_fetch_object($res);
  $quote = node_load($item->nid);
  return $quote;
}
```

Only the highlighted lines are new. All we are doing here is fetching the complete node object with `node_load()`, and then returning this object. (If `node_load()` is given a NULL value, it simply returns FALSE. We are relying on the `philquotes_block()` function to deal with empty results.)

What does this do in the context of our module? Let's look back at the lines of `philquotes_block()` that we worked on earlier:

```
$item = _philquotes_get_quote();
if(!empty($item)) {
  $content = theme('philquotes_quote',
    check_plain($item->body),
    check_plain($item->title));
```

The `$item` variable in `philquotes_block()` now contains the node object we just retrieved with `_philquotes_get_quote()` (the value of `$quote`). We have the data we need. Now we need to format it for display.

Next, we will look at the `theme()` function (and some related code), and how it handles turning our object into a themed string.

Theming Inside a Module

Once the `philquotes_block()` function has obtained the content of a quote, it must add some formatting and styling to the data. This is handled with functions that make use of the theme system. And the first stage is handled with the `theme()` function.

We took a look at the `theme()` function in the last chapter. But there we were primarily interested in creating themes. Here, we are working on a module. In the module, we want to provide some default theming, but in a way that makes use of the theme system. This provides more flexibility: theme developers can change the layout of our module without having to change any of our code.

> **Default Themes**
>
> Often, a module adds content that existing themes do not already provide layout information for. In such cases, the module developer should provide a **default theme**. A default theme should provide layout information for the new content that the module makes available.

The `theme()` function is called in `philquotes_block()` with three parameters:

```
$content = theme('philquotes_quote',
  check_plain($item->body),
  check_plain($item->title));
```

The first, `philquotes_quote`, tells the `theme()` function which theme hook should be executed. The `theme()` function will query the theme system to find an implementation of a function called `theme_philquotes_quote()` or a template called `philquotes_quote`.

Neither a matching function nor a matching theme exists in the default installation of Drupal. But in a moment, we will solve this problem by creating a default theme function that will be part of our module.

The next two parameters are the body and title of the quote we want to display. (Recall that `$item` is the object that contains the content of our random quote node.)

The `theme()` function itself does not do anything special with parameters after the first. Instead, they are passed on to the special theme hook (in this case, `theme_philquotes_quote()`).

Check the Content

In the last chapter, we looked at `check_plain()` and other content checking functions. Why do we use `check_plain()` here? The content of a quote may contain HTML content, and some of the HTML may not be safe. So before passing this data on to the theme system, it ought to be escaped. In this case, we want HTML-escaped text, so we use `check_plain()`. Failure to properly escape content can lead to security vulnerabilities.

Where will the `theme()` function, which now must find `theme_philquotes_quote()`, look for themes? One place it will look is inside the currently enabled theme. In our case, this is the Descartes theme we created in the last chapter. But there is no `philquotes_quote` function or template in that theme.

Drupal's theme system will also look among other **registered themes**. Modules can register their own theme functions, making these themes available to the theme system. If no theming is provided by the default theme, the module's theme will be used. Since our module is providing new content that needs some theming, we will need to register a theming function to provide default theming.

In Chapter 2, we created the Goodreads module. The output generated by that module was hard-coded HTML. To improve that module, we could make use of the theme system in much the same way that we are about to do for this module.

Registering a Theme

The `philquotes` module needs to register a theme function that takes a `quote` content item and formats it for display as an HTML block.

Essentially, when a theme is registered, it declares new theme hooks, which other parts of the theme system can use or override.

To register the module's default theme, we need to implement the theme registration hook (`hook_theme()`), following the naming convention `<modulename>_theme()`, where `<modulename>` is the name of the module:

```
/**
 * Implementation of hook_theme().
 */
function philquotes_theme() {
  return array(
    'philquotes_quote' => array(
      'arguments' => array('text' => NULL, 'origin' => NULL),
    ),
  );
}
```

In a nutshell, this function provides the theme system with a comprehensive list of what theme functions (hooks) are provided by this module, and how each function should be called.

There are a lot of different configurations that we might want for a theme hook. Unfortunately, the result of this is that the data structure that `hook_theme()` must return is a daunting series of nested associative arrays.

In the above example, the arrays are nested three-deep. Let's start with the outermost array.

The outermost array contains elements of the form `'theme_function_name' =>` `configuration_array`. In the above example, it looks as follows:

```
return array(
  'philquotes_quote' => array(
    // Contents of the array...
  ),
);
```

The `theme_function_name` string should be the name of a theme hook that this module implements or provides. In our theme, for example, we will provide a theme for `philquotes_quote`.

The actual name of the theme hook function will be `theme_philquotes_quote()`, but the `theme_` portion is omitted when we register the handler.

The value of this array element, `configuration_array`, is another associative array that provides Drupal with information about how this module handles the theme. We will look at this array in a moment.

The outer array may register more than one theme function. For example, we might register three different theme functions for a module as follows:

```
return array(
  'mytheme_a' => array( /* settings */ );
  'mytheme_b' => array( /* settings */ );
  'mytheme_c' => array( /* settings */ );
);
```

This code would register three theme hooks, each with an array of configuration options.

We are registering only one theme hook, though, and we can now take a closer look at the second level of associative arrays.

This array will contain configuration information about how this module implements the theme hook. Let's look at the configuration options that our `philquotes_quote` theme hook will have:

```
'philquotes_quote' => array(
  'arguments' => array( /* parameter info */ ),
),
```

The value for the `philquotes_quote` key in the outer array is itself an associative array. The keys that this array holds are well defined, and all the eight keys are explained in the `hook_theme()` API documentation (`http://api.drupal.org/api/function/hook_theme/`).

For example, the `template` key can be used to point to a template file that should be used instead of a theme function. Had we chosen to use a template file called `philquotes_quote.tpl.php`, we could have called the above as follows:

```
'philquotes_quote' => array(
  'template' => 'philquotes_quote',
  'arguments' => array( /* parameter info */ ),
),
```

When `theme_philquotes_quote()` is called with these parameters, it would look for a file called `philquotes_quote.tpl.php` inside the `philquotes` module directory. (The template file extension is appended automatically.)

In this example, the items in the `arguments` array would be passed in as variables to the template. To see an example of a module template, see Chapter 8.

Other similar directives exist for adding preprocessing functions, including other PHP files, and so on.

For our module, however, we will implement the hook as a function. The only directive we want in this array is `arguments`.

In the context of a hook function (as opposed to a template), this array entry is used to indicate what parameters will be passed to the function.

For our module hook, we only need two: `text` and `origin`.

```
/**
 * Implementation of hook_theme()
 */
function philquotes_theme() {
  return array(
    'philquotes_quote' => array(
      'arguments' => array('text' => NULL, 'origin' => NULL),
    ),
  );
}
```

Items in the `arguments` array are of the form `'argument_name' =>
default_value`.

Initially, we set both values to NULL; however, if we want to provide more robust default values, we could do so here.

Based on this array, we can now construct the method signature of our theme hook. It will be:

```
function theme_philquotes_quote($text, $origin)
```

The name of the function is the hook name with `theme_` prepended, and the two parameters here should correspond to the elements in the `arguments` array.

Now we are ready to create this function.

Creating a Theme Hook Function

We have just created a theme registration function, overriding the `hook_theme()` function for our module. In it, we have declared that this module implements a hook called `theme_philquotes_quote()` that takes two arguments, `$text` and `$origin`. Now we will create that function.

The goal of this function is to take the same content (a single quote) and configure it for display. Here is our first version of this function, which will provide a basic display of the quote:

```
/**
 * Theme function for theming quotes.
 *
 * @param $text
 *   The quote content as a string.
 * @param $origin
 *   The original source of the quote, as a string.
 * @return
 *   An HTML themed string.
 */
function theme_philquotes_quote($text, $origin) {
  $output = '<div id="philquotes-text">'. t($text)
    .'</div><div id="philquotes-origin">'. t($origin) .'</div>';
  return $output;
}
```

All we have done in this function is wrap the content of the `$text` and `$origin` variables in `<div/>` tags, each of which has an `id` attribute.

Looking back at our `philquotes_block()` function, we can see what happens from here: The string that this function returns will be rendered as a block item. When it is rendered, it should look something like this:

> **Pithy Quote**
> Purity of heart is to will one thing.
> S. Kierkegaard

The header, **Pithy Quote**, comes from `philquote_block()`, while the text and origin of the quote are rendered into two un-styled `<div/>` elements. We have taken our node content and formatted it as HTML.

The block might not show up for two reasons. First, if there are no published quotes, nothing will be displayed here. Second, the block cache may need to be cleared. The cache-clearing tool included with the Devel module can do this for you. See Chapters 1 and 3 for more on the Devel module.

But this formatting of our quote is not particularly attractive. We can improve it by adding a CSS stylesheet to our module.

Adding a Stylesheet

Earlier, the theme_philquotes_quote() function wrapped our quote's text and origin information inside of two <div/> tags. Each tag has a unique id attribute:

- philquotes-text
- philquotes-origin

Using those IDs, we can create a stylesheet that styles those two elements.

By convention, a module's main stylesheet should be named <module_name>. css (where <module_name> is the name of the module). As with all other module files, this file belongs inside the module directory (drupal/sites/all/modules/ philquotes, for this example). Our philquotes.css file looks as follows:

```
#philquotes-text:first-letter {
    font-size: 18pt;
    font-weight: bold;
}
#philquotes-origin {
  font-style: oblique;
  text-align: right;
  margin-right: 5px;
}
```

Here we have a simple stylesheet. When used, it will add some additional styling to our bland HTML.

However, simply having the stylesheet (and naming it correctly) is not enough to add this style to the default theme. Drupal does not automatically include a module's stylesheet when the page is rendered. We have to tell the theme system to include it.

Adding a stylesheet is done with a built-in function: `drupal_add_css()`. Using this function in our `theme_philquotes_quote()` hook, we can instruct the theme system to include the module's CSS file along with the other stylesheets Drupal will list in the HTML it sends to the client.

```
function theme_philquotes_quote($text, $origin) {
  $module_path = drupal_get_path('module', 'philquotes');
  $full_path =  $module_path .'/philquotes.css';

  drupal_add_css($full_path);

  $output = '<div id="philquotes-text">'. t($text)
    .'</div><div id="philquotes-origin">' . t($origin) . '</div>';
  return $output;
}
```

The above highlighted lines show the necessary modifications. Before Drupal can load the stylesheet, it must have the full path to the location of that stylesheet. The CSS file is located in our module, and we can construct the full path to this module using the `drupal_get_path()` function. Then we can append `/philquotes.css` to the string returned by `drupal_get_path()`.

`drupal_get_path()` is another useful function that is often needed for module development. It takes two arguments.

The first is the item type, which (for module developers) is usually either `theme` or `module`, depending on whether the path is part of a theme or a module. The second parameter is the name of the theme or module that this should get the path for. To get the path of the Descartes theme we created in the last chapter, then, we could use `drupal_get_path('theme', 'descartes')`.

> For the details of `drupal_get_path()`, see `http://api.drupal.com/api/function/drupal_get_path`.

We can now pass `$full_path` into the `drupal_add_css()`, which will include a link to our CSS file in the header of the HTML output when this module is used.

The output from our module should now look something as follows:

> **Pithy Quote**
>
> **P**urity of heart is to will one thing.
>
> *S. Kierkegaard*

With the addition of our stylesheet, the output of our `philquotes` module is now styled.

What we have done so far is created a default theme for our module. But why go through all of this trouble when we could have just hard-coded the HTML into the module?

Here is one very good reason.

By creating a default theme, we have ensured that our module can be displayed regardless of whether a theme developer created templates or theme functions specifically for our module.

Yet by using the theme system, we have also made it possible for a theme designer to override (or modify) our default theme. Thus, a theme developer can change the layout and styling for our module's content without having to edit a line of the module's code.

In the next section, we will see how this is done.

Overriding the Default Theme from a Theme

One of the chief advantages of using the theme system in a module is that it affords the theme developer the ability to use a module, but theme the module's contents as desired. Here we will take a look at theming module contents from a theme.

A Quick Clarification

We are now treading on the verges of terminological overload. The word 'theme' runs the risk of becoming ambiguous. So let's pause for just a moment and get clear on what we are about to do.

Thus far, we have been working on a *module*. In this module, we have created a *default theme*. This *default theme* has provided layout for this module's content. The default theme is used when the site's theme (be it Descartes, Bluemarine, Garland, or another theme) does not provide facilities for handling this module's content.

Now we are going to take a lateral step and work on a *theme*. We are switching directories from `drupal/sites/all/modules` to `drupal/sites/all/themes`.

In the previous chapter, we created the Descartes theme, which made use of PHPTemplate templates to render content into HTML. We are going to revisit that theme here (though this same process could be applied to any theme).

We will modify that theme, creating an alternative presentation of the quotes that are retrieved from our `philquotes` module. In other words, we are *overriding the module's default theme*.

We will look at two ways of doing this. One method will override the CSS styling only, and the other will make use of PHPTemplates to override the theme hook.

Overriding the Default Theme's CSS

If we look at in the `<head/>` section of a page that uses the `philquotes` block, we should see a link to the module's stylesheet:

```
<link type="text/css" rel="stylesheet" media="all"
  href="/drupal/sites/all/modules/devel/devel.css" />
<link type="text/css" rel="stylesheet" media="all"
  href="/drupal/sites/all/modules/philquotes/philquotes.css" />
<link type="text/css" rel="stylesheet" media="all"
  href="/drupal/themes/bluemarine/style.css" />
<link type="text/css" rel="stylesheet" media="all"
  href="/drupal/sites/all/themes/descartes/new.css" />
```

The highlighted link was added by the module's call to `drupal_add_css()`.

What if we want to override the styles from that file?

The placement of the CSS files is significant. Module CSS files are always loaded before theme CSS files. That way, theme files can use the CSS cascade rules to override or augment the styles specified in a module's CSS. (See the CSS2 specification for more information on the cascade: `http://www.w3.org/TR/CSS21/cascade.html`.)

Because of the order, the theme developer can override the module's default CSS by adding CSS statements to the theme's stylesheets.

So, for example, we could change the style of the `<div id="philquotes-text"/>` element simply by adding a few lines to the end of the `new.css` file we created for the Descartes theme:

```
#philquotes-text {
  color: pink;
}
```

This change doesn't directly override any of the styling added by the `philquotes.css`. Instead, it augments existing style.

Now, in addition to the styles already added by `philquotes.css`, the text of the quote will be rendered in a lovely shade of pale pink:

```
Pithy Quote

The life of man [is] solitary,
poor, nasty, brutish, and
short.
                    T. Hobbes
```

In this way, theme developers can override and extend the default CSS defined in the module.

Overriding Layout with Templates

In addition to being able to override CSS directives, a theme developer can also override the module's default theme hook. For example, we could create a simple template file in the Descartes theme to override the layout provided by the `philquotes` module's `theme_philquotes_quote()` function.

For the theme engine to recognize that this template is overriding the `theme_philquotes_quote()` hook implementation, it must be named `philquotes_quote.tpl.php`.

As an example, we can create a simple template in `drupal/sites/all/themes/descartes/philqyotes_quote.tpl.php` that looks as follows:

```php
<?php
// $Id$
?>
<div id="philquotes-text">
<?php print $text; ?>
</div>
<div id="philquotes-origin" style="background-color: #efefef">
<?php print $origin; ?>
</div>
```

This preserves the same basic structure as the previous module, but hard-codes in a background color. When rendered, the output would look something like this:

```
Pithy Quote
The life of man [is] solitary,
poor, nasty, brutish, and
short.
T. Hobbes
```

Note the light gray background in the origin section, as added in the preceding template.

But what happened to the other styles? Why isn't the origin in italics or the first letter of the quote's text in large caps?

The answer is found in the fact that the template overrode the `theme_philquotes_quote()` function. That function was responsible for the initial addition of the stylesheet with `drupal_add_css()`.

However, with the addition of the template, that function is no longer called and the stylesheet is no longer included. To include it, we would have to add the appropriate `stylesheets[all][]` directive to the theme's `.info` file.

```
stylesheets[all][] = style.css
stylesheets[all][] = new.css
stylesheet[all][] = philquotes.css
```

It is good for a module to provide a default theme, and when this is done correctly, it maximizes the effectiveness of Drupal's module and theme systems. A module will never be without a theme, but the theme developer will also be able to keep a module's look and feel consistent with the rest of the site.

Summary

In this chapter, we synthesized the knowledge of modules that we gained in Chapter 2 with the knowledge of the theme system from Chapter 3. We created a new module that provides a default theme.

In addition to this we worked with a simple custom content type and even made our first foray into the Drupal database API. At this point, we have a solid foundation for future module development.

In the upcoming chapters, we will start branching out, creating some more sophisticated modules. In the next chapter, we will continue developing the Philosophy Quotes module, integrating some sophisticated JavaScript and AJAX functionality. After that, we will turn to the administration interface, and create an administration module in Chapter 6. In Chapter 7, we will dive into the database API, creating a rich content type.

5
Using JavaScript and AJAX/ JSON in Modules

The module we created in the last chapter used the theme system to provide user-interface elements for our Philosophy Quotes module. In this chapter, we will pick up where we left off, and we will take steps toward a richer user interface.

In this chapter, we will use Drupal's JavaScript libraries (including the popular jQuery library) to add client-side features to the Philosophy Quotes module. We will also use AJAX (Aysnchronous JavaScript and XML) technology to dynamically change page contents without having to do a full page reload.

Here are some of the items we will cover while working on this module:

- Using the Drupal and jQuery JavaScript libraries
- Adding new locations (URLs) using `hook_menu()`
- Building a JSON (JavaScript Over the Network) service
- Fetching content using AJAX/JSON queries

Picking up Where We Left Off

In the last chapter, we built a module that read data from a custom content type, and displayed it as block content. This module made use of the Quote content type that we created. In order to provide layout information for our new content type, we created a default theme as part of the module. That theme code generated the necessary HTML and CSS for displaying quotes.

At the end of the last chapter, we overrode the module's default theme by adding a template to the Descartes theme. In this chapter, however, we will work on the default theme again. You will need to disable the `philquotes`-specific changes in the Descartes theme in order to work with the default theme again.

When our `philquotes` module is viewed as a block, a single quotation is displayed as the block's contents. The output looked somewhat as follows:

> **Pithy Quote**
>
> The only principle that does not inhibit progress is: anything goes.
> *P. Feyerabend, Against Method*

Now we will extend the `philquotes` module.

We will add features that make it possible to refresh the quotation without reloading the page. To do this, we will make use of several features of the Drupal JavaScript API, as well as the jQuery library.

So our module, when it is complete, should generate a block that looks as follows:

> **Pithy Quote**
>
> The only principle that does not inhibit progress is: anything goes.
> *P. Feyerabend, Against Method*
> **Next »**

Note the **Next >>** link at the bottom of this quote. When clicked, it should reload the origin and text of the quote above, choosing another random quote node from the database.

How will we get there from here? We'll start from our existing code. But most of that code will stay untouched. Our endeavor here will be additive.

The Philosophy Quotes module that we developed in the last chapter defined the following functions:

- `philquotes_help()`: An implementation of `hook_help()`. We will not make any changes to that function.

- `philquotes_block()`: An implementation of `hook_block()`. Since we will not change any of the block code, we will not do anything with this function, either.

- `philquotes_theme()`: An implementation of `hook_theme()`. This, too, is fine as it is.

They will not provide any new services for our update, though they do continue to perform an important role in the module. We will make use of the following functions:

- `_philquotes_get_quote()`: This private function handled the database query. Here, we will use the function in a different context.

- `theme_philquotes_quote()`: We will make some minor modifications to this function.

Of course, we will add some new functions to our module as we go. However, some of the big coding tasks in this chapter won't be in PHP. They will be in JavaScript.

> Debugging JavaScript can be a headache. The FireBug Firefox extension (`http://www.getfirebug.com/`) can be a big help. Along with a debugger, FireBug provides DOM (Document Object Model), HTML, and CSS browsing, an advanced logging facility, and command-line access to the JavaScript interpreter.

The first thing we will do is use some JavaScript to add some HTML into our page.

Introducing jQuery

jQuery is one of the most innovative JavaScript libraries to come around. Using an Object-Oriented design pattern called the **Fluent Interface**, jQuery makes it possible to chain a sequence of function calls together to construct elaborate queries.

What does jQuery query? Usually, it is used to query the DOM tree.

> A **DOM (Document Object Model) tree** is a data structure that defines the structure of a document—usually an HTML or XML document. The document is presented as a tree structure, where the first element is the root. The API is standardized (see `http://w3.org`).

DOM is known for its complex object model. jQuery provides an API that is more compact and easier to use.

However, it can be used for more than just querying. It has a suite of AJAX tools, tools for event handling, glitzy effects, and some very useful utility functions. We will use a little bit of everything in this chapter.

 For more information on jQuery, see `http://jquery.com`. A fantastic book entitled *Learning jQuery* by Karl Swedberg and Jonathan Chaffer (Packt Publishing, 2007), has received rave reviews as well.

The first thing we will do with jQuery is use it to find a particular location in the HTML generated by Drupal's template, and then insert some additional HTML elements into the DOM. This is the way we will add a link.

Modifying HTML with jQuery

The `philquotes` module's `hook_block()` implementation (in `philquotes.module`) creates a block of HTML that looks as follows:

```
<h2 class="title">Pithy Quote</h2>
<div class="content">
  <div id="philquotes-text">
    The only principle that does not inhibit progress is:
    anything goes.
  </div>
  <div id="philquotes-origin">
    P. Feyerabend, Against Method
  </div>
</div>
```

Two of the `<div/>` elements above, those with IDs `philquotes-text` and `philquotes-origin`, are created by the module's theme function, `theme_philquotes_quote()`.

Now we will begin writing some JavaScript code. This code will be part of our module, and it will go in its own file. Following standard naming conventions, the file will be stored in `drupal/sites/all/modules/philquotes/philquotes.js`.

The first thing that we want to do with our JavaScript is insert a **Next** link at the end of this block, just after the quote's origin.

jQuery provides the tools to do this simply and efficiently. With jQuery, this is a two-step process:

1. Find the `philquotes-origin` element
2. Insert a link after the element

The code is as follows:

```
$("#philquotes-origin").after("<a>Next &raquo;</a>");
```

This one line of code, at first glance, might appear to be both clean and confusing. Since we will be using jQuery several times in this chapter, we will devote a little time here to see what is going on.

The above line contains two function calls. The first function call looks like this: `$("#philquotes-origin")`. The function name, here, is `$()`. In JavaScript, the dollar sign ($) is a legal character when used in variable and function names. That means `countMy$()` and and `give$away()` are both valid function names in JavaScript. So is `$()`. By default, the jQuery library uses this function as a way to access the jQuery object. (You can also use the longer version, `jQuery()`, if you prefer.)

The `$()` function can be called several different ways, but the most common use of the function is to pass it a query, in the form of a CSS selector. (See `http://docs.jquery.com/Selectors` for a list of supported selectors.)

When jQuery is called this way, it searches the DOM tree for the current HTML and returns a jQuery object that contains a list of elements that match the query.

> The jQuery library is well documented. In addition to complete API documentation, there are also many tutorials on the topic. The best place to start is with the official jQuery documentation page: `http://docs.jquery.com/Main_Page`.

Looking back at our code above, the `$("#philquotes-origin")` call returns a jQuery object. Since the selector, `#philquotes-origin`, refers to an element ID, it will match no more than one element. According to our earlier HTML, it should match this element:

```
<div id="philquotes-origin">
  P. Feyerabend, Against Method
</div>
```

So our first call to `$()` returned a jQuery object. Making use of the fluent interface, we simply call the `after()` method on that returned object:

```
$("#philquotes-origin").after("<a>Next &raquo;</a>");
```

The `after()` method inserts content after the referenced element. In this case, it will put the content after the `<div/>` element above. So if we ran this query on a page with a quote on it, the resulting HTML would look like as follows:

```
<h2 class="title">Pithy Quote</h2>
<div class="content">
  <div id="philquotes-text">
```

```
    The only principle that does not inhibit progress is:
      anything goes.
  </div>
  <div id="philquotes-origin">
    P. Feyerabend, Against Method
  </div>
  <a>Next &raquo;</a>
</div>
```

While we don't make use of it in the code above, the `after()` function also returns a reference to the jQuery object, so we could continue chaining if we wanted.

> Using your browser's "View Source" feature will not show the newly inserted element. To see the source as it is modified by JavaScript, you will need FireBug or some other JavaScript development tool.

The jQuery object has a number of similar functions to `after()`. The `html()` function inserts HTML inside the selected element. The `before()` function inserts HTML before the selected element.

> **Getter or Setter?**
>
> One aspect of jQuery that can be startling at first is that one method may serve as both a getter and setter (or, an accessor and a mutator). That means that `html("<br/>")` will insert content into the current element and return a jQuery object, while `html()` (with no arguments) will not change anything, but will return the contents of the element.

What we have accomplished so far is the insertion of a small piece of HTML into our existing document. However, this little query alone may not work. Why?

There are two reasons:

- First, the browser may not support the requisite JavaScript. If this is the case, we don't want to insert this element at all.

- Second, the browser may execute the query before it has finished loading the HTML. In such a case, the query might not even find the `philequotes-origin` element.

We need to fix these two problems before moving on.

Checking for JavaScript Support with Drupal

For the first of our two steps we will use Drupal's JavaScript library.

The jQuery library introduced earlier is distributed with Drupal, but it contains no Drupal-specific code. JavaScript that is closely coupled with Drupal is stored in several different JavaScript files. The core functions, however, are all in `drupal/misc/drupal.js`.

Namespaces in JavaScript

All Drupal-specific JavaScript has a shared namespace in common. A **namespace** is an organized naming structure that signifies relationships between various pieces of code.

Without namespaces, function names are stored in the global namespace: `getURL()`, `toString()`, and so on. Such names, because they are common, are prone to collisions—multiple JavaScript libraries might use the same function name.

A namespace reduces the likelihood of this by using a distinctly named object or objects to serve as containers. Functions and variables are stored in that object, and accessed using the dot-notation.

Thus, the examples above would be called using the full namespace:

```
Philquotes.toString();
Philquotes.getURL();
```

Since the `toString()` and `getURL()` functions are contained by the `Philquotes` object, to access those functions, we must specify the complete namespace.

 Namespaces can be simple, as in the examples above. However, it is not uncommon to see namespaces used to produce organized hierarchies of objects, functions, and variables. Calling a function inside such a hierarchy might look something like this: `RSSFeeds.reader.getURL(rssUrl)`.

Drupal's Namespace

Drupal's JavaScript is organized into a hierarchically organized namespace. The top level of this namespace is `Drupal`. Commonly used JavaScript functions like the `t()` function and the `checkPlain()` function are stored directly under that namespace:

```
Drupal.t("Translate me!");
Drupal.checkPlain("<b>bold</b>");
```

> The `Drupal.t()` and `Drupal.checkPlain()` JavaScript functions perform tasks analogous to their PHP counterparts.

Many of the Drupal JavaScript functions that are designed to manipulate HTML content directly are stored in the `Drupal.behaviors` namespace. For example, the `Drupal.behaviors.teaser()` and `Drupal.behaviors.autocomplete()` functions are designed to alter HTML content from the client side.

In this chapter we will use functions directly under the `Drupal` namespace.

> **Respecting namespaces**
>
> The Drupal namespace is reserved for core Drupal JavaScript. Module developers should generally refrain from adding their own functions within the Drupal namespace. Instead, modules should have their own namespaces.

A Drupal Function: Drupal.jsEnabled()

The problem we are currently trying to solve is: We want to make sure that the jQuery query we created earlier only runs when the browser has the required level of JavaScript support.

If the browser does not support modern JavaScript and AJAX, we will not make any client-side modifications to the HTML.

Drupal's JavaScript library has a function for testing whether or not the client browser has the requisite level of JavaScript support. The function is named `Drupal.jsEnabled()`. This function returns `true` if the browser has adequate JavaScript support, and `false` otherwise.

The name is slightly misleading. `Drupal.jsEnabled()` checks for a specific level of support. A browser that has only some of the required features will *not* be marked by Drupal as JS-enabled. So a browser can support JavaScript, but not be considered by `Drupal.jsEnabled()` to be a JavaScript browser.

With this function, we can add to our `philquotes.js` file:

```
if(Drupal.jsEnabled) {
  $("#philquotes-origin").after("<a>Next &raquo;</a>");
}
```

Now the jQuery call will only be executed if the browser supports the modern JavaScript features needed by Drupal's JavaScript libraries.

We still have a problem, though. There is the distinct possibility that the jQuery call will be executed before the HTML is fully loaded. In that case, the new HTML may not be inserted.

Delaying JavaScript Execution with jQuery

There were two conditions we identified that would prevent our original HTML modification from working. The first, the issue of the browser's JavaScript support, was solved above.

The second problem was that the query might execute before the document was completely loaded. (A browser can start executing JavaScript as soon as the script is loaded—even if the entire page has not yet loaded.) We will solve that problem now.

Execution of the jQuery code must be delayed until the HTML is completely loaded (though we don't need to wait for the images or other files to load).

Again, jQuery provides a convenient method for handling this problem. It provides an event handling function, `ready()`, which executes a function only when the document is loaded.

The `ready()` function takes a function as a parameter. The function passed to `ready()` is then executed as soon as the page is loaded. Here's how we will use it:

```
if(Drupal.jsEnabled) {
  $(document).ready(
    function(){
      $("#philquotes-origin").after("<a>Next &raquo;</a>");
    }
  );
}
```

In the first highlighted line above, we use jQuery to select the document object: `$(document)`. In addition to using CSS selectors, jQuery can also select and operate on objects. The document object is the object that represents the DOM tree for the HTML page.

With the jQuery object returned by `$(document)`, we want to attach a new `ready()` event handler. Instead of creating a function elsewhere and then passing the function reference to `ready()`, the code in the example above creates an anonymous function.

```
$(document).ready(function() { /* Code here */ });
```

When the page is loaded and the DOM is ready for manipulation, the anonymous function will be executed.

Inside the anonymous function, we have inserted the HTML modification query that we created earlier.

In a nutshell, our script now does the following (in order):

- It checks to make sure adequate JavaScript support is enabled.
- Then, it adds an event listener that will be run when the document is loaded.
- When the document is loaded, it finds the element with the ID `philquotes-origin` and inserts a new link after that element.

The script file, `philquotes.js`, contains our code, and we are at a point where we can test out our JavaScript. However, we need to make sure that the JavaScript file is loaded.

Including JavaScript from the Module's Theme

We have a JavaScript file. But somehow we need to let Drupal know that whenever the `philquotes` block is used, a reference to the `philquotes.js` file needs to be inserted into the generated HTML.

Script files in HTML are referenced using the `<script/>` tag. Typically, this tag is inserted into the HTML's `<head/>` section, and that is where we want our script to go. However, the HTML that we directly control is a small portion of a block container nested somewhere in the page's body. How do we insert a script file reference into the header?

The answer to this question is similar to the strategy we used to include a CSS file. The script file is inserted inside the theming function, `theme_philquotes_quote()`, using a special Drupal function called `drupal_add_js()`.

Like its CSS counterpart, `drupal_add_css()`, the `drupal_add_js()` function notifies the theme system that a JavaScript file needs to be included in the header section.

Unlike its CSS counterpart, though, the `drupal_add_js()` function is considerably complex. This function can add a reference to a JavaScript file—which we will do shortly. However, it can also add arbitrary JavaScript, or even be used to extend the `Drupal.settings` JavaScript object. Here are some examples:

- `drupal_add_js("my.js")`: This will cause Drupal to insert a reference to the `my.js` file in the header. The file will be assumed to be a module's JavaScript file, which means that it will be loaded before any theme JavaScript files are loaded.

- `drupal_add_js('alert("Hello!")', 'inline')`: The second argument in this method, `inline`, tells Drupal not to treat the data in the first argument as a file name, but as a script. The script is then inserted as-is inside a `<script/>` tag: `<script>alert("Hello!")</script>`.

- `drupal_add_js(array("name" => "value"), 'settings')`: When the second argument is `settings`, then Drupal will attempt to take the associative array passed in the first value and append the key/value pairs to the `Drupal.settings` object. In the above example, then, a script referencing `Drupal.settings.name` would get the string `value`.

 As with other Drupal functions, the API documents describe this function in detail: `http://api.drupal.org/api/function/drupal_add_js/`.

Later in this chapter, we will use `drupal_add_js()` to extend the settings object. Now, however, we want to use the first version as we make a small modification to the `theme_philquotes_quote()` function of our module:

```
function theme_philquotes_quote($text, $origin) {
    $module_path = drupal_get_path('module', 'philquotes');
    $full_path =  $module_path .'/philquotes.css';

    drupal_add_css($full_path);
    drupal_add_js($module_path .'/philquotes.js');

    $output = '<div id="philquotes-text">'. t($text)
      .'</div><div id="philquotes-origin">' . t($origin) . '</div>';
    return $output;
}
```

The highlighted line above shows the use of `drupal_add_js()` to insert the reference to the `philquotes.js` file.

It is important to note that Drupal looks for the JavaScript file relative to the application's base path.

If we just used `drupal_add_js('philquotes.js')`, Drupal would create `<script/>` element looking something like `<script src="/philquotes.js"></script>` or `<script src="/drupal/philquotes.js">` (depending on where on your web server Drupal is installed).

Our script file, however, is located inside the `philquotes` module's directory. Rather than hard-code that path, we use the results of a call to the `drupal_get_path()` function described in the last chapter.

And now we are ready for the moment of truth. Reloading the page, the **Next** link should now show up.

```
Pithy Quote

The only principle that does
not inhibit progress is:
anything goes.
              P. Feyerabend, Against
                            Method
Next »
```

The **Next** link has been inserted dynamically by the JavaScript. The script file, `philquotes.js`, should be loaded somewhere in the HTML's head:

```
<script type="text/javascript"
  src="/drupal/misc/jquery.js"></script>
<script type="text/javascript"
  src="/drupal/misc/drupal.js"></script>
<script type="text/javascript"
  src="/drupal/sites/all/modules/devel/devel.js"></script>
<script type="text/javascript"
  src="/drupal/sites/all/modules/philquotes/philquotes.js"></script>
```

Notice that `jquery.js` and `drupal.js` are automatically included, as well. (`devel.js` comes from the Devel module described at the end of Chapter 1.)

But as it stands, the new `<a/>` element that is dynamically inserted does nothing. We are ready to take the next step.

What we want is: When the **Next** link is clicked, a new quote should be loaded and the new quote should be loaded without a full page reload. We can accomplish this with an AJAX request.

To make this happen, we have a fairly large task ahead of us. We need to write both ends of the AJAX service.

Writing a Drupal AJAX/JSON Service

AJAX stands for **Asynchronous JavaScript and XML**. AJAX refers to the practice of using JavaScript on the client side to retrieve XML from the server without requiring a page reload. This is typically done with the **XMLHttpRequest (XHR)** family of JavaScript objects.

However, the term is often used to capture a broader range of functionality than just XML over HTTP. For example the term AJAX is also used to describe retrieving fragments of HTML or JavaScript using XHR objects.

The JSON Format

One common alternative to using XML as the format for data exchange is to use the JSON format. **JSON (JavaScript Over the Network)** is a compact, easy-to-parse format that uses a syntax identical to JavaScript's array and object literal syntax.

 The JSON specification, along with numerous links to implementations and tutorials, can be found at `http://json.org/`.

For example, an XML document describing three British Empiricist philosophers might look as follows:

```
<empiricists>
  <name>
    <first>David</first>
    <last>Hume</last>
  </name>
  <name>
    <first>John</first>
    <last>Locke</last>
  </name>
  <name>
    <first>George</first>
    <last>Berkeley</last>
  </name>
</empiricists>
```

There's nothing wrong with this XML, but we might spare some processing time on both the server and the client by using a simplified format. JSON provides this.

The following code would be the JSON equivalent of the above:

```
{"empiricists":
  [
    {"name": {
      "first": "David",
      "last": "Hume"
    }},
    {"name": {
      "first": "John",
      "last": "Locke"
    }},
    {"name": {
      "first": "George",
      "last": "Berkeley"
    }},
  ]
}
```

The above may not be as easy for humans to read, but it is simpler for the JavaScript interpreter.

There are two basic data structures used in the above example:

- Arrays: These are denoted by square brackets, and contain a list of items separated by commas. For example: `["a","b","c"]`.

- Objects: These contain key/value pairs. Objects, in this case, work like dictionaries, maps, and associative arrays. These are denoted by curly braces and lists of colon-separated pairs individuated by commas. For example: `{"key 1": "value 1", "key 2": "value 2" }`.

Since JSON matches the JavaScript array and object notation perfectly, instead of parsing the contents with a sophisticated parse, the JavaScript `eval()` function can be used instead.

In regards to Drupal and jQuery, using JSON is even easier, since these libraries provide special tools for dealing with JSON data.

As we build our service, JSON will be our underlying data format. However, we will have to provide both server-side and client-side functions for passing this data.

Our Module Roadmap

As it stands now, `philquotes.module` contains the code necessary to display quote content as a block during the normal Drupal page rendering process.

However, there is no code either in our module or built into Drupal that will handle an AJAX request for just the contents of one quote. What do we need to do to make this happen?

We need to perform the following:

- Create a PHP function for serving a random JSON-encoded quote
- Map that PHP function to a URL handled by Drupal
- Create a JavaScript AJAX function for obtaining and displaying the quote
- Modify our existing JavaScript to call this function whenever the **Next** link is clicked

The first two tasks on the list are performed on the server side, and will be handled within our `philquotes.module` file. The third and fourth involve client-side scripting with JavaScript.

In the next section, we'll handle the PHP code and in the section following that, we will switch back to JavaScript to finish out the module.

Server Side: Defining a New Page

Two of our PHP programming tasks will be to first create a function to fetch a random quote and encode it into JSON format, and then map that function onto a particular URL that the client code can then use to make its request.

Creating a JSON Message

The first function will retrieve a random quote from the database, and then encode it into JSON and return it to the client.

The function we need to define will not implement a hook. Instead, we will use it later as a callback function from another hook. When it is called, it will return the JSON content directly to the client.

Following the module naming convention, we will create a new `philquotes_` function: `philquotes_item()`. The function needs to do only a few things:

- Get a random quote
- Set an HTTP header to let the client know what type of content to expect
- Print an appropriately formatted message to the client

By making use of existing functions, we can do these three things with
minimal coding:

```
/**
 * Callback to handle requests for philquotes content.
 * @return
 *   JSON data.
 */
function philquotes_item() {
  $item = _philquotes_get_quote();
  drupal_set_header('Content-Type: text/plain; charset: utf-8');
  printf(
    '{ "quote": { "origin": "%s", "text": "%s"}}',
    $item->title,
    $item->body
  );
}
```

The `philquotes_item()` function doesn't require any parameters.

The first thing this function does is retrieve a `quote` node object and store it in the
`$item` variable.

In the last chapter, we created a private function called `_philquotes_get_quote()`
that retrieved a node object that represented a random quote. Since this node
contains the content we want, we can make use of that function again.

Next, we need to notify the browser that the content that will be returned is not
HTML or XML:

```
drupal_set_header('Content-Type: text/plain; charset: utf-8');
```

The `drupal_set_header()` function is used to set an HTTP header. Headers are sent
at the beginning of the HTTP request and response messages, and contain information
used to help the user agent and server better determine how to communicate.

In this case, we are setting a header to tell the browser what type of content the
server is sending.

Ideally, we would use the MIME type for JSON (`application/json` as defined in
RFC 4627), but until that MIME type is widely used, it is safer to use the `text/plain`
MIME type. The browser will then hand the data to JavaScript without attempting to
parse it.

The last lines in the function handle the printing of the JSON data:

```
printf(
  '{ "quote": { "origin": "%s", "text": "%s"}}',
```

```
    $item->title,
    $item->body
);
```

The PHP built-in `printf()` function formats a string and then prints it. The first argument to this function is a format string containing a couple of placeholders (`%s`).

 The `sprintf()`/`printf()` family of functions was introduced in Chapter 2. See the PHP manual for details about these useful functions: `http://php.net/manual/en/function.printf.php`.

The rest of the parameters will be substituted for placeholders in order of appearance. `$item->title` will replace the first placeholder, and `$item->body` will replace the second placeholder. The result should be something as follows:

```
{ "quote": { "origin": "R. Descartes", "text": "Cogito, ergo sum."}}
```

Since `printf()` prints the data to the standard output, this data will be sent directly to the client.

That's all that there is to our JSON function. Next, we need to configure our module to map this function to a particular URL.

Mapping a Function to a URL

The second PHP function to add to our module will make it possible for our client-side AJAX function to connect to a specific URL and retrieve the JSON data.

Adding a new page with a distinct URL is not an uncommon task for Drupal module developers. As is to be expected in such a case, there is an existing hook designed to handle just such a case. This hook is called `hook_menu()`.

The basic purpose of `hook_menu()` is to allow module developers the ability to register a particular URI (or, more specifically, a relative URL path) and map that URI to a handling function. As the name suggests, this hook is often used to create menus for module administration. However, it can also be used for registering user-accessible pages, too.

 The `hook_menu()` mechanism is described in detail in the Drupal API documentation (`http://api.drupal.org/api/function/hook_menu`). The API even provides several example modules that implement this hook: `http://api.drupal.org/api/file/developer/examples/page_example.module/6`.

As with some of the other hooks we've seen so far, an implementation of hook_menu() is expected to return an array. In this case, it should return an array of menu items that will be registered with the Drupal core.

For the philquotes module, we need to register a path that the client can use to access JSON content. Our implementation of hook_menu() looks as follows:

```
/**
 * Implementaiton of hook_menu()
 */
function philquotes_menu() {
  $items['philquotes.json'] = array(
    'title' => 'Philquotes AJAX Gateway',
    'page callback' => 'philquotes_item',
    'access arguments' => array('access content'),
    'type' => MENU_CALLBACK,
  );

  return $items;
}
```

The associative array returned by the menu hook should contain one entry for each path that is registered. The key of the array should be the path being registered. The value is another associative array, which contains configuration parameters for the handler.

Based on these configuration parameters, Drupal will determine how to handle a client's request for the registered path. We will see how this works for the handler defined above.

The philquotes_menu() hook implementation registers one path: philquotes.json. When philquotes.json is registered, a handful of configuration parameters are defined for it:

```
$items['philquotes.json'] = array(
  'title' => 'Philquotes AJAX Gateway',
  'page callback' => 'philquotes_item',
  'access arguments' => array('access content'),
  'type' => MENU_CALLBACK,
);
```

The first entry in the configuration parameters is the title. This setting is *required*, and in many cases it will be used by other parts of Drupal to display, for example, a menu link to this page.

For our application, however, it is practically unused.

The second setting is the most important. `page callback` defines which function will be executed when this path is requested by a client.

The value of this parameter is the function name, with no parentheses at the end. In our case, this is the name of the function we defined earlier: `philquotes_item`.

The `access arguments` parameter lists what permissions a user must have in order to access this menu item. By default, the values in `access arguments` are passed to the `user_access()` function, which will check the permissions table to make sure that the requesting user has permission to access the menu item.

When used in conjunction with `hook_perm()`, a module can define and enforce permissions that administrators can customize using the **Administer | User management | Permissions** page.

The API documentation for `hook_perm()` and `hook_menu()` describes the specific roles for these functions, but the **Drupal Menu System** handbook provides a better overview of how the access control system works: `http://drupal.org/node/102338`

Our module, though, doesn't need any special access controls, and the array passed in here contains only the standard `access content` permission. This means any visitor who can access content can access this page.

Finally, the last of the four settings for this item is the `type`. Roughly speaking, this setting indicates what kind of item this page is. Based on the type, Drupal will determine how (and where) to display links to this item.

The situation is a little more complex. The value of `type` should be a bitmask defining specific characteristics of the item. Is it a root item? Should it be displayed in breadcrumb trails? Is this item modifiable by an administrator? By crafting a bitmask (a set of 1s and 0s), several such questions can be answered with one value.

Fortunately, most of the common bitmasks are already identified by constants. In fact, `drupal/includes/menu.inc` defines almost twenty such masks. The most important (and commonly used) ones are listed in the API docs (`http://api.drupal.org/api/function/hook_menu`).

The bitmask we have chosen, `MENU_CALLBACK`, simply makes this item accessible by URL. It does not, though, automatically create links to this item in the menu or anywhere else.

To summarize what we've just done, we have registered the path `philquotes.json`, providing Drupal's menu engine with the following information:

- The title of this path is "Philquotes AJAX Gateway."

- When the path is accessed by a client, the function `philquotes_items()` should be called.

- Permissions-wise, anyone who can view Drupal content (even non-authenticated users) should be able to access this resource.

- The resource should be accessible by direct URL, but should not be included in menus or other navigation.

As is evident, the menu system is powerful, and lots of features are packed in this compact settings mechanism. As we develop more sophisticated modules later in the book, we will revisit this hook, creating some more sophisticated mappings.

Now that our menu hook is finished, we can directly access the JSON content by entering the newly-registered URL in the browser:

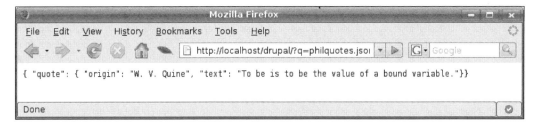

As the screenshot above shows, accessing the URL directly shows the raw JSON content. This is the content our client-side JavaScript will later parse and insert into the `philquotes` block area.

Note that the registered path (`philquotes.json`) is passed to Drupal with the GET parameter syntax (`http://localhost/drupal/q=philquotes.json`). This is the default Drupal setting. If you have Drupal configured to use Apache's `mod_rewrite` engine, the path will look something like this: `http://localhost/drupal/philquotes.json`.

> In this chapter, it is assumed that Drupal is configured without `mod_rewrite`. If `mod_rewrite` is enabled, you may want to adjust your URLs accordingly (though they should work using the GET parameter syntax).

We are almost done with the PHP coding for this module. In fact, our last change in this section will be a transitional effort, where we use PHP to generate JavaScript.

Passing PHP Settings to JavaScript

All we have left to do in `philquotes.module` is to provide a configuration parameter to the client-side JavaScript that tells it where to find the newly-registered `philquotes.json` page. This is done in `theme_philquotes_quote()`:

```
function theme_philquotes_quote($text, $origin) {
  $full_path = drupal_get_path('module', 'philquotes')
    .'/philquotes.css';
  drupal_add_css($full_path);
  drupal_add_js(drupal_get_path('module', 'philquotes')
    .'/philquotes.js');
  $opts = array('absolute' => TRUE);
  $json_url = url('philquotes.json', $opts);
  drupal_add_js(
    array('philquotes' =>
      array("json_url" => $json_url)), 'setting');
  $output = '<div id="philquotes-text">'. t($text)
    .'</div><div id="philquotes-origin">' . t($origin) . '</div>';
  return $output;
}
```

The highlighted lines above are the only addition. What do they do? These lines build a URL reference to the JSON page, and then store it in the JavaScript-side settings. Let's look at the lines more closely.

The first thing to do is create an absolute URL to the JSON data.

```
$opts = array('absolute' => TRUE);
$json_url = url('philquotes.json', $opts);
```

The Drupal function `url()` takes a Drupal path and an optional list of options. It returns a URL that the client can use to access the given path.

If a system uses `mod_rewrite`, the URL will be constructed to take advantage of this fact. Otherwise, the system will use the GET-style URL we saw earlier.

The options (`$opts`) parameter is an associative array that can contain additional information about how the URL should be constructed. Extra path information, anchors, and so on can be specified in this array.

 See the `url()` Drupal API documentation for details on all of the supported options: `http://api.drupal.org/?q=api/function/url`.

The only option we specify is the `absolute` option. We want the generated URL to be absolute, not relative: `'absolute' => true`. (By default, `url()` constructs relative paths.)

Once we have the URL, stored in `$json_url`, we just need a way to get this information to the JavaScript. To do this, we will once again use the `drupal_add_js()` function, but with a twist.

This time, instead of passing in a JavaScript file name, we want to modify Drupal's JavaScript settings. Drupal stores its JavaScript settings in the `Drupal.settings` JavaScript object. Using `drupal_add_js()`, we can modify this object from the PHP code (which generates JavaScript that it sends to the client).

We want to create a setting, `Drupal.settings.philquotes.json_url`, that our JavaScript can access later to find out what URL to connect to in order to get JSON data.

[
Why the long name?

Why choose `Drupal.settings.philquotes.json_url` instead of something shorter, like `Drupal.settings.json_url`? The answer is that we want to employ namespaces so that we reduce the likelihood of collisions with other modules.
]

The way to insert this configuration information into Drupal is to use the `'setting'` mode for `drupal_add_js()`. The syntax for this is `drupal_add_js($config_array, 'setting')`, where `$config_array` is an associative array of configuration parameters.

In our case, the function call looks as follows:

```
drupal_add_js(
  array('philquotes' =>
    array("json_url" => $json_url)),
  'setting');
```

The configuration array here is two levels deep: The value of the `'philquotes'` key is another associative array.

When Drupal renders this into JavaScript, the associative arrays will be converted into JavaScript objects, and will be inserted into `Drupal.settings`. Thus, `array('philquotes' => array("json_url" => $json_url))` will become `Drupal.settings.philquotes.json_url = http://localhost/drupal?q=philquotes.json`.

That's it for the PHP code.

Next, we will return to `philquotes.js` and finish coding this module.

Client Side: AJAX Handlers

Now that we have a service that provides quotes in JSON format, we need to develop some client-side JavaScript to dynamically retrieve this information.

Doing this will be a two-step process:

- Creating a JavaScript AJAX function for obtaining and displaying the quote
- Modifying our existing JavaScript to call this function whenever the **Next** link is clicked

The function we will create will have its own namespace. Since it is a module-specific function, we will define a module-specific JavaScript namespace, and then create this function within that namespace.

A JavaScript Function to Get JSON Content

Beginning where we left off, we will stub out our new function:

```
var Philquotes = {};

if(Drupal.jsEnabled) {
  $(document).ready(
    function(){
      $("#philquotes-origin").after("<a>Next &raquo;</a>");
    }
  );
  /**
   * A function to fetch quotes from the server, and display in the
   * designated area.
   */
  Philquotes.randQuote = function() {
    /* Code will go here. */
  }
}
```

The highlighted lines above show our new additions. On the first line, we define the new namespace. Recall that in JavaScript, a namespace is just an object. Creating a new namespace entails nothing more than creating a new (empty) object: `var Philquotes = {};`.

Several lines later, we define our first function in this newly-created namespace. `Philquotes.randQuote()` will be a function that fetches a random quote using the JSON structure we built in the preceding part of this chapter.

Why define the function inside a conditional?

The `Philquotes.randQuote()` function is inside the `if(Drupal.jsEnabled)` conditional. Why?

Since the function is only useful when the browser's JavaScript provides the necessary features. Defining the function outside of this conditional might cause browser errors or warning messages to be displayed.

Next, we can created the body of the `randQuote()` function. Thanks to jQuery, the body of this function is brief:

```
Philquotes.randQuote = function() {
    $.get(Drupal.settings.philquotes.json_url, function(data) {
        myQuote = Drupal.parseJson(data);
        if(!myQuote.status || myQuote.status == 0) {
            $("#philquotes-origin").text(myQuote.quote.origin);
                $("#philquotes-text").text(myQuote.quote.text);
        }
    }); // End inline function
}
```

The first line of `Philquotes.randQuote()` is the most complex. It uses jQuery's `get()` function, which handles simple AJAX requests.

The `$.get()` function takes two arguments: the URL that it should contact and a function to call when it is done communicating with the server.

Rather than hard-code the URL into the `get()` call, we can make use of the setting we created at the end of the last part. In the PHP code, we stored the absolute URL for the `philquotes.json` page using `drupal_add_js()`. Now, on the JavaScript side we can use `Drupal.settings.philquotes.json_url` to access that URL string.

That takes care of the first parameter. The second parameter to `get()` should be a function reference, which jQuery will call immediately after closing the connection to the remote server.

This function will be called with one argument (`data`), which will contain the data received from the remote server.

In the code above, this function is defined as an inline anonymous function that looks as follows:

```
function(data) {
    myQuote = Drupal.parseJson(data);
    if(!myQuote.status || myQuote.status == 0) {
```

```
      $("#philquotes-origin").text(myQuote.quote.origin);
      $("#philquotes-text").text(myQuote.quote.text);
    }
  }
```

As mentioned earlier, `data` will contain the data retrieved from the remote server. This *should* be a JSON document—unless an error occurs. Then it will be an HTML document.

Rather than parsing the JSON data by hand or calling the `eval()` function directly, we can use another built-in Drupal JavaScript function: `Drupal.parseJson()`. This function does some basic analysis of the data to ensure that it really is JSON data, and then transforms the JSON data into JavaScript data structures.

The results of the parsed JSON are stored in the `myQuote` object.

One feature of the `Drupal.parseJson()` function is that it provides some basic error handling, and we can take advantage of that to make sure that the data returned is JSON data.

If the data that comes back is not JSON data, then Drupal will return a status code (`myQuote.status`). If the returned status code is greater than zero, then an error occurred.

So, in the code, we do a simple check: If `myQuote.status` doesn't exist, then no error occurred. Or, if the status code exists, but is `0`, then no error occurred. (Normally, if the transmission was successful, the `status` object is not created.)

If status is anything other than `0`, then this function silently exits. No change is made, and the user will see the old quote.

Otherwise, a couple of jQuery statements set the text and origin of the quote:

```
      $("#philquotes-origin").text(myQuote.quote.origin);
      $("#philquotes-text").text(myQuote.quote.text);
```

Each line uses jQuery to select a specific element (`<div id="philquotes-origin"/>` and `<div id="philquotes-text"/>`) and assign new text content to that element.

The content it will assign these elements comes from the data returned by the server. Consider the case where the server returns this JSON content:

```
{ "quote": {
  "origin": "S. Kierkegaard",
  "text": "Purity of heart is to will one thing."
}}
```

When `Drupal.parseJson()` evaluates this, it will create an object called `quote`, and store in this two string objects, `origin` and `text`. So, to access the quote's text, we can use the JavaScript dot-object notation: `myQuote.quote.text`.

That is all there is to the `Philquotes.randQuote()` function. In fourteen lines of code, we retrieve and display a random quote from the server.

Now there is only one more thing to do. We need to connect the **Next** link to the `Philquotes.randQuote()` function.

Adding an Event Handler

The last change to make will be within the `ready()` event handler. We need to add a new event handler to the `<a>Next &raquo;</a>` link so that when it is clicked, it calls `Philquotes.randQuote()`.

Our last bit of code is just a small addition to the code we wrote earlier in the chapter:

```
$(document).ready(
  function(){
    $("#philquotes-origin").after("<a>Next &raquo;</a>")
      .next().click(Philquotes.randQuote);
  }
);
```

Only one line, highlighted above, needs to be added.

Let's start again with the query (`$("#philquotes-origin")`). This code selects the `<div id="philquotes-origin"/>` element and then, using `after()`, inserts a link after it.

The call to `after()` returned a jQuery object, so we can just continue to call methods on that object. Don't let the line break fool you. The `next()` function is called on the `jQuery` object returned by `after()`. In other words, the chain of functions looks like this:

```
$().after().next().click()
```

The role of the `next()` function might at first be confusing, so let's look at what's happening. What is the selected element that `after()` returns? It's not the `<a/>` element that we just inserted. It is still `<div id="philquotes-origin"/>`. Adding an element with `after()` doesn't result in jQuery automatically selecting that new element.

We want to add an event handler to the new `<a/>` element, though. Since this is the next sibling to the currently selected element, we can use `next()` to select it.

Now we have a jQuery object pointing to the `<a/>` element. We want it to be the case that when this link is clicked, the `Philquotes.randQuote()` function is called. All we need to do to make this happen is add a handler for the `click` event: `click(Philquotes.randQuote)`.

 Note that we pass click the function *reference*. Passing `Philquotes.randQuote()` instead of `Philquotes.randQuote` would pass the event handler the *results* of the function call, not the function itself.

Now we've created one long chain of jQuery commands: `$("#philquotes-origin").after("<a>Next &raquo;</a>").next().click(Philquotes.randQuote);`

When this chain is executed, the new HTML will be inserted in the appropriate place and the new event handler will be registered. Now, each time the **Next** link is clicked, `Philquotes.randQuote()` will be executed and a new quote will be displayed to the user.

Summary

The focus of this chapter was on JavaScript and integrating JavaScript services into Drupal modules. In the course of this chapter, we explored many of the features of jQuery and the Drupal JavaScript library. We also built on a previous module to create a JSON service for our module. We then linked that module to client-side JavaScript in order to add dynamic content to an existing block.

In the next chapter, we will build an administrative module. This module will provide new features for administrators, and will make use of some of the `hook_menu()` hook features introduced in this chapter.

6
An Administration Module

In this chapter, we will create a module with an administration interface. The module we create will provide a way for administrators to send email messages to users—all from within the administration section of Drupal.

This chapter has another intent, though. We will use a couple new hooks, the Forms API, and some other Drupal functions and constructs. These APIs are selected in part because they have undergone significant revision since Drupal 5. Thus, if you are already acquainted with Drupal 5 programming, this chapter will help the transition to Drupal 6.

In the course of creating our email module, we will perform the following:

- Take a closer look at hook_menu(), making use of access control settings
- Use the **Forms API** to create a form and handle the form's lifecycle
- Make use of Drupal's new mail subsystem and hook_mail() for sending messages to users
- Use hook_mail_alter() to add system-wide information to outbound email
- Implement hook_user() to add information to a user's profile page

We will start by defining the module's behavior.

The emailusers Module

The module we will create will provide an administration interface. It will make it easy for administrators to send a user an email message directly from the user's profile. This sort of module might be helpful in cases where administrators occasionally need to communicate with specific users through Drupal.

> There are already a host of mail-related modules available for Drupal. In fact, the **Contact module** bundled with Drupal provides similar functionality for user-to-user communication. (Ours is focused on administrator-to-user email). You can also browse the contributed modules by going to the Drupal module site and clicking on the **Mail** category: http://drupal.org/project/Modules/category/66

Given its function, we will name this module `emailusers`. We want this module to support the following features:

* An administrator will be able to send messages through a form-based interface.

* The form should be linked to the user's profile.

* Users who are not "user administrators" (administrators with access to user account information) should not be able to see or use the email form.

* Email messages ought to be delivered through the standard Drupal mail system.

As we develop this module, we will provide these features. Toward the end of the chapter, we will add another feature, too—cross-module feature. We will create an email footer that will be attached to any email leaving our Drupal installation—whether it goes through the `emailusers` module or not.

The Beginning of the Module

As with all modules, we will begin by creating a module folder, `emailusers/`. This folder will be located inside `drupal/sites/all/modules`.

Inside this folder, we will place the two required files: `emailusers.info` and `emailusers.module`. The info file is boilerplate:

```
; $Id$
name = "Email Users"
description = "Email a user from within the user administration
screen."
core = 6.x
php = 5.1
```

The fields here were described in Chapter 2, and nothing should be surprising.

We will start with a stubbed-out module, as well. It is always advisable to implement `hook_help()`, as we have done with the previous modules. Here's the beginning of our `emailusers.module` file:

```php
<?php
// $Id$

/**
 * This module provides an email interface for administrators.
 * Using this module, administrators can send email to a user from the
 * user's "view" page.
 * @file
 */

/**
 * implementation of hook_help()
 */
function emailusers_help($path, $arg) {

  if ($path == 'admin/help#emailusers') {
    $txt = 'This module provides a way for an administrator to send'.
      'email to a user. '.
      'It assumes that the Drupal mailer is configured.';
    return '<p>'. t($txt) .'</p>';
  }
}
```

Again, nothing in the implementation of this hook is new. Only the help text varies from our earlier implementations.

Mail Configuration

By default, Drupal sends email using the built-in PHP `mail()` command. The behavior of this command varies from operating system to operating system. For example, on Linux (by default) a call to `mail()` will invoke the `sendmail` command-line program. When PHP is running on Windows, in contrast, PHP will create direct SMTP socket connections to a mail server.

To configure how your system sends mail, you can edit your `php.ini` file.

The PHP `mail()` function has its limits, though and sometimes it is desirable to use an alternative mail library.

Drupal 6 allows extensions to the mail system. This is done by creating a custom mail library (not necessarily in the form of a module) which contains the `drupal_mail_wrapper()` function. By setting the value of the configuration variable `smtp_library` to point to the location of this mail library, you can cause Drupal to send mail through that library instead of through PHP's `mail()` function.

> The best source of information on this is the well-documented Drupal source code for `drupal/includes/mail.inc`, particularly the function `drupal_mail_send()`.

For our purposes, we will be using Drupal's default configuration.

Registering an Administration Page

Now that we have our basic module stubbed out, we will begin by registering a URL for the new page that we are going to create.

Our module will only need to register one new page. This is the page that will manage the email composition form. In the last chapter, we registered a JSON handler by implementing the `hook_menu()` function. We will use the same hook here as well. This time we are creating a page intended to be accessed by an administrative user.

```
/**
 * Implementation of hook_menu()
 */
function emailusers_menu() {
  // Need to pass User ID here:
  $items['admin/emailusers/compose/%'] = array(
    'title' => 'Compose a Message',
    'page callback' => 'emailusers_compose',
    'page arguments' => array(3), // <- userID (from % in node path)
    'access arguments' => array('administer users'),
    'type' => MENU_CALLBACK,
  );
  return $items;
}
```

As you may recall from the last chapter, the purpose of the menu hook is to register a URL. When we register a URL, we are mapping a URL or URL pattern to a function or page inside a Drupal module. In addition to registering the program, we also provide information to Drupal that indicates how the page is to be displayed and who has access to use this page.

An implementation of `hook_menu()` is expected to return an associative array where the keys in this array are paths and the values are associative arrays containing configuration information about each path. We covered many aspects of this in the last chapter, but in the present case we are using some different features. Let's take a closer look at the `$items` array created here.

```
$items['admin/emailusers/compose/%'] = array(
    'title' => 'Compose a Message',
    'page callback' => 'emailusers_compose',
    'page arguments' => array(3), // <- userID (from % in node path)
    'access arguments' => array('administer users'),
    'type' => MENU_CALLBACK,
);
```

A Detailed Look at the Path

The key added to the $items array is the string admin/emailusers/compose/%. This is the new path that we are registering and will be accessible with a URL as follows: http://example.com/drupal/?q=admin/emailusers/compose/1. (On hosts that have mod_rewrite support enabled, the ?q= could be omitted.)

Unlike the path we registered in the last chapter, this one uses a placeholder in the path. This placeholder is denoted by the percent sign (%). The placeholder indicates to Drupal that an additional (unspecified) argument is expected at the end of the path.

As the menu system interprets this path, the path is composed of four elements: admin, emailusers, compose, and whatever value is passed as %. It assigns each an integer value, starting with 0 (for admin), and ending with 3 (for the value of %).

> The % wildcard requires that some parameter value be passed. That space cannot be left empty. For example, if the browser requested a URL with the query string q=admin/emailusers/compose, the menu item above would not be invoked. Since there is no value to replace %, Drupal will not match the paths.

In our module, the % placeholder should be filled with a User ID, which is the unique integer that identifies a user. We will use this placeholder to find out to what user the mail should be sent.

Marking the Path as an Administration Page

There is another important thing to note about the path above. The first element of the path, admin, has special significance. It alerts Drupal that this URI is to be considered an administration page. Thus, the administration theme will be applied, and the page will be treated as part of the administration back end.

Note that the string admin *must come first in the path* for Drupal to treat the page as an administration page.

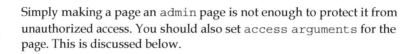

Simply making a page an `admin` page is not enough to protect it from unauthorized access. You should also set `access arguments` for the page. This is discussed below.

The path is the key to the `$items` array. The value to that key is another associative array—this one with configuration information related to that path. Let's look at that array.

Path Registration Parameters

We are now looking at the array of configuration information for our new menu item:

```
$items['admin/emailusers/compose/%'] = array(
    'title' => 'Compose a Message',
    'page callback' => 'emailusers_compose',
    'page arguments' => array(3), // <- userID (from % in node path)
    'access arguments' => array('administer users'),
    'type' => MENU_CALLBACK,
);
```

As we saw in the previous chapter, the `title` entry, which is required, should indicate the title of the link. For the most part, this value is used to generate menus. The page we are creating, however, will not be placed in an automatically generated menu.

There are a couple of other entries that can be set for a menu item. The Drupal API documents all recognized keys: `http://api.drupal.org/api/function/hook_menu/6`.

Also, as we saw in the last chapter, the value of `page callback` is the name of a function that Drupal will invoke when this URL is requested. In just a moment, we will create a function called `emailusers_compose()` which will be called when this menu item is accessed.

The `emailusers_compose()` function will take one argument: the User ID of the user to whom the module will send mail. Where do we get this ID? We will get it from the value of `%` from the registered path.

In order to pass arguments to the callback function, we set the `page arguments` entry: `'page arguments' => array(3)`. `Page arguments` takes an array of arguments. In our case, the array will have only one member: 3. What does this do? Let's take a look at the path again, as it would appear in the query string of a URL:

```
q=admin/emailusers/compose/1
```

As I mentioned earlier, this path appears to Drupal as four parameters: `admin`, `emailusers`, `compose`, and (in this case) 1. This last value indicates that we are dealing with the user whose User ID is 1.

Each of these parameters is associated with a number in ascending order from left to right. Thus, `admin` is 0, `emailusers` is 1, `compose` is 2, and the value of the placeholder (the User ID 1) is 3.

To pass the placeholder to the page callback function, then, we reference it by number. Thus `'page arguments' => array(3)` directs Drupal to pass the value of the fourth item in the URI (the placeholder) as an argument to the `emailusers_compose()` function.

The next line controls page access:

```
'access arguments' => array('administer users'),
```

We glanced at `access arguments` in the last chapter. It plays a more important role here, so we will look at it in more detail.

This entry tells the Drupal menu system who should have rights to access this page. The value of the argument is an array of permissions strings.

Permissions strings are managed through the administration pages. You can access them through **Home | Administer | User management | Permissions**. According to our access arguments, our new page should be accessible to any user with `administer users` permissions.

Looking at the **Permissions** page in **User management**, we can see what Drupal roles have this level of permissions:

Permission	anonymous user	authenticated user	site administrators
revert revisions	☐	☐	☐
view revisions	☐	☐	☐
system module			
access administration pages	☐	☐	☐
administer actions	☐	☐	☐
administer files	☐	☐	☐
administer site configuration	☐	☐	☐
select different theme	☐	☐	☐
taxonomy module			
administer taxonomy	☐	☐	☐
user module			
access user profiles	☐	☐	☐
administer permissions	☐	☐	☐
administer users	☐	☐	☑
change own username	☐	☐	☐

The second to last row (the one with the big arrow pointing to it) shows the **administer users** permission. Of the three defined roles, **anonymous user**, **authenticated user**, and **site administrators**, only the last group has permission to **administer users**.

 While **anonymous user** and **authenticated user** are built-in Drupal roles, **site administrators** is a custom role defined using **Administer | User management | Roles**.

By setting the `access arguments` entry for our new menu item, we have restricted access to only users with the `site administrators` role. (Remember that the Drupal administrator (User ID 1) is allowed access to all pages, regardless of roles. This user does not need to be assigned to the `site administrators` role to get administrative abilities.)

> **Define you own permissions**
>
> By implementing `hook_perm()` in your module, you can define permissions for your module. This hook is very easy to implement. See the API documentation at:
>
> `http://api.drupal.org/api/function/hook_perm/6`

The last configuration entry for our new page tells Drupal what type of page this is:

```
'type' => MENU_CALLBACK,
```

As with the JSON page created in the last chapter, this item is a menu item type `MENU_CALLBACK`, which means it will not automatically be included in any dynamically generated menu, or even in lists of items that can be included in menus. Typically, they are accessed by direct links from other pages. See the section *Mapping a Function to a URL* in the last chapter for more information on the `type` parameter.

Now we have a path registered. When Drupal receives a request for this resource, it will invoke the `emailusers_compose()` function, passing it the value of `%` as a parameter. Our next task is to create this callback.

> Since menus are frequently requested, Drupal will cache the generated menus. That means that updates to menu hooks may not be seen immediately. Using the Devel module, you can manually clear the menu router between code changes to your module using the **Rebuild menus** link.

Defining the Callback Function

Our callback function will have a simple task: Verify that the incoming parameter is a User ID, and then hand off control to the form generator.

```
/**
 * Compose a message.
 * This creates the form necessary to compose an email message.
 *
 * @param $to
 *   The address to send to.
 * @return
 *   HTML.
 */
function emailusers_compose($userid) {
  $userid = intval($userid);
  if ($userid == 0){
    return t('User ID must be an integer.');
  }
```

```
$account = user_load($userid);
if (empty($account)) {
   return t('No such user found.');
}
$to = $account->mail;
$sb =   '<p>'
   .t('Send a message to @email.', array('@email' => $to))
   .'</p>';
$sb .= drupal_get_form('emailusers_compose_form', $account);
return $sb;
}
```

The first five lines check the User ID and then attempt to load the user's account information. The `user_load()` function performs a database lookup to retrieve complete account information.

> As used above, the `user_load()` function takes a User ID and returns account information. However, the function is more robust than this. It can also take an associative array of values, and do a lookup based on those values. For example, to look up a user by email address, you can invoke the function as follows: `user_load(array('mail' => 'dave@example.com'));`.

Once the user information is loaded, a brief informative message is created and stored in `$sb`: **Send a message to @email**, where `@email` will be replaced with the value from the `$account` object. (If we so desired, we could hand this off to the theme system to theme the message. See Chapter 8 for an example of theming email messages.)

The next few lines are the most important of the function:

```
$sb .= drupal_get_form('emailusers_compose_form', $account);
return $sb;
```

To the `$sb` string is appended the output of `drupal_get_form()`, and then `$sb` is returned. The `drupal_get_form()` function is the workhorse of the Forms API. It is responsible for processing form definitions. We will start off the next section with a discussion of this function.

Handling Forms with the Forms API (FAPI)

Perhaps the most banal but time consuming aspect of web development is form handling. Typically, a form must be defined and prepared for display. Then, when form data is submitted to the server, various form processing tasks must be conducted to validate, manipulate, and store form data. Drupal has a special API for handling forms—the **Forms API (FAPI)**. FAPI automatically handles the mundane details of form handling, making it much easier for developers to quickly write forms.

Using the Forms API, developers can create a single form definition that is then used by Drupal to perform various aspects of form handling. The same data structure that is used to generate the form is also used to validate the form. And with a few simple functions, complex forms can be handled effectively. FAPI stands out as one of the gems in Drupal's crown because of these features.

In this section, we will implement a form using the FAPI.

 Regarding terminology, you may notice that in the Drupal documentation the forms library is variously called the Forms API, Form API, and FAPI. All refer to the same set of tools.

Of course, looking at a single simple form can hardly do justice to the powerful and complex Forms API. While we will return to some aspects of the API later in the book, if you are looking for an in-depth discussion beyond what this chapter has to offer, the Drupal website has some very good articles:

- The "quickstart" guide to the Forms API: `http://api.drupal.org/api/file/developer/topics/forms_api.html/6`

- The Forms API Quick Reference: `http://api.drupal.org/api/file/developer/topics/forms_api_reference.html/6`

- Form API changes between Drupal 5 and Drupal 6: `http://drupal.org/node/144132`

- The Form Generation API overview: `http://api.drupal.org/api/group/form_api/6`

Loading a Form with drupal_get_form()

Near the end of the `emailusers_compose()` function we created in the last section, we called the `drupal_get_form()` function:

```
$sb .= drupal_get_form('emailusers_compose_form', $account);
```

In its simplest form, the `drupal_get_form()` function takes a callback function and uses the results of that function to create a form structure and then manage handling of the resulting form. In the above example, it will return an HTML-formatted form.

While the `drupal_get_form()` function only makes use of one argument—the name of the callback function—it can take more arguments. Any additional arguments will simply be passed on to the functions that it calls.

In our case, we pass in the additional `$account` parameter, which contains the account information of the user we want to send an email.

The next thing to look at is the form "constructor" callback.

A Form Constructor

In Drupal parlance, the function that is used to create a form is called a **form constructor**. The term constructor has a narrow meaning here, and is not synonymous with the object-oriented programming term.

A form constructor creates an elaborate data structure that is used to construct, validate, and manage forms. In key ways it works like a hook: a particular naming convention is followed, and all form constructors are expected to return the same type of data structure.

Before we look at the form constructor, here's a list of the features we want our form to have:

- First, since we will need to use the `$account` object throughout form processing, we want to keep a reference to that object. Normally this is done with hidden fields in forms, but Drupal has a better way of handling these cases.

- Next, we need a couple of form fields to capture the subject and body of the email message.
    - The subject field will be a single-line text input.
    - The body field will be a multi-line text area.

- To keep our form well organized, we want to group the above using a field set (`<fieldset/>` in HTML).

- Since the administrator is sending this form through Drupal, he or she might like to have a copy of the message sent to him or her for archival purposes. So we will add a checkbox to indicate whether a BCC (blind carbon copy) of the message should be sent to the administrator.

- Again, to keep this form organized, we will create a "details" field set for the checkbox.

- Finally, we will need a submit button.

Now we can translate this list into a form constructor. The function is a little long simply because there are a lot of fields to create. However, it is not very complex to read:

```
function emailusers_compose_form($context, $account) {
  // This is a value only -- equivalent to a hidden field, except
  // that it is never rendered into the HTML.
  $form['to'] = array(
    '#type' => 'value',
    '#value' => $account,
  );
  // Create a fieldset for the body:
  $form['message'] = array(
    '#type' => 'fieldset',
    '#title' => t('Compose the Message'),
  );
  // Textfield for subject of the body
  $form['message']['subject'] = array(
    '#type' => 'textfield',
    '#title' => t('Subject'),
    '#size' => 50,
    '#maxlengh' => 255,
    '#description' => t('The subject of the email message.'),
  );
  // And a text area for the body.
  $form['message']['body'] = array(
    '#type' => 'textarea',
    '#title' => t('Message'),
    '#cols' => 50,
    '#rows' => 5,
    '#description' => t('The body of the email message.'),
  );
  // Create a fieldset for details
  $form['details'] = array(
```

```
        '#type' => 'fieldset',
        '#title' => t("Details"),
    );
    // Checkbox: if checked, CC the author, too.
    $form['details']['cc_me'] = array(
        '#type' => 'checkbox',
        '#title' => t('BCC Yourself'),
        '#default_value' => 1,
        '#description' =>
          t('If this is checked, the message will also be sent to you.'),
    );
    // Finally, a submit button:
    $form['submit'] = array(
        '#type' => 'submit',
        '#value' => t('Send Mail'),
    );
    return $form;
}
```

The general structure of this function should be familiar. It is very similar to other Drupal functions. The variable $form is an associative array, where each entry corresponds (roughly) to a form element. There are seven such form elements, and we will look at those in a moment.

The value of each entry in the $form array is another associative array containing configuration information for that element.

The function builds the $form array and then returns it. Other functions that call this function, such as drupal_get_form(), can then make use of this form definition for a variety of purposes, including creating an HTML representation of the form or performing rudimentary form validation.

Let's take a look at some of the items in the $form array. The first item stores the account information:

```
    $form['to'] = array(
      '#type' => 'value',
      '#value' => $account,
    );
```

This entry is a **value field**. Unlike the other elements we will look at, it does not correspond to a visual form element. Instead, it just holds a reference to a value (in this case, the $account variable) that the Forms API can use throughout form processing.

Since this is a short definition, it provides a good starting place. The key in the `$forms` array, `to` in this case, is used to reference data about this form. Thinking in terms of an HTML form, this is roughly equivalent to a form element's `name` attribute.

The value of this entry is an associative array that provides information about this form item. Given the complexity of forms, there is a wide variety of recognized values that can go in this array, but the two keys here are common to many form fields.

> For a complete list of supported parameters, see the Forms API Reference page: `http://api.drupal.org/api/file/developer/topics/forms_api_reference.html/6`. Along with the list of parameters it includes matrices indicating which parameters are supported by which form element types.

The first, `#type`, indicates what type of form element this is. There is a type for each HTML form element. There are also a handful of special form fields. The `value` type is an example of such an element. In many ways, it performs a role analogous to the `<input type="hidden"/>` HTML form field. It makes it possible to attach information to a form without providing the user with a way to modify the information. However, it is different in one important respect: the value is never sent to the client. It is stored on the server only.

> All the parameters used to define a form entry begin with the # sign. This is done to distinguish parameters from nested form fields. For example, see the discussion of field sets later.

The next parameter is the `#value` parameter. This, too, is used by a couple of different form types. It stores the value of the field for form types whose content cannot be modified by the user. In this case, it references the `$account` data.

> Most of the time, the value of a `#value` field should be an easily printable type (like a string or integer). However, when the `#type` is set to `value`, then `#value`'s referent can be any object.

> The repeated use of the term 'value' can get confusing here. There is a `#type` called `value`, which indicates what sort of form element is being described. There is also a `#value` element in the array. This indicates what the value of the form element should be set to. In our case, this leads to the unfortunate fact that we can say that the value of the `value` element is `#value`'s value.

This should provide a basic idea as to how a form element is defined. Now let's take a quicker look at some of the other entries in the `$form` array.

```
// Create a fieldset for the body:
$form['message'] = array(
   '#type' => 'fieldset',
   '#title' => t('Compose the Message'),
);
// Textfield for subject of the body
$form['message']['subject'] = array(
   '#type' => 'textfield',
   '#title' => t('Subject'),
   '#size' => 50,
   '#maxlengh' => 255,
   '#description' => t('The subject of the email message.'),
);
// And a text area for the body.
$form['message']['body'] = array(
   '#type' => 'textarea',
   '#title' => t('Message'),
   '#cols' => 50,
   '#rows' => 5,
   '#description' => t('The body of the email message.'),
);
```

Together, these three entries define a field set with the `Subject` text field and the `Message` text area.

The first entry of the three defines the field set (note that the value of `#type` is `fieldset`). The `#title` parameter can be used for most of the elements, and is used to create the legend for a field set and the labels for other form fields.

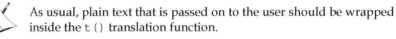 As usual, plain text that is passed on to the user should be wrapped inside the `t()` translation function.

The next entry defines the `Subject` text input area. In order to indicate that this field belongs inside the field set, the subject array is nested inside the `$form['message']` array as `$form['message']['subject']`. Using this nesting capability, complex forms can be structured in a logical way. When submitted form data is captured and presented by Drupal, you have the option of accessing it in a data structure identical to the one above.

The `textfield` type is rendered as a single-line text input box (`<input type="text"/>`) in HTML.

In this example, the `#size` and `#maxlength` parameters are used to set the visible field size and the maximum number of characters that this field can contain. In the case of `#maxlength`, not only is it used to generate the form, but when form data is uploaded, Drupal performs a server-side check to make sure the user-submitted data does not exceed this limit. The `#description` is rendered as help text for the input field.

Like the text field, the text area for the message body is defined as a sub-element of the `$form['message']` array. The text area will also be displayed inside the field set. Two new parameters are used here, `#rows` and `#cols`. These correspond directly to the identically named HTML attributes for the `<textarea/>` element.

Now that we have looked at a few fields, let's see how Drupal converts this data structure into a form. Rendered into HTML, these three entries look as follows:

In case of the field set, the title is embedded into the border. With the other two elements, the title is presented above the field, and the descriptive text is drawn below the field.

The last three definitions work in much the same way:

```
// Create a fieldset for details
$form['details'] = array(
  '#type' => 'fieldset',
  '#title' => t('Details'),
);
```

```
// Checkbox: if checked, CC the author, too.
$form['details']['cc_me'] = array(
  '#type' => 'checkbox',
  '#title' => t('BCC Yourself'),
  '#default_value' => 1,
  '#description' =>
    t('If this is checked, the message will also be sent to you.'),
);
// Finally, a submit button:
$form['submit'] = array(
  '#type' => 'submit',
  '#value' => t('Send Mail'),
);
```

In this section, a new field set is created for `Details`. The checkbox indicating that the sender should be BCC'd is added to the details field set. In the `cc_me` checkbox definition, the `#default_value` is used to indicate that the box should be checked by default (`1` = checked, `0` = unchecked). But a `#default_value` differs from `#value` in an important way: A `#default_value` indicates that the user may choose a different value if he or she wishes, while the value of a `#value` parameter cannot be changed by a user.

Finally, after the field set with its checkbox comes the form submit button. Here, again, `#value` is used—this time to add a label to the submit button.

At this point, if we were to access the page in a browser using a URL: `http://example.com/drupal?q=admin/emailusers/compose/3`, what would happen? First, the `emailusers_menu()` hook would cause Drupal to use the `emailusers_compose()` callback (passing it the integer 3). This function would load the user's account info (`$account`), generate a line of text, and then pass control to `drupal_get_form()`. The `drupal_get_form()` function would load the form constructor from `emailusers_compose_form()` and then render it into HTML, which would then be sent to the user.

> **When debugging, clear the cache**
>
> Forms and supporting form objects are cached. Sometimes, this caching can interfere with development. Using the **Empty cache** link on the Devel module's Devel block can save you frustration.

The user would be presented with a page that looks like the following screenshot:

Home » Administer

Compose a Message

Send a message to dave@localhost.

┌─ Compose the Message ──────────────────────────────────────┐
│   │
│ **Subject:**   │
│ ┌──────────────────────────────────┐   │
│ │   │   │
│ └──────────────────────────────────┘   │
│ The subject of the email message.   │
│   │
│ **Message:**   │
│ ┌──┐   │
│ │   │   │
│ │   │   │
│ │   │   │
│ │   │   │
│ │   │   │
│ │   │   │
│ └──┘   │
│ The body of the email message.   │
│   │
└──┘

┌─ Details ──┐
│   │
│ ☑ BCC Yourself   │
│ If this is checked, the message will also be sent to you. │
│   │
└──┘

┌──────────┐
│ Send Mail │
└──────────┘

But what happens when the form is submitted?

Handling Form Results

Drupal automatically handles submitted form data. It first checks the fields against the definition provided by the form constructor to ensure that the data is valid and in the expected form. It then executes a couple of callback functions.

The first, which should be the name of the form constructor with `_validate()` appended to the end (e.g. `emailusers_compose_form_validate()`) is used to perform additional validation on the data. We will forgo that function in this chapter, though we will make use of it in later chapters.

For more on the _validate() callback and other aspects of the Forms API, see the **Forms API Quickstart Guide** in the Drupal API: http:// api.drupal.org/api/file/developer/topics/forms_api. html/6. At the time of this writing, some of the material in this reference is out of date. You may want to consult the API docs for the Drupal form documents, as well as the release notes for your version of Drupal 6.

Once data validation is complete, Drupal issues a second callback — this time for a function with the name of the form constructor with _submit() appended to it. In our case, this function is named emailusers_compose_form_submit().

These functions are not hook implementations. There are no hook_validate() and hook_submit() functions in the Forms API.

The Form Submissions Callback

The responsibility of the _submit() callback is to determine what is to be done with the data. For example, a _submit() callback might store the form data in the database or turn it into a Drupal node. In our case, we want to format it as an email message and then send it.

Here is our submissions handler:

```
/**
 * Form submission handler, which functions like a hook.
 * Note that the params $form and &$form_state are new in D6. They
 * replace $form_id and $form_values.
 */
function emailusers_compose_form_submit($form, &$form_state) {
  $form_values = $form_state['values'];
  $account = $form_values['to'];

  drupal_mail(
    'emailusers',
    'composemessage',
    $account->mail,
    user_preferred_language($account),
    $form_values,
    variable_get('site_mail', null),
    true // Automatically send
  );
  $form_state['redirect'] = sprintf('user/%d', $account->uid);
}
```

When the Forms API calls the `_submit()` callback function, it passes the function two arguments: `$form` and `$form_state`. Since code elsewhere uses the values in `$form_state`, and the `_submit()` callback function often needs to modify that data, it is passed by reference (`&$form_state`). That way, any changes made to the values in `$form_state` will be available beyond the scope of this function.

> **Drupal and PHP references**
>
> In Drupal 6, more functions use PHP references to manipulate data without having to explicitly return modified objects. Along with being more efficient, this method is considerably more flexible. For example, three variables can be passed by reference, and all three can be modified by the function without having to return a complex object. For an explanation of how references work, see the PHP manual at: `http://www.php.net/manual/en/language.references.php`.

These two variables passed to the `_submit()` callback contain information about the form. The `$form` variable contains an associative array generated using the form constructor. But this time, all the information sent by the user (and all the information generated by Drupal's Forms API) is present in the array.

For example, `$form['to']` will contain the user's account information (since we set the value of `$form['to']` to be the contents of `$account` in our form constructor), and `$forms['#post']['subject']` will contain the user-submitted value of the `$forms['message']['subject']` field.

The `$forms` variable can be useful for extracting detailed information about the form. But the `$form_state` variable also holds a reference to the form data, and can be easier to use. In the `emailusers_compose_form_submit()` function opposite, we use the `$form_state` variable to retrieve the form information:

```
$form_values = $form_state['values'];
$account = $form_values['to'];
```

`$form_state` contains state-specific information about the form, including what information has been posted, and what should happen next in the form processing sequence. In advanced cases, it can be leveraged to create multi-page forms.

In the above two code lines, we use it for a simpler task—retrieve form information. All the form field values—both user-submitted and Drupal-generated—are stored in the `$form_state['values']` entry. Thus, `$form_state['values']['to']` holds the account object, `$form_state['values']['subject']` holds the user-submitted subject, `$form_state['values']['body']` holds the user-submitted body text, and so on for all of the fields we defined in the form constructor.

To simplify the code and keep things similar to Drupal 5 idioms, we use the variable `$form_values` to refer to the contents of the `$form_state['values']` array. If memory consumption is an issue, you may prefer to just use the `$form_state['values'][]` fields rather than making a copy of the form data.

Next, the submission function calls `drupal_mail()` to send an email message. We will look at that function in the next section, but for the moment let's skip to the last line of the submission function:

```
$form_state['redirect'] = sprintf('user/%d', $account->uid);
```

This line tells the Forms API that now that the submission process is over, the client browser should be redirected back to the user's account page (e.g. `http://example.com/drupal?q=user/3`).

How does this work?

First, `$form_state` was passed by reference. When we change the value of `redirect`, that value is accessible to other functions that also have access to `$form_state`. Some other function (in this case, `drupal_process_form()`) uses the contents of this variable to determine where to redirect the browser.

> **Is your redirect failing?**
>
> Is your form data being processed correctly, but the redirect is failing? Chances are good that the problem is that the `$form_state` variable was not passed by reference. Make sure your `_submit()` function looks like this: `example_submit($form, &$form_state)`.

So, by assigning the path `'user/<User ID>'` (where `<User ID>` is the user's unique integer identification number) to `$form_state['redirect']`, this function registers a redirection event that will occur after the form processing is complete. In our function, once an email message has been sent to the user, the administrator will be returned to `http://example.com/drupal/?q=user/3`.

As far as this module is concerned, we have now finished with the Forms API (though we will use FAPI in almost every remaining chapter in the book). From creation through processing, we have taken care of the complete lifecycle of our new form. Now we will move on to the mail API to examine how mail messages are sent from Drupal.

Sending Mail with the Mail API

The Drupal 6 Mail API is used to provide mail-sending services to Drupal modules. In most cases, using the Mail API is a two-step process:

1. Implement `hook_mail()` in your module.

2. Elsewhere in your module, use the `drupal_mail()` function to invoke your `hook_mail()` implementation and also do additional formatting and sending.

In the previous section, we briefly glanced at the `drupal_mail()` function. Here, we will start by looking at the function in more detail. Inside `emailusers_compose_form_submit()`, we called `drupal_mail()` with the following parameters:

```
drupal_mail(
    'emailusers',
    'composemessage',
    $account->mail,
    user_preferred_language($account),
    $form_values,
    variable_get('site_mail', null),
    true // Automatically send
);
```

Seven parameters! To get an idea as to what is going on here, let's look at each in turn.

The first parameter (`emailusers`) is the name of the module that contains an implementation of `hook_mail()`. Later, we will look at the `emailusers_mail()` hook that will be called when this `drupal_mail()` function is executed.

The second parameter, `composemessage`, is used as a key and passed on to the `hook_mail()` implementation. As we will see shortly, the mail hook can then determine how to treat the message based on the key. In other words, you can use one mail hook to handle various different mail-sending tasks simply by using different keys.

The third parameter should contain the destination address. In this case, an administrator will be sending the message to the email address for the account he or she is examining. This is stored in `$account->mail`.

The fourth parameter is the language that should be used by `t()` and other translation facilities when translating the message. Why is it necessary to specify this? Since the user receiving the message may prefer a different language than that of the system administrator who is sending the message.

Fortunately, the `user_preferred_language()` function, which takes an account object (like the one returned from `load_user()`), can return the appropriate locale information.

The fifth parameter holds an associative array of data that might be used when generating the message. This data is passed on to the `hook_mail()` implementation, and we will make use of it in a few moments. In this case, though, the data we want happens to be the values submitted through our form. So we pass `$form_values` here.

Moving to the sixth parameter, we need to specify a delivery address. Who is this message from? One of the values in Drupal's site-wide configuration is the administration email address. We can use this address by retrieving the setting: `variable_get('site_mail', null)`. This will attempt to get the `'site_mail'` setting. If no such setting is found, this will return the default value `null` (in which case the mailing library will attempt to assign an appropriate from address).

The last of the seven parameters is a Boolean flag to indicate whether or not the message should be sent. When `drupal_mail()` is executed, it will return a specially structured array, which can be passed to `drupal_mail_send()`. However, if this last parameter is set to `true`, then the `drupal_mail()` function will send the mail before returning. In that case, there is no need to call the `drupal_mail_send()` function or even capture the data returned from `drupal_mail()`.

What happens if mail can't be sent?

If the mailer is mis-configured or Drupal or PHP detect an error with the mailing subsystem, an error message will be printed to the screen. However, in cases where the mail is accepted for delivery by the underlying mail system, bad messages will be sent to the address indicated in the from parameter. For this reason, it is a good idea to create a mailbox (or an alias) to route mailer delivery errors.

When `drupal_mail()` is called, it goes through a series of steps to take the data passed in the seven parameters and create a suitable mail message. For example, it sets default RFC 2822 mail headers and makes sure that certain values (like a from address) are set.

Then it executes the `hook_mail()` implementation (if found).

After that, it proceeds through a few other steps, like executing any `hook_mail_alter()` implementations before it (optionally) sends the email and returns a formatted message.

So the mail hook is executed right in the middle of this process. What does it do? In a nutshell, it is responsible for setting appropriate fields (like the subject, CC, or BCC fields) as well as creating a formatted body for the message.

Formatting Mail with hook_mail()

Most of the work involved in sending a message from Drupal is standard enough that Mail API functions can perform the task without custom code. But right in the middle of this process, there comes the matter of formatting the message.

This task is one that requires some per-module (or even per-task) coding. To facilitate this, Drupal 6's Mail API includes the hook_mail() hook. Implementing this hook allows us to configure the email message headers and body to our liking before sending it off into the ether.

Earlier, we invoked drupal_mail() with a list of seven parameters. The first was the name of the module whose mail hook should be used: emailusers. Thus, when drupal_mail() gets to the appropriate point in its processing, it will look for a function called emailusers_mail(). We need to supply that function:

```
/**
 * Implementation of hook_mail()
 */
function emailusers_mail($key, &$message, $params) {

  // Just catch calls to this hook from compose form.
  if ($key == 'composemessage') {
    $language = $params['language'];
    $account = $params['to'];

    if ($params['cc_me']) {
      // Look up current user's email address:
      $my_account = user_current_load(null);
      $message['headers']['bcc'] = $my_account->mail;
    }

    $message['to'] =  $account->mail;
    $message['subject'] =
      t('Drupal Message: ', array(), $language->language);

    // If these were automatically-generated messages, they should be
    // run through t(), but since text is user-entered, don't use
    // t().
    $message['subject'] .= $params['subject'];
    $message['body'] = $params['body'];
  }
}
```

When a `hook_mail()` implementation is executed, it is passed three arguments:

- `$key`: A string key that can be used to determine information about how mail should be formatted.

- `$message`: The data structure that represents the email message as Drupal has constructed it so far. Note that this must be passed by reference (`&$message`) if you intend to modify it.

- `$params`: A collection of parameters passed from the module's invocation of `drupal_mail()`.

The first and third of these are passed unaltered from our call to `drupal_mail()`.

The `$key` parameter will contain the string we passed as the second argument to `drupal_mail()`. That is, it will contain the string `composemessage`. What is this for?

To understand, consider this case: You have a module that sends two differently formatted types of email messages, maybe a confirmation message and a monthly account reminder. The `hook_mail()` implementation should be able to handle both. But how can it distinguish them? Here's where the `$key` comes in. The module developer can set distinct keys that can be passed from the module code to the mail hook so that the mail hook can determine what rules to use when manipulating the message.

Another way to understand the role of `$key` is to compare it to the `$opt` parameter passed in `hook_block()`. We looked at `hook_block()` in Chapter 2. `$key` performs a similar role, but it is the module developer, not Drupal core developers, who determine what values are assigned to `$key`.

Taking a good look at the code, we can see the key used in this way (though we are only sending one type of message from our module):

```
function emailusers_mail($key, &$message, $params) {
  // Just catch calls to this hook from compose form.
  if ($key == 'composemessage') {
    // Do all processing here...
  }
}
```

The rules inside this `if` statement are only intended to apply to cases where mail is sent after data is collected from the composition form. So only those that pass in the `composemessage` key will be modified by the hook. Any other call to `emailusers_mail()` will return with no processing done.

The second parameter passed in to the mail hook, $message, is a reference to a partially-constructed mail message. $message is an associative array.

The drupal_mail() function has already populated the $message array with the information it already has accessible, such as the to and from addresses, the default mail headers, and some data used internally by Drupal. Even $message['body'] is set, though it is by default an empty array.

The intended job of an implementation of hook_mail() is to finish filling out the $message data. But for that, the hook will need access to the information it will use to fill out the form. In our case, for example, it will need access to the form submission results, and that is where the third parameter comes in.

The last parameter, $params, is another item passed through from drupal_mail(). The fifth argument we passed to drupal_mail() was an associative array of values. In our specific module, the array passed was $form_values, which contains the form data we collected with emailusers_compose_form() and passed on in emailusers_compose_form_submit().

The brunt of the emailusers_mail() function is spent taking data from the $params data, formatting it, and inserting it into the $message.

First off, a few parameters are assigned to local variables for convenience:

```
$language = $params['language'];
$account = $params['to'];
```

Next, the function determines whether to BCC the administrator who is sending the message.

```
if ($params['cc_me']) {
  // Look up current user's email address:
  $my_account = user_current_load(null);
  $message['headers']['bcc'] = $my_account->mail;
}
```

If the cc_me value, appearing in the form as a checkbox, is set, then we need to do two things: First, we need to load the account data for the current user (the administrator who is sending the message). This is done with the user_current_load() function.

Second, once we have that user's account object, we need to include that user's address in in the BCC field.

While the recipient (to) address is stored directly in the $message object, CC and BCC information must be added directly to the message headers. So instead of setting $message['bcc'] to the administrator's address, we must set $message['headers']['bcc'] instead.

> **Headers are strings**
>
> The values in the $message['headers'] array must all be strings. So if you want to set multiple CC or BCC recipients, you must convert the list to a string of comma-separated addresses: $message['headers']['cc'] = implode(',', array($addr1, addr2));

Other than MIME encoding and imploding the header array, Drupal will do no further processing to anything in the $message['headers']. You may set custom headers without worrying about Drupal's interference.

Next, the function simply does the basic formatting necessary for generating the message:

```
$message['to'] =  $account->mail;
$message['subject'] =
  t('Drupal Message: ', array(), $language->language);

// If these were automatically-generated messages, they should be
// run through t(), but since text is user-entered, don't use t().
$message['subject'] .= $params['subject'];
$message['body'] = $params['body'];
```

The recipient is set explicitly here, though if we omitted this, Drupal would use the correct ID (as gleaned from the parameters to drupal_mail()).

For the message's subject, we want to do two things: First, we want to include a hard-wired notification (Drupal message:) that the message was generated by Drupal. Then we want to append the user-submitted subject line. There is an important difference in the way we do these two tasks.

When we set the automated subject line, we want to do so in a way considerate to the recipient. Since the Drupal message: message is hard-coded, it should be made available to the translation subsystem. So we will wrap it in the t() function.

But in order to get t() to work on behalf of the recipient, we need to make sure we pass it information about what language to translate the message into. This is done by passing in the $language value of the $language object (which we obtained originally from the recipient's account record): t('Drupal Message: ', array(), $language->language).

While you should use `t()` as often as it is practical, it should not be used in cases where the text is supplied by the user or another source that is external to Drupal. Thus, when we append the user-submitted subject to the hard coded value, we do it simply by appending the string as-is. And the same goes for the message body:

```
$message['subject'] .= $params['subject'];
$message['body'] = $params['body'];
```

Here, the two values are simply retrieved as-is from the `$params` array and assigned to their respective fields in the `$message` array.

At this point, we have done all we need to do to complete the `$message`. Since it was passed by reference, it is not returned at the end of the function.

When the mail hook returns, the Drupal Mail API will do the necessary encoding of information, execute any `hook_mail_alter()` hooks, and then send the message. A message sent from this would look something like this:

```
Return-Path: <www-data@example.com>
X-Original-To: dave@example.com
Delivered-To: dave@example.com
Received: by mail (Postfix, from userid 33)
    id 8C59AF85CB; Fri, 14 Dec 2007 15:27:16 -0700 (MST)
To: dave@localhost
Subject: Drupal Message: Content editor?
MIME-Version: 1.0
Content-Type: text/plain;
  charset=UTF-8;
  format=flowed;
  delsp=yes
Content-Transfer-Encoding: 8Bit
X-Mailer: Drupal
Errors-To: root@example.com
Sender: root@example.com
Reply-To: root@example.com
From: root@example.com
Message-Id: <20071214222716.8C59AF85CB@mail>
Date: Fri, 14 Dec 2007 15:27:16 -0700 (MST)

Dave,

You've been very active in our community. Would you be interested in
taking on an even more active role by becoming a content editor?

Let us know,
Matt
```

Headers that are generated directly by the Drupal Mail API (including `hook_mail()`) are highlighted. Those headers can all be altered in the `$message` data passed into the mail hook. However, a module can also alter them after a mail hook has been called using the **mail alter hook**.

Altering Messages with hook_mail_alter()

As we have seen, `drupal_mail()` calls only one specific mail hook. But what if we want to write a mail message post-processor or a mail hook that is invoked every time `drupal_mail()` is called?

This can be accomplished by implementing another hook—`hook_mail_alter()`. Drupal's Mail API invokes all instances of `hook_mail_alter()` immediately after it has executed the specified mail hook.

Before implementing our own mail altering hook, we will take a quick look at altering as a concept in Drupal.

Altering Hooks

There are a handful of hooks provided in Drupal whose purpose is to allow module developers to intercept and alter data after a main hook has been called. These are called **alter hooks** or **altering hooks**.

The following are a few of the main hook/altering hook pairings:

- `hook_mail()`/`hook_mail_alter()`: Format mail message/alter mail message before it is sent.
- `hook_link()`/`hook_link_alter()`: Create a list of links/alter a list of links before they are sent to the user.
- `hook_menu()`/`hook_menu_alter()`: Register Drupal paths/alter the list of paths before Drupal routes them.

All of these are documented in the Drupal API (`http://api.drupal.org/api/group/hooks/6`). But this selected list ought to give an idea as to how altering hooks provide the ability to intercept some bit of data and do a little extra processing.

To demonstrate how this works, we will use the `hook_mail_alter()` hook to add a standard footer to an email message. But be wary when using this hook—it will operate not only on mail from our `emailusers` module, but also on any email sent through the Mail API.

Adding a Mail Footer

To add a standard footer to all email messages leaving our Drupal installation, all we need to do is alter the mail message after the mail hook has been executed, and this is easily done by implementing `hook_mail_alter()`.

Here's how we can implement this:

```
/**
 * Implements hook_mail_alter().
 */
function emailusers_mail_alter(&$message) {
  $append = "\n=======================\n"
    ."This message was sent from !site_name (!website). "
    ."If you believe this message to be a case of abuse, "
    ."please contact !site_email.\n";

  $args = array(
    '!website' => url('', array('absolute' => true)),
    '!site_email' => variable_get('site_mail', null),
    '!site_name' => variable_get('site_name', 'Unknown'),
  );

  $message['body'] .= t($append, $args);
}
```

An implementation of the mail altering hook is passed only one argument: `$message`. Just as was the case with `hook_mail()`, `$message` should be passed by reference (`&$message`) so that any changes made within the body of the function will be available outside the scope of this function.

This theme's function is simple: Append a standard message to the end of the message body. To do this, we first create the footer message:

```
$append = "\n=======================\n"
  ."This message was sent from !site_name (!website). "
  ."If you believe this message to be a case of abuse, "
  ."please contact !site_email.\n";
```

There are three placeholders in this message: `!site_name`, `!website`, and `!site_email`. (Recall that using `!` in a placeholder instructs Drupal not to perform encoding or escaping for these values. Since the message is in plain text, we don't need HTML Escaping.) When this string is passed to the translation function, those should be replaced.

Next, we need to define the replacement values for the three placeholders:

```
$args = array(
  '!website' => url('', array('absolute' => true)),
  '!site_email' => variable_get('site_mail', null),
  '!site_name' => variable_get('site_name', 'Unknown'),
);
```

According to this array, the !website placeholder will be replaced by the base URL of the website (which is generated by the calling url() with an empty string and the absolute flag, which generates an absolute URL).

Both !site_email and !site_name will be replaced by values from the site configuration. The site_email value, as we saw earlier, is the main email address for the site, and the site_name value is the name of the site. Both these values are set through the administration interface using **Administer | Site configuration | Site information**.

Finally, we append these to the existing message body:

```
$message['body'] .= t($append, $args)';
```

We pass this through the translation function since the message is static text. Note also that we are appending (.=) the string to the existing text. If the equals (=) operator were used instead, it would replace whatever message was created by the original mail hook (emailusers_mail(), in our case).

Let's see how this hook takes effect when we send email. The email generated from the compose form we created earlier in this chapter will now have an additional footer:

```
Return-Path: <www-data@example.com>
X-Original-To: dave@example.com
Delivered-To: dave@example.com
Received: by mail (Postfix, from userid 33)
  id 8C59AF85CB; Fri, 14 Dec 2007 15:27:16 -0700 (MST)
To: dave@example.com
Subject: Drupal Message: Content editor?
MIME-Version: 1.0
Content-Type: text/plain;
  charset=UTF-8;
  format=flowed;
  delsp=yes
Content-Transfer-Encoding: 8Bit
X-Mailer: Drupal
Errors-To: root@example.com
Sender: root@example.com
Reply-To: root@example.com
```

```
From: root@example.com
Message-Id: <20071214222716.8C59AF85CB@mail>
Date: Fri, 14 Dec 2007 15:27:16 -0700 (MST)
Dave,
You've been very active in our community. Would you be interested in
taking
on an even more active role by becoming a content editor?
Let us know,
Matt
========================
```

This message was sent from Philosopher Bios (http://example.com/ drupal/). If you believe this message to be a case of abuse, please contact root@example.com.

The footer, highlighted above, is the result of our new `useremail_mail_alter()` hook.

To gain additional flexibility, we could have used the theme system to do the formatting of this message (and the same could be said for `hook_mail()` implementations). In fact, in Chapter 8 we use the theme system for just this purpose.

There is one final thing to keep in mind about using hooks of this sort: since they will apply to *all* outgoing email, they should be constructed carefully. For example, it is entirely possible that some instance of `hook_mail()` might format a message in HTML or encode the message in another way. If this is the case, then the hook implementation above might actually break existing markup. Thus, a production-grade hook would need a series of additional checks on the contents of the `$message` data to make sure that the footer was inserted appropriately (if at all).

Incorporating the Module into Administration

So far, we have registered a new path for our mail composition form, implemented that form with the Forms API, and used the Mail API to send the results as an email message. But our module is missing one component. As it currently stands, the only way to access this composition form is to access the appropriate URL directly.

Our last step is to incorporate this module into the administration interface. This module targets administrators who need to send an email message to a particular user. We want the administrator to be able to go directly from a user's profile to the message composition form.

We can do this by implementing another hook.

Modifying the User Profile with hook_user()

By default, every registered user can visit the **My account** page for his or her own account. The URL to access this page is usually something like this: **http://example. com/drupal/?q=user/3**. The page looks like the following screenshot:

```
Home
dave
    View        Edit



History
Member for
2 weeks 3 days
```

An administrator (with the appropriate permissions) can also visit this page. In fact, an administrator can visit the account page for any user on the system. This is the main interface for user administration.

Much of the content for the page above is generated by the hook_user() hook. By implementing this hook in our module, we can use this page to tie the rest of our module to the user administration interface.

Actually, the hook_user() hook does a lot more than paint the user's account page. In Drupal 6, there are thirteen registered operations that this hook might perform. It is invoked in cases ranging from addition, modification, or deletion of a user to a user's logging in or logging out of Drupal. (And, of course, the API docs are the place to go to learn about these thirteen different operations: http://api.drupal.org/ api/function/hook_user/6.)

Here, though, we are only concerned about the operation that is used to display the main user page. This is the view operation. Our user hook looks as follows:

```
/**
 * Implementation of hook_user().
 */
function emailusers_user($op, &$edit, &$account, $category) {

  if ($op == 'view' && user_access('administer users')) {
    // Create the outer "block"
    $account->content['EmailUsers'] = array(
      '#type' => 'user_profile_category',
      '#attributes' => array('class' => 'user-member'),
```

```
    '#weight' => 0,
    '#title' => t('Contact user'),
  );

  // Create the content of the block
  $account->content['EmailUsers']['EmailLink'] = array(
    '#type' => 'user_profile_item',
    '#title' => t('Send a message to this user from the site '
      . 'administrator.'),
    '#value' => l(
      'Email',
      'admin/emailusers/compose/'. $account->uid
    ),
  );
}
}
```

This code is responsible for generating a chunk of text that will point an administrator to the email composition form. When an administrator views a user's profile page, she or he will see an additional chunk of content:

```
Home
dave
  View    Edit




Contact User
Send a message to this user from the site administrator.
Email

History
Member for
2 weeks 3 days
```

Let's take a closer look at the above code to see how this new content is added.

A hook_user() implementation will receive as many as four parameters:

- $op: The name of the operation (Examples: view, login, delete). There are thirteen possible operations.

- $edit: An array containing any values submitted from a form. This is used by operations that handle posted data (like insert). It is intended to be passed by reference.

- $account: The account object for the given user. This is the same kind of account object we have looked at elsewhere in this chapter (constructed by load_user()). It is also intended to be passed by reference.

- $category: A few of the operations (and the view operation is not one of them) use additional category information to determine what part of a profile's data should be used for the transaction.

This last parameter, $category, is never passed during the view operation, so we have omitted it from our function declaration.

The first line of the function body sets a few constraints on when this function should perform its task.

```
if ($op == 'view' && user_access('administer users')) {
```

Since we are only concerned with the view operation, we want our hook to do its work only when the $op parameter is set to view. (Of course, the hook could handle more than just the view operation using more conditionals or a switch statement. But this module does not require anything else.)

There is a second constraint that we want to check before doing any further processing. The email link should appear only if the user accessing the page is an administrator. Recall that when we registered the path for admin/emailuser/compose/% using emailusers_menu(), we set the access arguments parameter to restrict access to administer users. Basically, we are implementing the same restriction here. But this time, we do so with an explicit call to the user_access() function.

The user_access() function checks to see if the given permission is available for a given user (by default, the current user). It is usually called like this: user_access($permission_string, $account). And if $account is omitted, the current user account is used. It returns Boolean TRUE if the user does have this permission, and FALSE otherwise.

So, according to the conditional that opens our function, the operation must be 'view' and the user must have the administer users permission. If these two conditions are satisfied, the message we saw in the screenshot is constructed.

Constructing the Content

The next thing to do is construct the content that will be displayed on the user profile. Accomplishing this is done in a surprising way.

Recall that the $account object is passed in by reference. $account contains an attribute, $content, that is used to display the user profile.

To modify the information displayed on the user profile page, we modify the user's `$account` object.

> This modification is only temporary, and is not written to the user's permanent database record.

Moreover, `$content` is an array structured analogously to the form constructors we looked at earlier in the chapter. Each entry in the array has a name, and contains a handful of values. These values may be parameters (strings beginning with a hash sign (#)) or another associative array. This is similar to the way that forms support nesting elements.

We want to create a two-tiered entry: a **profile category** (which, roughly speaking, defines an area of similar information, like a field set), and a **profile item**, which belongs to the category.

Here's a closer look at the first of these two tiers:

```
// Create the outer "block"
$account->content['EmailUsers'] = array(
  '#type' => 'user_profile_category',
  '#attributes' => array('class' => 'user-member'),
  '#weight' => 0,
  '#title' => t('Contact user'),
);
```

The above creates the profile category for this new section, and it works in much the same way as the form declarations we developed earlier in the chapter. The `#type` field is set to `user_profile_category`, which is the correct category for a profile category in the `hook_user()` hook.

The `#attributes` field is used for adding HTML attributes to the rendered HTML elements. In this case, it will add an attribute that looks like this: `class="user-member"`. When the CSS stylesheet is applied to the rendered HTML, this class declaration is used to style the element.

The `#weight` field is used to indicate roughly where in the generated list of user profile items this particular one should go. The heavier the weight, the lower on the list it goes (and thus the closer to the bottom of the page). Think of it this way: The heavier the weight, the lower it sinks. Negative numbers may be used as well (they "float up"). Zero is the default weight and we will leave it at that.

Finally, the `#title` field is used to give this profile category a title. The section will have the title **Contact user**.

Inside this profile section, we want to add a single item, which will point to the email composition screen that we created earlier in this chapter. Just as we did when adding form fields to a field set, here we will add a profile item to a profile category:

```
// Create the content of the block
$account->content['EmailUsers']['EmailLink'] = array(
  '#type' => 'user_profile_item',
  '#title' => t('Send a message to this user from the site '
    . 'administrator.'),
  '#value' => l(
    'Email',
    'admin/emailusers/compose/'. $account->uid
  ),
);
```

The profile category was stored in `$account->content['EmailUsers']`. Now, we are adding a new element to the `EmailUsers` array:
`$account->content['EmailUsers']['EmailLink']`.

The `#type` for this item is `user_profile_item`, and just as with the profile category, we need to assign it a `#title`. We are taking some liberties, though, by using the title a little more like a description, since it will appear immediately below the profile category's title: **Send a message to this user from the site administrator**.

The `#value` entry should contain text that will display after the title. In this case, we just want to create a link to the composition form. We do that with the `l()` function introduced in Chapter 2. This link points to the path that we registered with `emailusers_menu()`, appending the user's ID (`$account->uid`) to the end.

Drupal will generate a URL that looks something like this: `http://example.com/drupal?q=admin/emailusers/compose/3`. This URL maps onto the path we registered in the menu hook, and when an administrator clicks on the link, he or she will be taken to the email composition form.

Summary

In this chapter, we explored the administration side of Drupal. We created a module that allows an administrator to send an email to a user directly from the user's account profile in Drupal. While creating this module, we took another look at `hook_menu()`, and also looked at a handful of new hooks. We created a new form plus form handling utilities using the Forms API. Using the Mail API we created and sent an email message, and looked at how to use altering hooks as well. Finally, using `hook_user()`, we added this new module to the user profile.

In the next chapter, we will continue building on the material we started here, but with a new module. We will create a new content type from scratch, and that will involve working more closely with the database layer.

7

Building a Content Type

In Chapter 5, we created a simple content type using the Drupal administration interface. In this chapter, we will write a module that defines a more complex content type. Doing so will allow us to explore some new APIs including the database and schema APIs. We'll also revisit some of the hooks and APIs we used in the previous chapters.

The module we will create in this chapter will define a biography content type. As we create it, we will perform the following:

- Create a module installation file
- Use the **Schema API** to define a new database table
- Implement a host of new hooks, mostly from the **Node API**
- Use the **Database API** to execute queries against the database
- Revisit some already-used APIs and hooks such as the access control hooks and the Forms API

We will start by defining the module's behavior.

The biography Module

The name of our fictional website is "Philosopher Bios". So far, we have created a host of modules, but nothing related to the idea of a biography. In this chapter, we will create the biography module.

This module will define a new content type (sometimes called a node type) that will contain specialized fields for storing a simple biographical profile.

What should a biographical profile look like? Well, for us it will have the following fields:

- The name of the person the biography is about
- A brief summary of what makes that person notable
- The date of birth and date of death
- A history of the person
- A list of notable works or achievements of that person

While we can use the default **title** and **body** fields available to all nodes, we will need to create additional fields for the rest of the data.

The Content Creation Kit

In this chapter, we are creating our new content type by coding a module.

However, there is another way we could create a new content type. One of the most prolific Drupal add-on modules is the **Content Creation Kit (CCK)**. CCK provides a visual interface for creating custom content types.

> **The future of CCK and Views**
>
> It is very likely that CCK will be incorporated into the core in Drupal 7. Why? Because it is a robust, well-written, useful module that is among the most frequently used, and it provides a set of features desirable in a CMS framework. A similarly popular module, the **Views module**, is also likely to be incorporated.

When creating a content type of moderate complexity, CCK is usually the right tool for the job. However, there are a few reasons why we will write a module instead of using CCK:

1. Writing a content type from scratch gives us more insight into internals, and provides the opportunity to examine several powerful APIs. By writing this low-level module, we will have a good excuse to examine the database API, access control APIs, the new Schema API, and take another look at some of the libraries we've worked with already.

2. There is a good argument to be made for coding custom content types when they are directly related to modules. Custom content types are often easier to maintain this way, and users do not need to worry about tinkering with content types through the administration interface. And, of course, there is no dependency on the CCK module.

3. At the time of this writing a production-quality Drupal 6 version of CCK has not yet been released, but a beta version has been released. Hopefully, by the time this book is published, a stable version of CCK will be available for Drupal 6.

Although CCK would be capable of creating a biography content type such as the one we are defining, we will write a module to provide our new content type.

The Starting Point

As with the other modules, we will start by creating our new biography module. As usual, we will put this module in the drupal/sites/all/modules/biography directory. Also, as with other modules, we will immediately create the biography. info and biography.module files.

The biography.info module includes nothing new or notable:

```
; $Id$
name = "Biography Content (Node) Type"
description = "This provides a custom content type to store simple \
online biographies."
core = 6.x
php = 5.1
```

As with the other modules, we will start our biography.module by implementing the hook_help() hook:

```
<?php
// $Id$
/**
 * Provides the biography content type.
 * @file
 */
/**
 * implementation of hook_help().
 */
function biography_help($path, $arg) {

  if ($path == 'admin/help#biography') {
    $txt = 'A biography is a textual description of a '
      .'person\'s life and works. The summary should give '
      .'a brief overview of the person explaining why the '
      .'person is important. The \'dates\' area should '
      .'provide information on birth date and death date for '
      .'the person. This field is free-text, and might look '
```

```
        .'like this: \'c. 500 BCE-450 BCE\'. \'Life\' should '
        .'provide a biography of the person, and \'Works\' '
        .'should contain a list of this person\'s works.';
    $replace = array();
    return '<p>'. t($txt, $replace) .'</p>';
  }
}
```

Now that we have the boilerplate material complete, we will turn to a new task. We will create an installer.

The Module Installation Script

Our new module is going to create a new content type. This new node type will need some additional data fields that the default node implementation does not provide.

Where will these fields be stored?

Answer: In a custom database table.

Thus, when our `biography` module is first enabled (in **Administer | Site building | Modules**), we need to make sure that a new table is created. Likewise, when this module is uninstalled (from the **Uninstall** tab of **Administer | Site building | Modules**), we need to make sure that the database table is removed.

To accomplish this, we will create a new file, `biography.install`. When Drupal first enables a module, it looks in the module's directory for a file named `<modulename>. install`. If it finds this file, it will load it and then check to see if the installation hook, `hook_install()`, is implemented. If it is, Drupal will execute it.

To create a new table, then, we simply have to implement `hook_install()` with code for creating a database table.

Drupal also has a `hook_uninstall()` hook for tasks that should be performed when a module is uninstalled. `hook_update_N()` provides a function for specifying changes that should be made when a module is upgraded from a previous version.

> The `hook_update_N()` hook is named like this: `<modulename>_ update_<revision number>`, where revision number is a four digit code. The first digit corresponds to the core Drupal release: 6. The second digit is the module's major release number. The last two digits are for sequential update numbers. For example, our first module update may be 6100 (Drupal 6, our module version 1, and the first update, 00) and we would implement `hook_update_6100()`. A subsequent bugfix release would be 6101.

While we don't have any updates, we do want to configure an installation process and an uninstallation process.

So the beginning of our `biography.install` file looks as follows:

```php
<?php
// $Id$
/**
 * Install the biography module, including it's content (node)
 * type.
 * @file
 */
/**
 * Implementation of hook_install().
 */
function biography_install() {
  drupal_install_schema('biography');
}
/**
 * Implementation of hook_uninstall().
 */
function biography_uninstall() {
  drupal_uninstall_schema('biography');
}
```

The two functions, `biography_install()` and `biography_uninstall()` implement the installation and uninstallation hooks. Both simply call existing Drupal functions to install and uninstall existing schemas. We will take a closer look at this idea.

We only have one major task for our installer to do. We want it to add a new table. In older versions of Drupal, this required writing SQL inside of the `hook_install()` implementation. But now, in Drupal 6, we can make use of a powerful new API: the Schema API.

In the following section, we will see how a new table is defined with the schema. But for now, it is sufficient merely to understand what the two Drupal schema functions do.

- `drupal_install_schema()` installs a module's schema. It takes only the module's name (here, `biography`) as a parameter. Drupal then invokes `hook_schema()` to retrieve the schema information. Once it has the schema, it converts the schema to SQL and executes the SQL against the database.

- `drupal_uninstall_schema()` also takes a module name (`biography`), and loads that module's schema by invoking `hook_schema()`. It then takes that schema and generates the appropriate table-deletion SQL, which is then executed in the database.

The installer performs only one simple task—it creates a new table in the database.

Likewise, the uninstall process is also simple. The table is dropped.

However, since we have a schema, there is no need to hand-author any SQL.

As mentioned, both `drupal_install_schema()` and `drupal_uninstall_schema()` cause Drupal to invoke the `hook_schema()` implementation for this module. Let's turn now and look at this hook.

The Schema API: Defining Database Structures

The next task in our module installation process is the defining of our new table.

In previous versions of Drupal, a module author wrote SQL DDL (Data Definition Language) to define any new database structures. However, this caused portability problems. Since SQL DDL is not particularly transferable from one DBMS (DataBase Management System) to another, modules that worked on, say, MySQL could not then be installed on PostgreSQL.

Database abstraction is a good goal

In the past, Drupal has been tightly integrated with MySQL, with moderate support for PostgreSQL. But as Drupal continues to evolve, it is likely that support may be extended to other databases. Oracle, MS SQL Server, and others have been suggested as database platforms for Drupal. For this reason, Drupal developers are starting to emphasize the desirability of portable SQL. Database-agnostic APIs and generic SQL are desirable for keeping modules portable.

To rectify this situation—and also simplify database management tasks—Drupal developers added a new API. This Schema API provides the facilities for defining abstract database structures, and then converting them to DBMS-specific SQL DDL. In other words, the API allows you to define tables, indexes, and so on as PHP code. Then, as necessary, the Schema API can translate these PHP data structures into SQL specific to the particular database engine. From a single schema, Drupal can then create MySQL and PostgreSQL versions (or, indeed, versions for any supported DBMS).

The Schema API overview describes the API and provides links to all of the functions in the Schema API:
`http://api.drupal.org/api/group/schemaapi/6.`

Also, once Drupal has a complete schema, it can perform different operations. For example, a table schema can be used to create or drop a table (as well as its indexes).

Practically speaking, then, we will use the `hook_schema()` hook to define a new schema, and let Drupal do the conversions to SQL as required.

A First Look at the Table Definition

For our new content type, we only need to create a single table, so our hook implementation will be fairly straightforward:

```php
/**
 * Implementation of hook_schema().
 */
function biography_schema() {
  $schema['biography'] = array(
    'fields' => array(
      'vid' => array(
        'type' => 'int',
        'unsigned' => TRUE,
        'not null' => TRUE,
        'default' => 0,
      ),
      'nid' => array(
        'type' => 'int',
        'unsigned' => TRUE,
        'not null' => TRUE,
        'default' => 0,
      ),
      'dates' => array(
        'type' => 'varchar',
        'length' => 127,
        'not null' => TRUE,
        'default' => '',
      ),
      // Note: On MySQL, text fields cannot have default values.
      'life' => array('type' => 'text', 'not null' => FALSE),
      'works' => array('type' => 'text', 'not null' => FALSE),
    ),
    'indexes' => array(
      'nid' => array('nid'),
    ),
    // Version is primary key. Could do nid, vid.
    'primary key' => array('vid'),
  );

  return $schema;
}
```

A `hook_schema()` implementation is expected to return an associative array, where the top level of each array is a table name. Consider a simplified version of the second line of `biography_schema()`:

```
$schema['biography'] = array();
```

The `$schema` array will be the associative array we will return. This line indicates that we are defining a table named `biography`.

However, this isn't a complete schema. We need to add information about each column in our table.

Our table is to have five columns: `vid`, `nid`, `dates`, `life`, and `works`. Let's talk about the purpose of each of these, and then we will revisit the code.

- `vid`: This is the **version ID** of the entry in this table. VIDs are unique to the table, and will serve as the primary key. In a Drupal installation that supports versioning, each version of a document will result in a new line being created in this table. This field is required for a content type extension table.

- `nid`: The **node ID** tracks the unique ID of a particular node (specified in the `node` table). When Drupal retrieves a node, it will retrieve the latest available `vid` for the requested `nid`. This field is required for a content type extension table.

- `dates`: This will be a free-form text field for entering date information. Why free-form text instead of a date selection field? Because we need to allow less than precise dates like "Circa 500 B.C.E. to 450 B.C.E" or "Unknown to 368 C.E.".

- `life`: This field will contain free-form text content (actually, restricted HTML text) that will describe the individual's life.

- `works`: This will also be used to hold restricted HTML text. This field is used to store bibliographic information.

Now that we know basically what each column is supposed to do, let's take a closer look at the schema.

Defining Fields (Columns)

Inside the array of the `biography` schema, there are three main arrays:

```
$schema['biography'] = array(
  'fields' => array()
  'indexes' => array()
  'primary key' => array('vid'),
);
```

These arrays provide various aspects of the table's definition.

- `fields`: This array contains a definition for each of the columns in the table. Since our table will have five columns, this array will contain five entries.

- `indexes`: This array contains an entry for each index that is to be added to the table.

- `primary key`: This array contains entries for each component of a primary key.

In addition to these three, the schema API defines two more:

- `unique key`: This array contains entries for each unique (non-primary) key in a table.

- `description`: This allows you to attach a textual description to the schema definition.

Let's look at a couple of the definitions in the `fields` array:

```
'nid' => array(
  'type' => 'int',
  'unsigned' => TRUE,
  'not null' => TRUE,
  'default' => 0,
),
'dates' => array(
  'type' => 'varchar',
  'length' => 127,
  'not null' => TRUE,
  'default' => '',
),
```

Here are the definitions for the `nid` column and the `dates` column. The NID (Node ID) is a positive (unsigned) integer that can never be null. The purpose of this field is to correlate our extended table with the main nodes table. A `nid` in this table will always correspond to the `nid` field in the `node` table. Hence, we don't need to configure it to increment automatically.

If we were to take this definition and convert it to MySQL-brand DDL, it would look as follows:

```
CREATE TABLE `biography` (
  `vid` int unsigned NOT NULL default '0',
  `nid` int unsigned NOT NULL default '0',
  `dates` varchar(127) NOT NULL default '',
  `life` text,
```

```
    `works` text,
    PRIMARY KEY  (`vid`),
    KEY `nid` (`nid`)
)
```

The `nid` array key becomes the column name, and the contents of the array are combined to create the definition. All this transformation is done under the hood by the schema API.

 Each of the possible fields that can be used in a schema definition is documented in the Schema API manual: `http://drupal.org/node/146939`. For the most part, the Schema API names follow the naming patterns used by MySQL.

Likewise, the `dates` entry also represents a column, though in this case the type is `varchar` instead of an `int`. Since we know a date field is short, even when expressed in text, we can limit the length of the field to `127` characters. To express the size limit, instead of defining `type` as `varchar(127)`, we define the `type` as `varchar` and set `length` to `127`.

There are a number of predefined sizes, such as `small`, `big`, `tiny`, and so on. (These sizes are commonly used with `int`s in MySQL.) If no size is specified, or if `size` is set to `normal`, then the defaults of the underlying database system are used.

The text type and default values

MySQL does not allow columns of type `text` to have default values. When the Schema API encounters a default value for a text column, it simply ignores the definition. This, however, can cause unexpected errors if SQL statements assume that a default will be set. For this reason, it is better to insert empty strings into text fields in a Drupal database. (We will see an example of this later in the chapter.)

The other field definitions follow the same patterns. Rather than belaboring the point, we will skip the other fields and take a look at the next two entries in the definition: `indexes` and `primary key`.

Defining Keys and Indexes

As we noted earlier, there are three items in the `$schema['biography']` array: `fields`, `indexes`, and `primary key`. Above, we looked at the field definitions, which are used to define columns in a database table. Now we will look at the other two:

```
'indexes' => array(
   'nid' => array('nid'),
),
'primary key' => array('vid'),
```

The `indexes` array is used to define database indexes. To ensure good performance, you should define indexes on fields used to match rows in a database query. The rule of thumb for this is that fields that are frequently used in the WHERE clause or in JOINs in your SQL are those that make good candidates for indexes.

Defining an index is fairly simple. Every index needs a name and a list of fields to index. The name can be the same as the indexed fields.

In the example above, we define an index on Node IDs (`nid`), since that field is frequently used in retrieving information from the table. The index is defined as `'nid' => array('nid')`. The array key, `nid`, will be the name of the index, and the array that it references, `array('nid')`, is the list of fields indexed here.

To improve performance on some queries, we could change this index to include cases where `nid` and `vid` (Version ID) were both used in the WHERE clause of a query. Consider an index like this: `'nidvid' => array('nid','vid')`. This defines an index named `nidvid` that will optimize for queries against Node ID and Version ID. (For example a query like: SELECT * FROM {biography} WHERE nid=10 AND vid=11;.)

> **MySQL and multi-column indexes**
>
> With MySQL, the `nidvid` index would not only be used for cases where both columns were accessed in the WHERE clause, but also for cases where the first of the columns (`nid`) is used. In other words, this one index can function as two different indexes—one on `nid` alone, and one on `nid` and `vid`.

Finally, a `primary key` entry indicates which field or combination of fields is to be treated as the table's primary key. A primary key must be unique and can never be null.

In most content type extension tables (like ours), the `vid` should be treated as the primary key. (Optionally, you can use the combination of `nid` and `vid`, but it is not clear that this offers any benefit.)

Once a field is identified as a primary key (or even a unique key, see the description above) then the field should not be indexed. Attempting to do so will cause database errors.

The structure of the primary key definition is simpler than the index definition: `'primary key' => array('vid')`. Primary keys do not need names. Consequently, all the `primary key` entry requires is an array of fields to treat as the key. The `unique keys` definition also follows this same pattern.

Now we have created a complex data structure representing our schema definition. Any time the `hook_schema()` hook is called on this module, this schema definition is returned. Also, in our installation file, the scheme is retrieved twice—once by `drupal_install_schema()` and once by `drupal_uninstall_schema()`.

At this point, we are done with the `biography.install` file. The three functions, `biography_install()`, `biography_uninstall()`, and `biography_schema()`, are the only functions we need to install this module.

Now we are ready to return to `biography.module` and make use of our newly defined database table.

Correlating the New Table with Nodes

The install script defined a new table. But how does Drupal know that this table is to be treated as part of a content type? In fact, how is Drupal to know that we are defining a content type at all?

 In the first chapter, we discussed nodes. From the developer's point of view, each piece of content is backed by a node and (perhaps) some extensions to that node. What extensions are used depends on the content type of that piece of content. The table we just created represents extensions to the node for our `biography` content type.

The hook function `hook_node_info()` is used to register a new content type. Other functions that we will look at shortly (namely, our implementation of `hook_load()`) will provide Drupal with information on how we have augmented the node with our custom fields.

An implementation of the `hook_node_info()` hook must return an array of information about the node. This information is basic, and does not include details about the table we have created. Most of the options, in fact, deal with how the basic content authoring form is displayed.

Hence, we will take a quick look at the content authoring form for a `Story` content type before looking at the `hook_node_info()` code for our `biography` module. This will give us the basis for a visual comparison.

Home ⁕ Create content
Create Page
Title: *

▸ Menu settings

Split summary at cursor

Body:

The **name** of this content type is **Story**. The **description** of a Story, which appears on the **Create content** page, reads as follows:

A story, similar in form to a page, is ideal for creating and displaying content that informs or engages website visitors. Press releases, site announcements, and informal blog-like entries may all be created with a story entry. By default, a story entry is automatically featured on the site's initial home page, and provides the ability to post comments.

> By default, the **Create content** page is accessible from the main site navigation, or through a URL like this: `http://example.com/drupal/?q=node/add` (replacing `example.com` with your domain).

The title and body fields (labeled **Title** and **Body** in the above form) are both enabled for the Story content type. The four fields—name, description, title, and body—are fields that we will set for our biography content type.

Now we are ready to look at `biography_node_info()`, our implementation of `hook_node_info()`.

```
/**
 * Implements hook_node_info().
 */
function biography_node_info() {
```

```
    return array(
      'biography' => array(
        'name' => t('Biography'),
        'module' => 'biography',
        'description' => t('A biography of a person.'),
        'has_title' => TRUE,
        'title_label' => t('Biography of'),
        'has_body' => TRUE,
        'body_label' => t('Overview'),
      )
    );
  }
```

This hook is expected to return an array describing all the content types that our module provides. Our implementation only provides one, a content type named biography. The content type's name is used as an array key. In Drupalish style, the value of that array entry is another array: an associative array loaded with information about the content type:

```
biography' => array(
  'name' => t('Biography'),
  'description' => t('A biography of a person.'),
  'has_title' => TRUE,
  'title_label' => t('Biography of'),
  'has_body' => TRUE,
  'body_label' => t('Overview'),
  'module' => 'biography',
)
```

Most of these fields determine how our new content type will appear on the **Create content** list and for the content creation form (like the one in the previous screenshot) for our content type. Let's look at them in order:

- name: This will be the content type's name, as displayed to the user.

- description: A sentence or two describing the content type. This is displayed on the **Create content** page. For brevity's sake, we will use a short label: A biography of a person. Usually, something a little more descriptive is appropriate.

- has_title: This takes a Boolean value. If it is set to FALSE, no title form field will be displayed. If it is set to TRUE, the title form field will be displayed, along with the label set in title_label. We want a title entry field, so we set this to TRUE.

- title_label: This should be the user-friendly label for the title form field. By default, this is Title. We will use this as the field to display who the biography is about. So our label is Biography of. Note that we must run this through the t() translation function.

- has_body: If this is set to TRUE, a text area will be displayed. Users creating content will be able to enter the node's main content through this form. If it is set to FALSE, no text area will be displayed. We will use this field, so we set it to TRUE.

- body_label: Like title_label, this specifies the label to be used for the body section (if has_body is set to TRUE). By default, this is Body. We will use this field to display a short summary of our biography, so the label is set to Overview.

The last field is in some ways an exception. The fields above deal with the look and feel of this new content type. This last field, though, plays a functional role in the node subsystem:

- module: The computer-friendly name of this module (biography). This will be used to construct hook function calls for this content type. In rare cases, you may need to set this to something other than the name of this module. But we will define all of the necessary hooks below.

There are a few other fields that we have not used in our hook_node_info() implementation. These are help for help text, min_word_count to specify the minimum number of words in the body, and lock to indicate whether an administrator can override the labels we have given this content type.

In Chapter 4, we created the **Quote content type**. We changed the title_label and body_label through the **Administer | Content management | Content types** interface.

To take a look ahead, we have set up the labels so that the content creation form would look like this:

Home * **Create content**

Create Biography

Biography of: *

▸ Menu settings

Split summary at cursor

Overview:

▸ Input format

However, until we implement `hook_form()`, the form will not display. Now we will take a look at that hook.

The Content Creation Form

In Chapter 4, we created the Quote content type. Creating new content was easy. The form displayed in **Create content | Quote** was the same form used by **Create content | Page** and **Create content | Story**.

Now, however, we have a more complex content type. We need a form that will display all the biography fields: **Biography of** (stored as the document's title), **Overview** (stored in the document's body), **Dates**, **Life**, and **Works**.

To specify how the form for our new content type ought to look, we will implement `hook_form()`. Drupal will call this hook whenever a user creates a new biography.

In the last chapter, we looked at the **Forms API (FAPI)** in some detail. Here, we will make use of many of the same features. Since we have seen this API before, I will keep the explanation brief.

```php
/ **
 * Implementation of hook_form().
 */
function biography_form(&$node) {
  $type = node_get_types('type', $node);
  // Existing files: title (Biography of) and body (Overview)
  if ($type->has_title) {
    $form['title'] = array(
      '#type' => 'textfield',
      '#title' => check_plain($type->title_label),
      '#required' => TRUE,
      '#default_value' => $node->title,
      '#weight' => -5,
    );
  }

  if ($type->has_body) {
    $form['body_field'] = node_body_field(
      $node,
      $type->body_label,
      $type->min_word_count
    );
  }

  // Our custom fields: Dates, Life, Works.
```

```
  // (See FAPI docs for specification)
  $form['dates'] = array(
    '#type' => 'textfield',
    '#size' => 50,
    '#maxlengh' => 127,
    '#title' => t('Dates'),
    '#description' => t('Birth and death dates.'),
    '#default_value' => isset($node->dates) ? $node->dates : '',
  );

  $form['life'] = array(
    '#type' => 'textarea',
    '#title' => t('Life'),
    '#cols' => 50,
    '#rows' => 15,
    '#description' => t('A description of this person\'s life.'),
    '#default_value' => isset($node->life) ? $node->life : '',
  );
  $form['works'] = array(
    '#type' => 'textarea',
    '#title' => t('Works'),
    '#cols' => 50,
    '#rows' => 5,
    '#description' => t('An annotated bibliography of this person\'s
works.'),
    '#default_value' => isset($node->works) ? $node->works : '',
  );

  return $form;
}
```

Our `biography_form()` hook implementation is passed one parameter. The `$node` variable (which is passed by reference) will contain the base *node object* for our new content. This node is initialized with default information.

Part of the job of this hook is to override existing defaults with defaults more appropriate for our content type.

Also, at this point Drupal doesn't have any biography-specific fields set. Therefore, the second purpose of this function will be to configure extra default data for a biography content type.

Let's start with the first.

Overriding hook_form() Defaults

Most of the contents of this function should look familiar. It is the first section, if anything, that should appear uncommon for a form definition. The following code is responsible for overriding existing defaults.

```
$type = node_get_types('type', $node);

// Existing files: title (Biography of) and body (Overview)
if ($type->has_title) {
  $form['title'] = array(
    '#type' => 'textfield',
    '#title' => check_plain($type->title_label),
    '#required' => TRUE,
    '#default_value' => $node->title,
    '#weight' => -5,
  );
}
if ($type->has_body) {
  $form['body_field'] = node_body_field(
      $node,
      $type->body_label,
      $type->min_word_count
    );
}
```

The first thing this code does is retrieve information about the type of node that we are working with.

At first, this might seem silly. After all, we know that this node is a `biography` node. But the object returned by `node_get_type()` is richer than that. It returns an object that contains some important information about the configuration of the biography content type.

The `$type` object contains attributes matching those we created in `biography_node_info()`. But the values of these fields might be different. While our `biography_hook_info()` function sets the defaults for `title_label`, `body_label`, `has_body` and so on, an administrator can override these values.

Using `node_get_type()`, we can get the latest information about this content type's configuration—including any changes the administrator has made over and above our initial setup with `biography_hook_info()`.

With this information, we can begin to define the first two fields of our form. If this form is to have a title (that is, if `$type->has_title` is `TRUE`), then we define the title's text field:

```
if ($type->has_title) {
  $form['title'] = array(
    '#type' => 'textfield',
    '#title' => check_plain($type->title_label),
    '#required' => TRUE,
    '#default_value' => $node->title,
    '#weight' => -5,
  );
}
```

Note that we use `$type->title_label` to set the field's title. If an administrator has not made a change, the `#title` field should be set to `Biography of`.

A similar setup is used for the body (`Overview`) field. If `$type->has_body` is `TRUE`, then a form field is configured for the body, as well.

Drupal uses a sophisticated set of elements to display the body field—elements including a separator bar to delimit what part of the body is to be treated as the **Summary**, a text area field, and the **Input format** submenu. To conveniently create all of these fields, Drupal provides the `node_body_field()` function.

> Generally speaking, the `node_body_field()` function should only be called to create the node's body field. It is not suitable for use to create additional custom fields. For more information on `node_body_field()`, see the Drupal API notes: `http://api.drupal.org/api/function/node_body_field/6`.

Now the title (`Biography of`) and body (`Overview`) fields are correctly configured. Next, we need to add a few new fields to our form.

Adding New hook_form() Form Elements

As we saw earlier, the first purpose of the `hook_form()` hook was to give us a chance to override Drupal's defaults for our new content type.

The second purpose is to give us the opportunity to specify form elements for our content type.

Accomplishing this is simply a matter of using FAPI to define the desired form elements:

```
$form['dates'] = array(
  '#type' => 'textfield',
  '#size' => 50,
  '#maxlengh' => 127,
  '#title' => t('Dates'),
  '#description' => t('Birth and death dates.'),
  '#default_value' => isset($node->dates) ? $node->dates : '',
);
$form['life'] = array(
  '#type' => 'textarea',
  '#title' => t('Life'),
  '#cols' => 50,
  '#rows' => 15,
  '#description' => t('A description of this person\'s life.'),
  '#default_value' => isset($node->life) ? $node->life : '',
);
$form['works'] = array(
  '#type' => 'textarea',
  '#title' => t('Works'),
  '#cols' => 50,
  '#rows' => 5,
  '#description' => t('An annotated bibliography of this
                      person\'s works.'),
  '#default_value' => isset($node->works) ? $node->works : '',
);

return $form;
```

The form elements created above do not differ markedly from the forms we created in the last chapter. In a nutshell, this code creates three additional form fields:

1. A text field for entering a person's dates (`Dates`)
2. A text area for adding a biography (`Life`)
3. A text area for adding a bibliography or list of accomplishments (`Works`)

These three fields correlate to the three identically named columns we created in the bibliography database at the beginning of this chapter.

Once the form data structure is complete, we return it. When Drupal renders it, it will look something like the following screenshot:

(Note that the text areas were sized down to fit in the screenshot)

The content entry form is now complete. But what happens to the data when it is submitted?

The short answer is—lots of things.

Permissions are checked, form data is validated, extra processing tasks are performed, and then the data is inserted into the database. We are only concerned with a couple of these tasks, though.

First, we will examine the permission checking features. Then, we will move on to the database API.

Access Controls

In the last chapter, we took a quick look at access controls as a way to allow some users the ability to send email messages, while denying others such capabilities.

Here, we will be doing something similar. We will create one hook to register three new permissions, and then we will create a second hook that will test a user to see if she or he can access a biography.

First, let's look at hook_perm(), which is responsible for registering new permissions:

```
/**
 * Implements hook_perm()
 */
function biography_perm() {
  return array(
    'create biography node',
    'edit biography nodes',
    'delete biography nodes',
  );
}
```

An implementation of hook_perm() simply returns an array of permission strings. Our implementation, biography_perm(), registers three new permissions: create biography node, edit biography nodes, and delete biography nodes.

These permissions will now show up on **Administer | User management | Permissions**:

Permission	anonymous user	authenticated user	site administrators
biography module			
create biography node	☐	☐	☐
delete biography nodes	☐	☐	☐
edit biography nodes	☐	☐	☐
block module			
administer blocks	☐	☐	☐
use PHP for block visibility	☐	☐	☐

Using this screen, an administrator can choose which roles to assign these permissions to.

Roles and permissions were introduced in Chapter 1 and covered again in Chapter 6. The `email_user()` function we created in Chapter 6 used the `user_access()` function (an implementation of `hook_access()`) to determine if a user could `administer users`.

Though these three permissions strings are meaningful to us, by themselves they have no special meaning for Drupal. We could have named them A, B, and I like butterflies, and it would not make a functional difference.

For Drupal, the purpose of these strings is determined by the context in which Drupal invokes the `hook_access()` hook.

For example, when a user tries to create a new biography entry, Drupal will try to invoke `biography_access()`, passing it the operation `create`. If the function returns TRUE, then Drupal will allow the user to create the biography node. But a FALSE return will prevent the user from creating new biography nodes.

We can use our hook implementation to only grant `create` rights to users who are members of a role with `create biography node` permissions.

Permissions are assigned to roles. Users are members of roles. Any access control, then, is based on a user's role.

Here is our `biography_access()` hook implementation:

```
/**
 * Implements hook_access()
 */
function biography_access($op, $node, $account) {
  switch ($op) {
    case 'create':
      return user_access('create biography node', $account);
    case 'update':
      return user_access('edit biography nodes', $account);
    case 'delete':
      return user_access('delete biography nodes', $account);
  }
}
```

Three arguments are passed into this function:

- `$op`: The name of the operation Drupal will perform if this function returns TRUE. In our case, we are concerned with three operations: `create`, `update`, and `delete` — all of which have to do with manipulating nodes with our biography content type.

- `$node`: The node that Drupal will act on if this form returns TRUE. This is passed in to allow for advanced checking. We could, for instance, make a determination based on whether the user was the owner of that node.

- `$account`: The user's account object. We looked at the `$account` object in the last chapter. Here, we can use it to find out about a user's permissions.

Our function maps the permissions we created with `biography_perm()` to the names of the three operations. The `create` operation is permitted for a user only if that user's `$account` object has the permission `create biography node`. Similarly, `modify` attempts return `true` only if the user has `modify biography nodes` set; `delete` attempts are allowed only if the user has the `delete biography nodes` permission.

Calling another hook implementation

Rather than replicating the permissions testing logic, which would require getting a user's role and then checking the permissions in that role, our code above calls another instance of `hook_access()`. `user_access()` already contains the requisite logic, so we use that instead of writing redundant code.

As this example illustrates, there is no reason why one hook implementation cannot call another hook implementation.

What happens if the `hook_access()` function does not handle the `$op` operation? Drupal does not simply assume that the user does not have permissions. Instead, Drupal examines the `node_access` table in the database and tries to determine whether the user should be allowed to perform the requested operation. This may lead to situations where users are granted permissions that were not intended. See `http://api.drupal.org/api/group/node_access/6` for a description of the node access system. (This document also explains what happens if `hook_access()` is not defined for a module.)

Now we have configured the permissions and access control aspects of our new content type. Next, we are going switch to a lower-level task. We are going to implement a handful of database hooks, which will be responsible for dealing with the underlying database.

Database Hooks

When we created the installer, we used the Schema API to define how our new biography content type table looks. However, the Schema API is abstract enough that we wrote no SQL, and we didn't directly call any database functions.

Now we will create four functions that deal with the database at a low level, and we will write SQL statements to perform database operations.

We need to define functions to perform the following:

- Insert a new biography entry into the biography table.
- Remove an unwanted entry from the biography table.
- Update an existing entry in the biography table.
- Remove a particular version (or revision) from the biography table.

Keep in mind that the biography table that we created earlier is an auxiliary table. Much of the content type's data is stored in the node table. Only identification information and data that is specific to our content type (like dates, life, and works) is stored in our custom table.

The functions that we define will only need to operate on our custom table. Drupal already contains functions for manipulating entries in the node table.

We will begin with the insertion code.

Database Inserts with hook_insert()

When a user submits a new biography (as defined by biography_form()), Drupal will go through a checking and cleaning procedure, and then it will attempt to store the data.

Part of the storage procedure involves calling the appropriate hook_insert() implementation for the module specified by hook_node_info(). Our biography_node_info() set 'module' => 'biography', so Drupal will look for the biography_insert() function to handle the task of inserting biography data into custom tables.

biography_insert() is passed one parameter, $node, which contains the data that the user submitted. All the default node fields will be present, as will the fields that we set up in $biography_form().

Our responsibility will be to take the appropriate subset of information from the $node object and use it to populate the custom biography table.

```
/**
 * implements hook_insert().
 */
function biography_insert($node) {
  if (!isset($node->life)) {
    $node->life = '';
  }
  if (!isset($node->works)) {
    $node->works = '';
  }
  db_query(
    'INSERT INTO {biography} (vid, nid, dates, life, works) '
      ."VALUES (%d, %d, '%s', '%s','%s')",
    $node->vid,
    $node->nid,
    $node->dates,
    $node->life,
    $node->works
  );
}
```

What do we do with the $node object passed in? We put the requisite fields into an SQL statement and run it. This is all done in one step. The Drupal db_query() function handles most of the mundane database preparation.

> **Checking text fields**
>
> In the first few lines of the above function, we add a default value (if necessary) to $node->life and $node->works. Both these fields are stored in the database using the text type. So it is necessary to set defaults because MySQL cannot set default values for text fields. The dates field (which is a varchar field) already has a default, so we don't need to define one here. This was noted when we created the schema at the beginning of this chapter.

The db_query() function takes the SQL statement, and then any number of arguments that it will format and insert into the SQL. Let's begin by looking at the SQL statement. As a plain old string, it looks as follows:

```
INSERT INTO {biography} (vid, nid, dates, life, works)
  VALUES (%d, %d, '%s', '%s','%s')
```

This statement is a basic SQL insert that sets values for vid, nid, dates, life, and works.

Before passing this string on to the database to be executed, Drupal does some interpolation. The first things it will examine are the table names.

The table name is enclosed in curly braces: {biography}. This additional punctuation informs Drupal that this is a table name. Under some circumstances, Drupal will need to rewrite the table name. For example, it is possible to configure Drupal to add a prefix to every table. The db_query() function handles this for us, rather than the developer handling prefixes.

Any table name surrounded by curly braces will be automatically adjusted according to table configuration rules for Drupal. (This actually happens behind the scenes in the Schema API, too.)

The next thing to look at is the series of placeholders. In the code, there are two instances of the %d placeholder, and three instances of the %s placeholder.

When db_query() executes, it will replace each of the placeholders with the remaining arguments. Since there are five placeholders, it will expect five additional parameters to be passed in:

```
db_query(
    'INSERT INTO {biography} (vid, nid, dates, life, works) '
      ."VALUES (%d, %d, '%s', '%s','%s')",
    $node->vid,
    $node->nid,
    $node->dates,
    $node->life,
    $node->works
);
```

The five $node attributes (vid, nid, dates, life, and works) are substituted for placeholders in order. So $node->vid will replace the first %d, and $node->nid will replace the second. Then, each of the three remaining parameters will replace (in order) the three %s placeholders.

 A string with placeholders in it, especially one intended to be used by the printf()/sprintf() family of functions, is called a **format string**.

So what's with the `%d` and `%s` things? These placeholders identify the data type of the variable that will be substituted in. Briefly, the following are the common placeholders:

- `%d` represents an integer (one or more digits, but no decimals).
- `%s` represents a string.
- `%b` represents a binary number.
- `%f` represents a floating point number (digits and decimals).
- `%%` escapes a percent sign. In other words, it is converted to `%`.

Drupal's substitution mechanism does not support the more advanced patterns (like `%2.5f`) that PHP's `sprintf()`/`printf()` family of functions provide. Only these five simple placeholders are supported. Thus, if you want to round a decimal before inserting it, you will need to do the rounding in code, instead of relying upon `db_query()`.

> Note that when we use the `%s` placeholder for a value, we surround it in quotes. But integers (`%d`) and floats (`%f`) don't need to be quoted. This is a function of SQL, not of Drupal's library, though. For example, if you enclose an integer in quotation marks, yet insert it into an integer field, MySQL will automatically convert it to an integer.

Why use the placeholder function instead of just concatenating strings? Why not just write SQL like this: `'SELECT ' .implode(', ', fields) . ' FROM {mytable};'`? (Do not *ever* write your Drupal code this way!)

There are two reasons why the above is frowned upon. First, it is more difficult to read concatenated strings than it is to read a format string. This leads to errors, some of which are hard to detect.

Second, and more importantly, using the placeholder method is more secure. Drupal's `db_query()` function does more than just format the string. It also performs a series of checks and escapes on the data.

Values earmarked to replace `%d` are converted to integers and those replacing `%f` are converted to floats. Binary values (`%b`) are encoded with the Drupal `db_encode_blob()` function, and strings are escaped with the `db_escape_string()` Drupal function.

>
> `db_encode_blob()` and `db_escape_string()` are wrapper functions. The underlying database libraries will use the strongest available escaping algorithms to prepare data for database queries. For example, `db_escape_string()` will use `pg_escape_string()` on PostgreSQL, and `mysqli_real_escape_string()` for MySQL (with the MySQLi library).

These measures provide vital protection against accidents, mistakes, and malicious attempts to subvert the system. For that reason, you should *always* use placeholders for your data (especially for user-submitted data).

When `biography_insert()` is run, a new row will be added to the biography table. The `nid` (Node ID) and `vid` (Version ID) will correlate to the matching `nid` and `vid` in the node table. That is how the `title` (`Biography of`) and `body` (`Overview`) data, which is stored in the node table, retains its connection with the data in the biography table.

In order to introduce the features of Drupal's `db_query()`, we've lingered over the `hook_insert()` hook. Now we'll move along faster.

Updating and Deleting Database Records

With a general idea of how database queries work, we can move along faster through the remaining database functions.

We already have a function to perform inserts. Next, we need to create one to update existing data:

```
/**
 * implements hook_update().
 */
function biography_update($node) {
  if ($node->revision) {
    biography_insert($node);
  }
  else {
    db_query("UPDATE {biography} "
        ."SET dates = '%s', life = '%s', works='%s' "
        ."WHERE vid = %d",
      $node->dates,
      $node->life,
      $node->works,
      $node->vid
    );
  }
}
```

This function handles updates.

Actually, it does just a little more than that. This function might be called for a row that does not already exist. When a new revision is created for an existing node, the revision is handled by `hook_update()` instead of `hook_insert()`. So the first thing we need to do is see if the `$node->revision` flag is set. If it is TRUE, then we treat the update as an insert, and pass the `$node` on to `biography_insert()`.

Otherwise, we assume that the existing row is to be modified, and we perform an SQL update. In the update itself, we use the `vid` (which is the table's primary key) to locate the row that should be changed. Since `nid` will remain static, we don't bother with it at all in this operation.

Next, we need to define a function for deleting a node. When a node is deleted, all rows containing that node's ID (`nid`) should be removed. If Drupal is tracking revisions (using `vid`), that may mean that more than one row is deleted from our table:

```
/**
 * Implements hook_delete().
 */
function biography_delete($node) {
  db_query(
    'DELETE FROM {biography} WHERE nid = %d',
    $node->nid
  );
}
```

While we update using the `vid`, `hook_delete()` should delete using the `nid` because we want to delete *all* the versions of this node.

But what if we need to delete just a revision of a particular node? There is no hook for doing that, so we have to implement `hook_nodeapi()`, a general purpose hook for handling nodes.

The `hook_nodeapi()` hook works like other Drupal functions we've seen. It is passed three parameters:

- `$node`: The *reference* to the current node
- `$op`: The name of the operation to perform
- `$teaser`: The teaser parameter (when `$op` is `view`) or form parameter (when `$op` is `validate`)
- `$page`: The page parameter when `$op` is `view`

While there are over a dozen different possible `$op` values, we are only concerned with one: `'delete revision'`. That is the operation that is requested when only one `vid` should be deleted.

```
/**
 * This implementation just handles deleting node revisions.
 * Implements hook_nodeapi().
 */
function biography_nodeapi(&$node, $op, $teaser, $page) {
  if ($op == 'delete revision') {
    db_query(
```

```
        'DELETE FROM {biography} WHERE vid = %d',
        $node->vid
    );
    }
}
```

When the `delete revision` operation is passed, we delete the row with the primary key stored in `$node->vid`.

> `hook_nodeapi()` is a veritable Swiss army knife of tools for dealing with nodes. As with most other Drupal hooks, `hook_nodeapi()` is documented, and the documentation can be viewed at: `http://api.drupal.org/api/function/hook_nodeapi/6`.

At this point, we have finished with the majority of the database code (we still have a `SELECT` coming up).

When developing modules with low-level database code like we have used here, it is important to keep security in mind. In many cases, simply by using the correct functions (like `db_query()`) correctly (by using placeholders), a module developer can avoid the common pitfalls associated with SQL development.

We've implemented half a dozen hooks already, but we've still got more to go in order to create a fully functional content type. The next class of hooks is those used to assist in loading and viewing the content.

Hooks for Getting Data

We're getting close to the end, now. We have only three more functions to go.

So far, we've created an installer, implemented hooks to create the database tables, implemented access controls, created a form, and developed functions for maintaining our custom tables.

In this section, we will look at functions used for accessing our content. And once again, we will be moving back toward the familiar. We will start by implementing `hook_load()`, then we will take a look at `hook_view()` and `hook_theme()`.

> In the subsection *Getting the Node's Content* in Chapter 4, we used the function `node_load()` to load the contents of a node. That function is an implementation of `hook_node()`. In that chapter we also looked carefully at adding theme support to a module, covering `hook_theme()` as well.

Loading a Node with hook_load()

The `hook_load()` hook provides a chance for extended content types, like the one we are creating, to load additional data. This extra information is combined with the existing node data to return a custom node object.

While this sounds confusing, in fact it is fairly straightforward. Any content type is going to have an entry in Drupal's node table. So any time Drupal loads a node, it will first fetch data from the node table.

Let's refer to our node object as `$node`. When Drupal first loads `$node`, it will contain the fields set in the node table and its supporting tables.

But our content type, `biography`, has some additional fields that are not stored in the default tables, and so do not get initially added to `$node`.

That's where `hook_load()` comes in. While loading the node, Drupal will call the appropriate `hook_load()` for that node type. In our example, then, that would be `biography_load()`. In general, the responsibility of this function is to load and prepare any additional data for the biography content type. We will do this by selecting some data out of our biography table.

```
/**
 * Implementation of hook_load().
 */
function biography_load($node) {
  $result = db_query(
    'SELECT dates, life, works FROM {biography} WHERE vid = %d',
    $node->vid
  );
  return db_fetch_object($result);
}
```

A `hook_node()` implementation is passed a `$node` object that has been partially built. All its fields have been loaded from the `node` table (and any supporting tables), and the object is initialized.

Why do I say `$node` is *partially* built? Because the fields that we are going to fetch from the database will eventually become part of this object, as well.

This function is not exactly daunting. The $node that is passed into biography_ load() has a vid, and that is all we need to select our fields from the database. (It also has a nid, so we don't need to fetch that from the database.) We only need to create a basic SELECT statement to retrieve the data:

```
'SELECT dates, life, works FROM {biography} WHERE vid = %d'
```

Again, keep in mind that {biography} is treated as a placeholder for the biography table name and %d will be replaced with the vid.

Our use of db_query() here differs a little from our previous cases. Here, we capture the return value of db_query(), which is a database-specific resource ID. (Its content differs between PostgreSQL and MySQL.)

Earlier, we didn't need to capture this return value because we had no need of returned data. But after executing a SELECT, we want to access the returned rows.

The ID returned from the query can be used to fetch this data using db_fetch_object().

Capturing results with db_fetch_* functions

There are two different functions for fetching the results of a database query: db_fetch_object() and db_fetch_array(). The first, db_ fetch_object(), returns on object representing the returned values. These values are accessed as members: $obj->my_column_name. db_ fetch_array() returns an associative array whose values are accessed this way: $arr['my_column_name']. There are other methods of accessing returned data, like db_result(), but the two db_fetch_* functions are the most frequently used.

We simply return the results of db_fetch_object() at the end of the function. Drupal will take care of combining this object with the existing $node.

When we later work with the resulting $node object, we will find that it contains all the fields from the node table, as well as these that we've added from the biography table.

We're working our way from low-level DB work up to a theme. Next, we'll look at the process of preparing the node for display.

Preparing the Node for Display with hook_view()

The `hook_view()` hook is called once a `$node` object has been loaded, but before the `$node` has been displayed. It gives us a chance to prepare that node for display before passing it on to the theme engine.

Why do we need a function like this? Because Drupal doesn't know what to do with the extra fields of our content type.

For example, our data has not been checked and escaped for display in the browser.

In addition, the theme system does not have any information regarding how it should display our content. We need to supply information about theme rendering, as well.

With this in mind, let's look at the function:

```
/**
 * Implementation of hook_view().
 */
function biography_view($node, $teaser = FALSE, $page = FALSE) {
  $node = node_prepare($node, $teaser); // get it ready for display

  $dates = check_plain($node->dates);
  $life = check_markup($node->life);
  $works = check_markup($node->works);

  // Add theme stuff here
  $node->content['biography_info'] = array(
    '#value' => theme('biography_info', $dates, $life, $works),
    '#weight' => 1,
  );

  return $node;
}
```

The function is passed three arguments:

- The fully initialized `$node`, which now contains the extra fields from our biography database.

- A flag, `$teaser`, telling us whether the article should be displayed as a teaser only.

- A flag, `$page`, telling us whether the article is on its own page. This effects theme rendering.

For our module, we won't be doing much with $teaser or $page—we'll just pass them on to other functions that will take care of any specific formatting.

In some cases, though, you might want to use these flags in order to better control the display of your content type.

The first thing this function does is call node_prepare(). The node_prepare() function handles a variety of boilerplate preparation tasks. It makes sure that a **read more** link is added if the node is displayed in teaser form (i.e. if $teaser is TRUE). It does some safety checking on the title (Biography of) and body (Overview) fields that have been retrieved from the node table. Specifically, it runs check_markup() on both of these.

Safety-checking HTML with check_markup()

The check_markup() function handles formatting of user-entered text. By default, it checks to make sure that any HTML tags used in the field are allowed tags. (Some tags, like <script/>, are not allowed for security reasons.) It also does a certain amount of cross-platform conversion and other cleanup. check_markup(), along with check_plain(), is one of the most important functions in a module developer's toolbox. It should always be used when sending user-submitted HTML to the client. See the API documentation for more details at: http://api. drupal.org/api/function/check_markup/6. We will look at this function again in the next chapter, as well.

Finally, $node_prepare() begins the process of building the $node object's content field. This field is used by the theme API to display the node.

After doing the base node preparation with node_prepare(), we need to do some additional work to prepare the biography fields.

```
$dates = check_plain($node->dates);
$life = check_markup($node->life);
$works = check_markup($node->works);
```

We want to make sure that all the three fields are safe for display on the user's browser. To do this, we use check_* functions on our fields.

It is absolutely critical to do this checking. Failure to do so opens the door for a malicious user to attempt a Cross Site Scripting (XSS) attack using your site.

The check_plain() function, which we have seen before, removes all HTML from a string. check_markup() allows "safe" HTML only. Both do some additional formatting of the data. See the tip **Safety-checking HTML with check_markup()** earlier for more information on check_markup().

Finally, the function finishes up by preparing the content for the theme engine and returning the finished node:

```
$node->content['biography_info'] = array(
   '#value' => theme('biography_info', $dates, $life, $works),
   '#weight' => 1,
);

return $node
```

The first section above continues the process of building the $node->content array, which will eventually be used to display the content in the node template or theming function.

We will add an element to the content array and element named biography_info. This element itself must have a #value (the formatted content to display) and a #weight (to indicate roughly where this data will be placed in the rendered page).

The documentation for hook_view() is a good starting point for learning more about preparing node contents for theming:
http://api.drupal.org/api/function/hook_view/6.

The #weight field determines how high on the page a field will display. Putting it at 1 will ensure that it displays after the title and body.

We discussed using weights in the last chapter. Remember, the higher the number, the "heavier" the object, and the lower it will sink on the list. You can use the theme examining features in the Devel module to examine the effect of weights on the output.

To generate the #value, we will connect our module to the theme engine. We are going to create a biography_info theme, which will function a lot like the theming we did at the end of Chapter 4.

Let's move on and look at the theming of our new content type.

Theming Biography Content

We are at the last step of developing our custom content type. The code presented in the last section handled the process of retrieving the information from the database, preparing it, and then handing it off to the theme layer.

Here, we just need to implement the theme layer.

We took our first look at coding themes in Chapter 3. Since then, we have interacted with the theme layer in subsequent chapters. Once again we will make use of the theme layer. We will provide a default theme for our content type.

Actually, we will be doing a little less than that. We will provide a default theme *only for the custom fields* of our biography content type. The standard node fields already have theme support, and there is no particular reason why we (as module developers) would want to override those. After all, we are only providing defaults. We'll leave more serious theming to the theme developers.

This time around, we are going to use a template for our theme instead of writing a theming function. So creating our default theme will be a two-step process:

- Register a theme by implementing `hook_theme()`.
- Create a theme template in `biography.tpl.php`.

Since we have already taken a look at the theme system (Chapter 3) and also implemented a default theme (in Chapter 4), we will move quickly, here.

Registering a Theme

The last thing we need to do in `biography.module` is register the theme that this module is going to implement.

At the end of the previous section we looked at this snippet of code from `biography_view()`:

```
$node->content['biography_info'] = array(
  '#value' => theme('biography_info', $dates, $life, $works),
  '#weight' => 1,
);
```

In this code, we build the `$node->content` array. Already, that array has the standard node content (which was added by `node_prepare()`). But we need to format our custom fields, `$life`, `$works`, and `$dates`, and add those to the content. Formatting work is handled by themes, so we used the theme function: `theme('biography_info', $dates, $life, $works)`.

This function will use the `biography_info` theme function or template to render our additional content. `$dates`, `$life`, and `$works` will be passed on to the theme.

As it stands now, though, there is no such theme as `biography_info`. We will start out by registering this theme:

```
/**
 * Implements hook_theme().
 */
function biography_theme() {
  return array(
    'biography_info' => array(
      'template' => 'biography_info',
      'arguments' => array(
        'dates' => NULL,
        'life' => NULL,
        'works' => NULL,
      ),
    ),
  );
}
```

As you may recall from Chapter 4, `hook_theme()` is used to register new themes. An implementation of this hook should return an associative array where the keys are the names of the newly registered themes, and the values are arrays that describe how each theme should be executed.

In our example, we want to register one theme, `biography_info`, and we want to create a template (instead of a function) to do our theming. To do this, we will need to add two items to the `biography_info` entry:

```
'biography_info' => array(
  'template' => 'biography_info',
  'arguments' => array(
    'dates' => NULL,
    'life' => NULL,
    'works' => NULL,
  ),
```

The first item, `template` points to the name (without the `.tpl.php` extension) of the template file. So in this case, we are registering a template named `biography_info`. Actually, the file must be named `biography_info.tpl.php`, but `.tpl.php` is added automatically.

The second item, `arguments`, indicates what information should be passed on to this theme. Since we are using a template, what this setting does is determine what variables will be available in our template. We want $dates, $life, and $works to be variables in our template.

Now we have registered the default `biography_info` theme and tied it to a template named `biography_info.tpl.php`. The last thing to do in this chapter is create the template.

The biography_info.tpl.php Template

We looked at a handful of templates in Chapter 3. Because of the small scope of our current theme, which only needs to present three variables, this template will be even simpler than those we have looked at already.

To create our template, we simply create a new file in our module's directory. The name of the template we registered is `biography_info.tpl.php`. Here are the contents of that file:

```php
<?php
// $Id$
/**
 * Template to display biography nodes.
 *
 * Fields available:
 * $dates: cleaned plain text string
 * $life: cleaned HTML string
 * $works: cleaned HTML string
 */
?>
<div class="biography_info">
  <h2><?php print t('Dates');?>:</h2>
  <?php print $dates;?>
  <h2><?php print t('Life');?>:</h2>
  <?php print $life;?>
  <h2><?php print t('Works');?>:</h2>
  <?php print $works;?>
</div>
```

The first thing that should stand out is the fact that the comments are almost as long as the template file. The template we are adding is a default theme. We recognize that a theme developer may very well want to override our implementation to provide a better (less generic) display of biography info. Providing detailed comments here is simply a way of making the theme developer's life easier.

Otherwise, this template consists of some very basic HTML and template code:

```
<div class="biography_info">
  <h2><?php print t('Dates');?>:</h2>
  <?php print $dates;?>
  <h2><?php print t('Life');?>:</h2>
  <?php print $life;?>
  <h2><?php print t('Works');?>:</h2>
  <?php print $works;?>
</div>
```

The template simply prints out three sections—one for `$dates`, one for `$life`, and one for `$works`. Each one gets a header, translated with the `t()` function. That's simply all there is to it.

The Results

Earlier, we took a look at the forms we created for adding content. Now that we've finished the theme, we can see what a biography entry will look like when viewed.

Home

Thomas Reid

Submitted by matt on Mon, 01/21/2008 - 00:12

The Scottish philosopher Thomas Reid is famous for advocating a "common sense" approach to philosophy grounded in a realist metaphysics.Often, he is cited for his strong opposition to David Hume's skeptically tinged empiricism.

Dates:

April 26, 1710 – October 7, 1796

Life:

Reid studied at the University of Aberdeen. After a brief period as a minister, he taught at Kings College, Aberdeen. Twelve years later, he moved to University of Glasgow, taking a more prestigious chair.

Works:

An Essay on Quantity

An Inquiry into the Human Mind on the Principles of Common Sense

Essays on the Intellectual Powers of Man

Essays on the Active Powers of Man

The top part of this page (from **Thomas Reid** to the end of the first paragraph) is generated by the default theme for a node. In this case, it is generated from the `node.tpl.php` file from the Descartes/Bluemarine theme we worked with in Chapter 3.

The lower half of the screenshot, though, is generated from our `biography_info.tpl.php` template.

Any time a biography node is viewed, it will be laid out like this (assuming the theme isn't changed). All of our custom fields will be displayed automatically.

Similarly, a biography node will be treated like all other nodes. Biographies can be promoted to the front page; they will be visible in RSS feeds, and so on. In short, by building a custom content type, we have fully integrated biographies into the Drupal framework.

Summary

In many ways, this chapter has been the most difficult. We looked at several APIs, including the Schema API, the Node API, the database API, the Forms API, and the theming system. We implemented many hooks from these APIs.

We moved from installation (with a module install file) to content creation, and on to content viewing. And we moved back and forth from high-level user interface APIs (like FAPI and the theme system) down to the lowest database APIs.

In the end, we created a fully integrated custom content type. In the process, we got a very good view of Drupal's inner workings, learning how to make use of some of the most fundamental APIs.

The next chapter will continue building upon existing knowledge. In that chapter, we will explore some of the advanced features of Drupal's module system.

8
Filters, Actions, and Hooks

In this chapter, we will build a module that will automate the process of sending a newsletter email to all of the users on our system. In Chapter 6, we looked at the email features. In this chapter, we will focus on three other important topics: building content filters, creating an action and assigning a trigger to the action, and creating a hook that other modules can implement.

Along the way, we will revisit some of the other topics we have already explored, but we will focus our attention on these three new topics. During the course of this chapter we will perform the following:

- Assign a dependency to a module
- Create a simple content type
- Create content filter and an administrative interface for that filter
- Add a new action
- Define a custom hook and implement it
- Revisit the mail API — this time to send a message to all users
- Use the theme system to theme plain-text email
- Create a trigger

This is a lot of ground to cover. But this chapter illustrates how complex module programming tasks can be accomplished efficiently in Drupal.

As usual, we will begin with a brief description of what we want this new module to do.

The sitenews Module

In this chapter, we will build a module that handles sending an email message containing site news to users of the system. The module will send an email message about the latest content and features on our site. The message will be made up of the following components:

- **The introduction**: An administrator will compose a message that will be placed at the top of the site news message. This message, which we will call a news brief provides a way of tailoring a message to the system's users. We will also make this content available on the website.

- **Zero or more update sections**: While the news brief will provide an introduction to the newsletter, these sections will consist of automatically generated messages. Modules will be able to define their own sections. We will use the hook mechanism to define a hook that modules can implement.

In a nutshell, then, every site news email that goes out will have exactly one news brief item, and zero or more other sections generated automatically by other modules.

This brief description explains the content of the site news message, but we will also create a process. We will design code that handles the collecting, composing, and sending of site news. Also, we will write this code in such a way that an administrator will be able to determine when the code is executed. To do this, we will use the Actions API, and configure a trigger to execute that action.

When the appropriate trigger fires, Drupal will send the site news as an email message to all users of our system.

> While it might be desirable in some scenarios to have an opt-in or opt-out scheme allowing users to decide for themselves whether they will receive the site news mailing, we will not be creating this feature. Adding an opt-in checkbox to a user profile would not be difficult. See Chapter 5.

There's another desirable feature of the news brief content type that we will implement. By default, Drupal content is targeted toward web browsers. But our site news will be emailed. To respect the wide variety of email clients, we will format the content as plain text, not HTML.

While we format text, there is another task we can accomplish. Sometimes it is nice to insert some generic placeholders in the body of the news brief, and have Drupal replace those placeholders with generated text as needed.

To accomplish these to formatting tasks, we will use the content filter system from the Filter module.

By the end of the chapter, we will have a module that performs the following series of steps:

- When a certain event occurs, a site news action will be triggered (and this action is the sending of the email message). The event, for us, will be the publishing of a news brief node.
- The main site news message will be prepared for sending.
  - Part of this preparation will be the filtering of this node through a series of custom filters.
- Then the other blocks of content, gathered from modules that implement our hook, will be formatted, as well.
- Once all of this content is formatted, it will be inserted into an email message, which will then be sent to all the site subscribers.

This module will provide a mostly-automated process for creating a new newsletter or site updates system without requiring significant labor from the site administrators or content creators.

As we have done with our other modules, we will begin with the .info file and the rudiments of our new sitenews.module file.

Getting Started

Our new module will be called sitenews, and will be stored in the drupal/sites/all/modules/sitenews directory.

Citing Dependencies in the .info File

While the .info files we've been using differ only in name and description, here we will make use of a new field.

```
; $Id$
name = "Site News"
description = "Send an email message of site news to all users."
core = 6.x
php = 5.1
dependencies[] = "trigger"
```

The `sitenews.info` file should look largely familiar. The last line is the only one with a new directive.

This last line is used to indicate what dependencies a modules has. That is, it tells Drupal which other modules must be installed before this module can function appropriately.

Since it is not uncommon for a module to have multiple dependencies, the `dependencies` directive is multi-valued. As we saw in Chapter 2, its syntax is basically like that of a PHP array assignment:

```
dependencies[] = "trigger"
```

If we need to add a second dependency, we would simply add another similar line:

```
dependencies[] = "trigger"
dependencies[] = "othermodule"
```

Why set a dependency? There are a couple of reasons one might choose to do this.

The most common reason is that the code in one module uses code defined in another module. But that will not be the case for us.

Another reason is that a module might basically be unusable without the other module. This is not necessarily a code dependency so much as a process dependency. This is the case for our module. In order to make it possible for an administrator to assign an event to module's main action, we need to have the Trigger module installed and enabled. This will become more apparent as we proceed.

> The **Trigger module** is part of the core Drupal distribution. You should have it already, though it is not enabled by default.

> Since there is no code dependency between our module and the trigger module, we *could* have left off the `dependencies[]` directive. However, this would not provide the best experience for our user, who would have a module that is impossible to configure out of the box.

Other than this new dependency setup, this `.info` file should look familiar. Let's move on to the first few lines of our new `.module` file.

The Beginning of the .module File

Our `sitenews.module` file will begin in the same old way. After an initial documentation section, we implement the `hook_help()` hook, providing administrative help:

```php
<?php
// $Id$
/**
 * The sitenews module.
 * This module adds a content type (News Brief), and
 * provides an action (Send site news) that allows
 * administrators to send periodic updates (via email)
 * about the latest happenings.
 *
 * It also defines a new hook (hook_sitenews()) and
 * defines a new filter (News Brief Placeholders).
 *
 * @file
 */
/**
 * Implementation of hook_help().
 */
function sitenews_help($path, $arg) {
  if ($path == 'admin/help#sitenews') {
    $txt = 'Keep users up-to-date by sending them a status '
      .'report about the latest site happenings. To use this '
      .'module, you will need to assign a trigger to the '
      .'"Send site news as email to all users" action. It '
      .'is recommended that the node publish event be tied to this'
      .'action, as that will result in the site news being sent'
      .'whenever a new "news brief" node is published.';
    $replace = array();
    return '<p>'. t($txt, $replace) .'</p>';
  }
```

Other than the fact that the help text is a little longer, here, nothing should be surprising in the above block of code.

> **Good help is hard to find**
>
> The help text is briefly presented in this book. But when writing production modules, it is best to write good help text. A quick look at the core modules gives an idea of how help text ought to look.

We will move on to our first pair of functions defining our new content type.

A Simple Content Type, Defined in Code

In Chapter 4, we created our first custom content type. There, we created the new type through Drupal's administration interface.

In Chapter 7, we created a much more advanced content type. This content type included additional content stored in additional tables.

Here, we will create a simple content type like the one in Chapter 4, but we will do it programmatically. Since we are adding no fields beyond the standard node content, we can create our content type with only two functions (and no database manipulation).

We have covered the techniques for creating content types already, so we will proceed rapidly.

Our new content type will be the **news brief** content type. This content type will be used to provide some editorial content at the beginning of a new site news email message. Adding such a simple content type in code requires implementing two hooks, both of which we saw in the last chapter:

- `hook_node_info()`: Set the defaults for the content type.
- `hook_form()`: Create the basic form for editing a new news brief node.

Let's begin with the implementation of `hook_node_info()`.

```
/**
 * Create the 'newsbrief' content type.
 * Implements hook_node_info().
 *
 */
function sitenews_node_info() {
  return array(
    'newsbrief' => array(
      'module' => 'sitenews',
      'name' => t('News Brief'),
      'description' => t("A news brief about the state of the site."),
      'has_title' => TRUE,
      'title_label' => t('Title'),
      'has_body' => TRUE,
      'body_label' => t('News Brief'),
    )
  );
}
```

In the preceding code, we create a new content type named `newsbrief`. This new content type belongs to our `sitenews` module, and will have two fields: the **Title** of the brief, and a body.

> For a detailed discussion of `hook_node_info()` see the previous chapter.

One thing that makes implementing a simple content type in code more difficult than creating it through the administration interface is that the code must also create a form for the content (using the Forms API and `hook_form()`).

```
/**
 * Create the form for editing News Brief nodes.
 * Implements hook_form().
 *
 */
function sitenews_form(&$node) {
  $type = node_get_types('type', $node);
  if ($type->has_title) {
    $form['title'] = array(
      '#type' => 'textfield',
      '#title' => check_plain($type->title_label),
      '#required' => true,
      '#default_value' => $node->title,
      '#weight' => -5,
    );
  }
  if ($type->has_body) {
    $form['body_field'] = node_body_field(
        $node,
        $type->body_label,
        $type->min_word_count
      );
  }
  return $form;
}
```

This form simply defines fields for the title and body of a news brief node. For all practical purposes, it is an abbreviated version of the form we looked at in Chapter 7.

Now we've defined our new content type. There's nothing special to do in the module's `.install` file, and we aren't going to create any special access rules for this type. We are ready to move on to the next task.

Next, we will look at a way to pass the contents of this node through a series of filters.

Creating Filters and an Input Format

Earlier, we created a new content type for the news brief that will be included at the top of each site news message.

However, there are a few things that we want to change about the content of a news brief node:

1. When we send the content out in an email message, we want to make sure that the HTML is removed from the news brief. In short, we want plain text. Drupal's `check_plain()` function seems a likely candidate for this task, but it escapes HTML instead of removing it. We want to *remove* the HTML.

2. There are a couple of common pieces of information that will likely appear in all of our content, but which we might want to change periodically. For example, the greeting and the name of the newsletter. We want to create placeholders for this information, and have Drupal replace the placeholders with meaningful text as needed.

The first task involves removing unwanted content. The second task involves adding content. But both of these can be done with filters.

The filtering API is provided by the **Filter module**.

Using this system, we will define a new **input format.** An input format is a set of filters (formatting rules) determining what markup or code is allowed in a piece of text. Drupal provides two of these out of the box: **Filtered HTML** and **Full HTML**. These two formats determine what HTML tags and constructions are allowed inside of a piece of text.

> **Other input formats**
>
> The filters used by the two built-in formats are not the only ones available in the default Drupal distribution. The PHP module also provides another type for filtering PHP code. Other filters are available on the Drupal website as contributed modules. Later in this chapter, we will discuss creating custom input formats with their own lists of filters.

We will create a new one called **Tagless text**, which we will use to remove tags and other unwanted markup from a piece of text.

An input format can be passed to Drupal's built-in `check_markup()` function to instruct Drupal as to how a piece of content should be filtered before it is sent to the client.

In spite of the name, input filters are rarely used to filter content when it is first put into Drupal. For the most part, text is stored as entered by the user. No filtering is done before the storage. It is only sent the filters when being displayed.

An input format itself doesn't perform any of the filtering. An input format is more like a container. Particular **filters** are assigned to the input format, and it is the job of a filter to perform the necessary manipulation of the text.

For example, the default Filtered HTML input format is assigned the following filters:

- **HTML corrector**: Fix mistakes in HTML markup
- **HTML filter**: Remove unwanted tags
- **Linebreak converter**: Replace line breaks with `<br/>` and `<p/>` tags
- **URL filter**: Convert URLs into hyperlinks

While an input format functions as a container, each filter is backed by a piece of code (an implementation of `hook_filter()`) that performs the actual text processing.

Creating Filters

We are going to create two filters:

- **News Brief Placeholders**: This will replace special placeholders, `{{salutation}}` and `{{brief name}}`, with a greeting message and the name of the site news message, respectively.
- **Remove All HTML/XML Tags**: This filter will remove anything that looks like an HTML or XML tag.

We will create the main logic for both of these filters with one function. It is one of the most complex functions in this book. We will glance at the function as a whole, and then take a closer look at the parts.

```
/**
 * Implements hook_filter().
 */
function sitenews_filter($op, $delta = 0, $format = -1, $text = '') {
  global $user;

  if ($op == 'list') {
    $list = array(
      0 => t('News Brief Placeholders'),
      1 => t('Remove All HTML/XML Tags'),
    );
```

```
      return $list;
  }
  switch ($delta) {
    //Delta 0 is for replacing placeholders:
    case 0:
      switch ($op) {
        case 'description':
          return t('Replaces {{salutation}} with the news brief '
          .'salutation, and {{brief name}} with the news brief '
          .'name.');
        case 'prepare':
          return $text;
        case 'process':
          $text = str_replace(
            '{{salutation}}',
            variable_get('sitenews_salutation', 'Dear Community
                  Member'),
            $text
          );
          $text = str_replace(
            '{{brief name}}',
            variable_get('sitenews_name', 'Site News'),
            $text
          );
          return $text;
        case 'settings':
          $form['sitenews_filter'] = array(
            '#type' => 'fieldset',
            '#title' => t('Site News Filters'),
            '#collapsible' => true,
            '#collapsed' => false,
          );
          $form['sitenews_filter']['sitenews_salutation'] = array(
            '#type' => 'textfield',
            '#description' => t('The greeting'),
            '#title' => t('Salutation'),
            '#default_value' => variable_get('sitenews_saluation',
              'Dear Community Member,'),
          );
          $form['sitenews_filter']['sitenews_name'] = array(
            '#type' => 'textfield',
            '#description' => t('Title of the site news'),
            '#title' => t('Site News Name'),
            '#default_value' => variable_get('sitenews_name', 'Site
```

```
              News'),
        );
        return $form;
    }
  case 1:
    switch ($op) {
      case 'description':
        return t('Removes all tags (HTML or XML elements).');
      case 'prepare':
        return $text;
      case 'process':
        return strip_tags($text);
    } //end switch for $op
  } // end outer switch

}
```

A `hook_filter()` function receives four parameters: `$op`, `$delta`, `$format`, and `$text`. `$text` contains the text to be filtered, and `$format` contains the integer ID of the input format that called this filter. (We will return to input formats later in this section.) For a moment, though, we will focus on the `$op` and `$delta` parameters.

The bulk of this code is nested inside `switch` statements—one for `$delta`, and then each case has a switch statement for `$op`.

In this function, `$delta` and `$op` work the same way as they do in `hook_block()` functions. The `$op` parameter indicates what operation is being requested. There are six operations that an instance of `hook_filter()` may implement:

- `list`: Returns the list of filters provided by this hook implementation.
- `no cache`: If this operation returns TRUE, caching of the filter's output is disabled. By default, filtered content is cached to reduce the rendering time for nodes.
- `description`: Should return a human-friendly description of what the filter does.
- `prepare`: Do any necessary preprocessing and escaping before the `process` operation is performed.
- `process`: Perform the actual filtering.
- `settings`: Return a form for setting preferences for this filter.

The preceding example uses all of these except `no cache`.

The $delta parameter is easiest to understand if we first look at the handler for the list operation:

```
if ($op == 'list') {
  $list = array(
    0 => t('News Brief Placeholders'),
    1 => t('Remove All HTML/XML Tags'),
  );
  return $list;
}
```

A list operation should return an indexed array of filtering operations that this hook provides. In our case, we are going to create two filters, so we return a two-element index.

I've made the mapping explicit to draw attention to the numbering: Drupal will refer to the News Brief Placeholders filter as delta 0, and the Remove All HTML/XML Tags filter as delta 1.

While $delta doesn't ever impact the list operation, any hook_filter() implementation with more than one filter should use $delta to find out what filters should be run.

For the rest of the operations, we first create a switch statement to find out which value of $delta was passed. Then, inside each $delta case, there is another switch statement for handling the operations. So the overarching structure looks like this:

```
switch ($delta) {
  //Delta 0 is for replacing placeholders:
  case 0:
    switch ($op) {
      case 'description':
      //...
      case 'prepare':
        //...
      case 'process':
        //...
      case 'settings':
        //...
    }
  case 1:
  switch ($op) {
    case 'description':
      //...
    case 'prepare':
      //...
```

```
      case 'process':
        //...
    } //end switch for $op
  } // end outer switch
```

Now we are ready to look at each of the two filters.

The First Filter: News Brief Placeholders

Let's take a look at the `News Brief Placeholders` case where `$delta` is 0. The first operation in our function is the description:

```
case 'description':
  return t('Replaces {{salutation}} with the news brief'
  .'salutation, and {{brief name}} with the news brief '
  .'name.');
```

This operation simply returns some useful content that will be displayed on the configuration screen for an input format (**Administer | Site configuration | Input formats**):

```
Filters
Choose the filters that will be used in this filter format.

☑ HTML corrector
Corrects faulty and chopped off HTML in postings.

☑ HTML filter
Allows you to restrict whether users can post HTML and which tags to filter out. It will also
remove harmful content such as JavaScript events, JavaScript URLs and CSS styles from
those tags that are not removed.

☑ Line break converter
Converts line breaks into HTML (i.e. <br> and <p> tags).

☑ News Brief Placeholders
Replaces {{salutation}} with the news brief salutation, and {{brief name}} with the news
brief name.

☐ Remove All HTML/XML Tags
Removes all tags (HTML or XML elements).

☑ URL filter
Turns web and e-mail addresses into clickable links.
```

Notice that in this list, both **Remove All HTML/XML Tags** and **News Brief Placeholders** are present, and they can be set separately. Even though one hook implementation provides both filters, Drupal will treat them as independent of one another.

> The preceding screenshot displays the input format for **Filtered HTML**. By checking the **News Brief Placeholders** checkbox and saving this form, we have added the new filter to the **Filtered HTML** input format.

Providing a `description` is highly recommended, since filters are configurable by administrators.

The next two operations are closely related, and so we will cover them together.

```
case 'prepare':
  return $text;
case 'process':
  $text = str_replace(
    '{{salutation}}',
    variable_get('sitenews_salutation', 'Dear Community Member'),
    $text
  );
  $text = str_replace(
    '{{brief name}}',
    variable_get('sitenews_name', 'Site News'),
    $text
  );
  return $text;
```

The required `prepare` operation is used to perform any preprocessing on the `$text` before the `process` operation is called. This is often used when certain HTML or XML-like tags need escaping before the filter is run. For our purposes, though, we don't need to do any preprocessing, so we simply return `$text` unaltered.

> The `prepare` operation is both required *and* must return some text. Otherwise, neither `process` nor any other downstream code will receive any text. The result will be missing content on the user's screen.

Once the `prepare` operation is complete, the filter handling code will invoke the hook with the `process` operation, which is expected to do the actual filtering of the `$text`.

While the preceding example might initially look complex, it is in fact fairly basic. First, $text is searched for any instance of the placeholder {{saluatation}}. If one is found, it is replaced with the value of the site variable sitenews_salutation.

 Site variables are stored in Drupal's variable table, and can often be set using tools in the administration web interface.

To fetch the site variable, we use the variable_get() function:

```
variable_get('sitenews_salutation', 'Dear Community Member'),
```

This attempts to get the configured value for sitenews_salutation, but if none is set, it uses the default value, Dear Community Member.

This same sort of substitution process is then run to replace {{brief name}} with the value of sitenews_name. The default there is Site News.

So what would happen if we passed the following text to this filter?

```
{{saluatation}},
Welcome to {{brief name}}.
```

Assuming no administrator has set other values for 'sitenews_salutation' and 'sitenews_name', the text would be transformed into the following:

```
Dear Community Member,
Welcome to Site News.
```

This is the basic way that filtering works. The returned $text is then passed along to the rest of the content rendering system, where it may be run through other filters before it is eventually themed and sent to the client.

The last operation is the most complex. The settings operation is used to build a form (using the Forms API, of course) for the administration section. We want to allow site administrators to set values for the 'sitenews_salutation' and 'sitenews_name' variables, so we create a simple form for this:

```
case 'settings':
  $form['sitenews_filter'] = array(
    '#type' => 'fieldset',
    '#title' => t('Site News Filters'),
    '#collapsible' => true,
    '#collapsed' => false,
  );
  $form['sitenews_filter']['sitenews_salutation'] = array(
    '#type' => 'textfield',
    '#description' => t('The greeting'),
```

```
          '#title' => t('Salutation'),
          '#default_value' => variable_get('sitenews_saluation',
            'Dear Community Member,'),
      );
      $form['sitenews_filter']['sitenews_name'] = array(
          '#type' => 'textfield',
          '#description' => t('Title of the site news'),
          '#title' => t('Site News Name'),
          '#default_value' => variable_get('sitenews_name', 'Site News'),
      );
      return $form;
  }
```

This creates a form with a field set and two input text fields. The first text field is for the salutation, and the second is for the site news name.

Drupal handles storing the values for these fields; so there is no need to write any more form handling code. This form-generating operation is then invoked when creating a "Configure Input Format" screen:

Notice that the field set that we created is rendered as one component in a larger form. All of that is provided by Drupal, and there is no need for us to code it.

The Second Filter: Remove All Tags

The second filter is similar to the first in structure, but it is considerably shorter. This filter will remove all tags from the given text:

```
case 1:
  switch ($op) {
    case 'description':
      return t('Removes all tags (HTML or XML elements).');
    case 'prepare':
      return $text;
    case 'process':
      return strip_tags($text);
}
```

As we saw with the last filter, `description` returns a human-friendly message indicating what the module does.

Since there is no preprocessing work to be done, `prepare` returns `$text` unaltered.

The `processing` operation does the filtering. PHP has a built-in function for removing tags, `strip_tags()`. Using that makes this filter quick and easy.

At this point, our filters are working. However, there is one more hook that we ought to implement: `hook_filter_info()`. This hook provides content creators with some help text to tell them how the filter impacts their content. Here's an implementation for our filters:

```
/**
 * Provides formatting tips to users who are creating content.
 * Implements hook_format_info().
 */
function sitenews_filter_tips($delta, $format, $long) {
  switch ($delta) {
    case 0:
      $text = "Instances of {{brief name}} will be "
        ."replaced by the global name for site news."
        ." {{salutation}} will be replaced with the global "
        ."greeting message.";
      if ($long) {
        $text .= "Site News name and salutation text "
        ."can be configured from the administration "
        ."interface.";
      }
      return $text;
    case 1:
      return "HTML and XML tags will be removed from the "
        ."final output.";
  }
}
```

An implementation of `hook_filter_info()` is passed three arguments:

- `$delta`: The delta of the filter. Using this, we can match help text to the filter being used.

- `$format`: The input format ID.

- `$long`: A Boolean flag indicating whether to provide verbose help text (`$long` = TRUE) or brief help text (`$long` = FALSE).

As in the `sitenews_filter()` function, we use a `switch` statement to select the right delta. That way, the applicable help text is returned.

If the longer version of help text is requested (`$long == TRUE`) and `$delta` is set to `0`, a longer help message is returned. However, if the delta is `1`, the same text is returned regardless of whether `$long` is set to `true`. The generated help text:

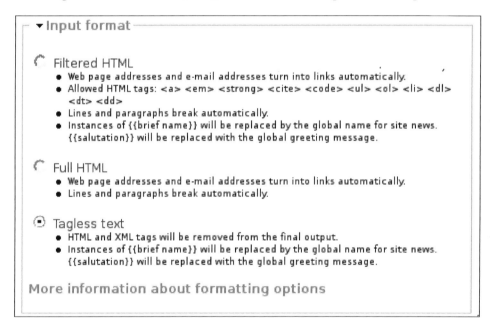

Clicking on the **More information about formatting options** link will display the long version:

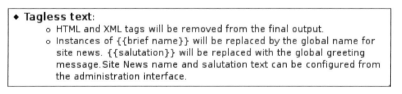

While our long version is still only a few lines, more complex filters often have long tips that span several paragraphs.

Now we've written our two hooks and implemented a pair of filters. How do we make use of these filters?

One way is to use the administration web interface to assign the filters to an input format. This is done on the **Administer | Site configuration | Input formats** screen. There, we could create a new input type, or assign the filters to an existing input format.

However, this method is not particularly friendly to the module installer. It would be more convenient to automatically add a new input format when the module is installed.

Adding an Input Format

We want to create a new input format—one especially for the site news that we will be sending via email. Also, we want to configure this new input format to use the two filters we have created.

While we could add this all by manual configuration through the web interface, it is more convenient to have the module do this for us. This sort of task ought to be done during module installation.

To install this, we need to create a `sitenews.install` file and implement `hook_install()` inside that file.

 In Chapter 7, we covered the module `.install` file and some of the hooks used in that file.

Here are the contents of our `sitenews.install` file:

```php
<?php
// $Id$
/**
 * Install the sitenews module.
 * @file
 */
/**
 * Implements hook_install().
 */
function sitenews_install() {
  $name = 'Tagless text';
```

```
// Check to see if format already exists.
$res = db_query(
  "SELECT name FROM {filter_formats} WHERE name = '%s'",
  $name
);
$has_format = db_result($res);

// Create format
if (!$has_format) {
  db_query(
    "INSERT INTO {filter_formats} (name) VALUES ('%s')",
    $name
  );
}
$res = db_query(
  "SELECT format FROM {filter_formats} WHERE name = '%s'",
  $name
);
$format = db_fetch_object($res);
$q = "INSERT INTO {filters} (format, module, delta, weight) "
  ."VALUES(%d, 'sitenews', %d, %d)";
// First, insert the "News Brief Placeholders" filter:
db_query($q, $format->format, 0, 10);
// Second, insert the "Remove All HTML/XML Tags" filter:
db_query($q, $format->format, 1, 0);
}
```

The `.install` file contains only one function, `sitenews_install()`, which implements `hook_install()`.

 In the filter module, the term *input format* is sometimes abbreviated to *format*. This is fine within the context of the filter module, but since the term *format* is used elsewhere in Drupal and PHP, it is best to reduce the ambiguity by referring to these as *input formats*, not just *formats*.

This function proceeds through four steps:

- Check to see if the input format already exists.
- If it does not, create it.
- Get the format ID for this input format.
- Add the two filters (created above) to this input format.

Here's the first step:

```
$name = 'Tagless text';
// Check to see if format already exists.
$res = db_query(
  "SELECT name FROM {filter_formats} WHERE name = '%s'",
  $name
);
$has_format = db_result($res);
```

Here, we look in the `filter_formats` table—the filter module's table for storing information about input formats. It is possible that there is already an input format named `Tagless text`. So we check for its existence first.

The `db_result()` function returns the data from our query. Unlike `db_fetch_array()` and `db_fetch_object()`, it assumes that there is only one row of content returned. For our purposes, that is sufficient. Since it returns FALSE if no data is found, we can use it in a Boolean context.

If the input format does not exist, we create it.

```
// Create format
if(!$has_format){
  db_query(
    "INSERT INTO {filter_formats} (name) VALUES ('%s')",
    $name
  );
}
```

For the most part, we want to accept the defaults for the `filter_formats` table, but we do need to set the `name` field to `Tagless text`.

Now that we have the new field inserted, we need to retrieve the format ID of this new input type.

```
$res = db_query(
  "SELECT format FROM {filter_formats} WHERE name='%s'",
  $name
);
$format = db_fetch_object($res);
```

The `format` column in the `filter_formats` table contains the unique integer ID of an input format. We want that ID for the input format we just created.

> Since we want to keep the database API portable across multiple databases, we do not use any special MySQL or PostgreSQL SQL to retrieve the ID of the last inserted row.

Once we have that, we can perform another insert into another table. We can assign filters to our new input format.

To do this, we insert rows into the filter module's `filter` table. To be specific, we insert one row per filter. Since we are adding two filters, we will need to perform two separate inserts:

```
$q = "INSERT INTO {filters} (format, module, delta, weight) "
    ."VALUES(%d, 'sitenews', %d, %d)";
// First, insert the "News Brief Placeholders" filter:
db_query($q, $format->format, 0, 10);
// Second, insert the "Remove All HTML/XML Tags" filter:
db_query($q, $format->format, 1, 0);
```

This code uses the same SQL query twice, substituting different values in each time.

There are four values that we need to set when adding a filter to an input method:

- `format`: The ID for the input format. This is the format ID that we retrieved from the database in the previous step. It is stored in the `format` property of the `$format` object.

- `module`: The name of the module that contains the filters. In our case, it will be sitenews for both rows.

- `delta`: The delta for the filter. This corresponds to the delta integer returned by the `list` operation for `hook_filter()`. We looked at this in the last section.

- `weight`: Filters are executed in order. As with other Drupal systems, filters are ordered by weight. The heavier the weight, the later in the series of filters this filter will be executed. We want News Brief Placeholder to be run late, so we assign it a heavy weight, 10. But we want the tag removal filter to run very early, so we assign it a weight of 0.

Why does filter ordering matter?

It is in our best interest to run our filters quickly and securely. The order in which filters are executed can make a difference. For example, we want to remove tags early because it will cut down on the amount of text that other filters will have to process. And we want to run the substitution filter (News Brief Placeholder) late because we don't want to perform substitutions in text that is going to be removed by subsequent filters.

When we first install our new `sitenews` module, these database operations will be run. We should be able to see our new input format in the **Administer | Site configuration | Input formats** page:

Home » Administer » Site configuration

Input formats

| List | **Add input format** |

Input formats define a way of processing user-supplied text in Drupal. Each input format uses filters to manipulate text, and most input formats apply several different filters to text, in a specific order. Each filter is designed to accomplish a specific purpose, and generally either removes elements from or adds elements to text before it is displayed. Users can choose between the available input formats when submitting content.

Use the list below to configure which input formats are available to which roles, as well as choose a default input format (used for imported content, for example). The default format is always available to users. All input formats are available to users in a role with the "administer filters" permission.

Default	Name	Roles	Operations
⊙	Filtered HTML	All roles may use default format	configure
⊙	Full HTML	No roles may use this format	configure delete
⊙	Tagless text	No roles may use this format	configure delete

| Set default format |

In the above screenshot, we can see the **Tagless text** input method included along with the other two default input methods. Clicking the configure link would show us a list of filters for this input method, and there would be only two filters enabled—the two we just added in our code.

> **What if the input format isn't there?**
>
> If there is a problem with the `.install` file, the appropriate database entries may not have been inserted. When developing installation hooks, the best way to test and re-test `.install` file is with the **Devel module's Reinstall module** tool.

Our input format is defined. Later, we will make direct use of this input format. Right now, though, we will add one utility function.

While Drupal's filter module provides a handful of functions for working with input formats, they all use the input format's ID. However, the ID will vary depending on when it was inserted into the database. If there are already several formats defined, our new one might have a higher ID than if only the few built-in filters are defined.

Here is a quick function to get a format ID by the format's name:

```
/**
 * Get a format ID by name.
 * This returns an Input Format ID that can be passed to
 * check_markup() to filter content.
 *
 * If a format isn't found matching the given name, the
 * default format is returned.
 *
 * @param $name
 *   String name of the format
 *
 * @return
 *   The ID (an integer) of the format.
 */
function sitenews_get_format($name) {
  $res = db_query(
    "SELECT format FROM {filter_formats} WHERE name = '%s'",
    $name
  );
  $format = db_fetch_object($res);
  if ($format) {
    return $format->format;
  } else {
    return FILTER_FORMAT_DEFAULT;
  }
}
```

This checks the `filter_formats` table to see if an input format named `$name` exists. If it does, that format's ID is returned. Otherwise, the default input format ID is returned. (`FILTER_FORMAT_DEFAULT`, the default format ID, is `0`).

Later, we will use this function to invoke our special input format for outbound mail.

We have now finished defining our two filters and our new input format. We will now move on to our next major topic: Defining an action.

The Beginning of an Action

We have a content type (News Brief) that will be included in our site news mailing. We also have an input format, complete with a pair of filters, which we will use to prepare the site news for sending to our users' email accounts. Now we need to start the processes of assembling the site news message.

To do this, we are going to create an **action**. In Drupal parlance, an action is a particular task that can be executed in response to a particular event. Using the **Trigger module**, administrators can tie particular events (such as a node being published or a new user joining the system) to a particular action.

What we will be doing is defining a new action that will bring all the pieces of our site news message together, and then send it to users. Later, we will create a trigger to run the action *whenever a news brief is published*.

We will begin by registering the new action.

Implementing hook_action_info()

The first step in creating an action is to implement the `hook_action_info()` hook in order to register the action or actions that our module will provide.

This hook works similarly to `hook_menu()`. The idea is to provide Drupal's action subsytem with some information about the action, including what function should be called when the action is executed. (Compare this to the menu function, where a function is mapped to a path instead of an action name.)

[*note* For an introduction to `hook_menu()`, see Chapter 5.]

Here's what `sitenews_action_info()` looks like:

```
/**
 * Implements hook_action_info().
 */
function sitenews_action_info() {
  watchdog('action',"Called sitenews_action_info");
  $actions['sitenews_send_action'] = array(
    'type' => 'node',
    'description' => t('Send site news as email to all users.'),
    'configurable' => FALSE,
    'hooks' => array(
      'nodeapi' => array('insert', 'update', 'presave'),
```

```
        )
    );
    return $actions;
}
```

A function implementing `hook_action_info()` must return an associative array where the key is the name of the action, and the value is an associative array of settings.

At the time of this writing, the API documentation for `hook_action_info()` is nested inside the documentation for `actions_list()`. `http://api.drupal.org/api/function/actions_list/6`.

In the preceding code, we define an action named `sitenews_send_action`, and then set properties for this new action. The action name doubles as a callback. That is, the action subsystem will expect a function to exist named `sitenews_send_action()`. We will create that function shortly.

The associative array defined as the value to `$action['sitenews_send_action']` contains settings for this action. There are four possible properties that can be defined in this array:

- `type`: The Drupal type that this action operates upon. The built-in types are `node`, `comment`, `user`, `taxonomy`, and `system`. This setting is used for several things, but most importantly, it is used to determine what sort of object should be passed in as a parameter to the callback function. We will see this shortly.

- `description`: A human-readable description of what this action does. This is used for display in the actions and triggers administration pages.

- `configurable`: This takes a Boolean value to indicate whether administrators can use this to create an advanced action.

- `hooks`: This setting takes an associative array of modules and hooks that this action can interact with. For example, an action intended to work with user hooks might have a hooks section like this: `'user' => array('login', 'logout', 'view')`.

Drupal's core modules implement `hook_hook_info()` as a way of providing information about type and hooks. The array returned by a `hook_hook_info()` implementation is structured like this: `$info[$type][$hook_key][$hook_value]`. Unfortunately, as of this writing `hook_hook_info()` is not documented in the API.

These settings in our module look as follows:

```
$actions['sitenews_send_action'] = array(
   'type' => 'node',
   'description' => t('Send site news as email to all users.'),
   'configurable' => FALSE,
   'hooks' => array(
      'nodeapi' => array('insert', 'update', 'presave'),
   )
);
```

This action will be tied to a particular news brief node, so our `type` is `node`. Also of note, the `hooks` array references only hooks implemented by `nodeapi`. This array indicates to the actions subsystem that our module only deals with Node API events—specifically, the `insert`, `update`, and `presave` events. (`presave` is an event that is fired before either an insert or an update of a node).

At this point, the new action should be visible in the Drupal administration interface (though it won't work without the callback). In **Administer | Site configuration | Action**, the new action should appear at the end of the list:

Action type	Description
comment	Unpublish comment
node	Publish post
node	Unpublish post
node	Make post sticky
node	Make post unsticky
node	Promote post to front page
node	Remove post from front page
node	Save post
user	Block current user
user	Ban IP address of current user
node	Send site news as email to all users

Actions available to Drupal:

Make a new advanced action available

Choose an advanced action ▾   Create

The last item on the list above is a **node** action type named **Send site news as email to all users**. That name should sound familiar. It's the value of the `description` field we returned from `sitenews_action_info()`.

The new action is also available in the drop-down boxes on the triggers configuration screen at **Administer | Site building | Triggers**. Later in the chapter we will look at that screen.

The action is registered. Now we need to create a function that will perform the action.

The Action Callback

Now that we've provide the actions subsystem with a definition of what our action will look like, we need to implement the `sitenews_send_action()` callback:

```
/**
 * Action: Send an email message to all users.
 */
function sitenews_send_action(&$object, $context) {
  // If not a published sitenews, skip.
  if (!$object->status || $object->type != 'newsbrief') {
    return;
  }
  // Get addresses
  $q = "SELECT mail, status FROM {users} "
    ."WHERE status != 0 AND uid > 0";
  $results = db_query($q);
  $addresses = array();
  while ($obj = db_fetch_object($results)) {
    $addresses[] = $obj->mail;
  }
  if (count($addresses) == 0) {
    watchdog(
      'sitenews',
      'No user email addresses were found',
      array(),
      WATCHDOG_ERROR
    );
    return;
  }
  // Execute hook_sitenews()
  $content = module_invoke_all('sitenews');
  // Build params
  $params = array(
    'node' => $object,
```

```
        'to' => implode(', ', $addresses),
        'subject' => $object->title,
        'context' => $context,
        'additional content' => $content,
    );
    $message = _sitenews_do_message($object, $params);
    watchdog(
        'actions',
        'Site News "Send" action fired. Sending to !mail',
        array('!mail' => $params['to'])
    );
}
```

This function is simpler than it looks.

An action callback is passed at least two parameters: `&$object` and `$context`. The contents of both of these will vary based on what `type` is set to in the `hook_action_info()` implementation.

For example, if `'type' => 'user'`, then when this callback is executed, `&$object` will contain a user object, and the `$context` will contain information on the hook and operation called, as well as some additional data (perhaps from a user profile form).

In our case, `&$object` will be a node. The `$context` will contain information about what was happening when this callback was called. It will also contain another copy of the node. For our purposes, it is the node object that is important.

The first thing our callback function does is check to see if the passed-in node is one that we want:

```
// If not a published sitenews, skip.
if (!$object->status || $object->type != 'newsbrief') {
    return;
}
```

Our action should be performed only on published news brief nodes. We don't want to accidentally send a site news email with a message that isn't ready. Nor do we want every new node to be sent to our users. Therefore, if the node isn't published (that is, if `$object->status` is 0) or if it isn't of the `newsbrief` content type, this function returns immediately.

The next piece of code retrieves the email addresses of the users to whom we will send our site news:

```
// Get addresses
$q = "SELECT mail, status FROM {users} "
  ."WHERE status != 0 AND uid > 0";
$results = db_query($q);
$addresses = array();
while ($obj = db_fetch_object($results)) {
  $addresses[] = $obj->mail;
}
if (count($addresses) == 0) {
  watchdog(
    'sitenews',
    'No user email addresses were found',
    array(),
    WATCHDOG_ERROR
  );
  return;
}
```

In the highlighted portion above, we retrieve the email addresses for all of the users that are currently active. Also, to avoid sending mail to the "anonymous" user, whose uid is 0, we select only users with UIDs greater than 0.

In the second half of this function, we check to make sure we will be sending this report to somebody. If we have no users, there is no point in trying to construct and send a message. However, we do log the event with the watchdog() function.

Once all of this is done, we are ready to begin building the message.

We already have the news brief. It was passed in as &$object. But we also need to get any additional content. To do that, we call this bit of code:

```
$content = module_invoke_all('sitenews');
```

This single line of code illustrates one of the most powerful features of Drupal. This function invokes the hook_sitenews() hook in all installed modules. The content returned from all of the implementing hooks is stored in $content.

 We will return to this line of code in the next section. We've hit an important concept, and it deserves a section of its own. But before we cover hook definitions in detail, let's finish looking at this function.

We have all of our content, now. The next thing to do is package it up, and then send it to a function that can do the mailing:

```
// Build params
$params = array(
   'node' => $object,
   'to' => implode(', ', $addresses),
   'subject' => $object->title,
   'context' => $context,
   'additional content' => $content,
);
$message = _sitenews_do_message($object, $params);
```

The `$params` array will contain all of the parameters that are needed to build and send the message.

 The `$addresses` array is imploded and added to the `$params['to']` field. This will allow us to send the message to all of the addresses at once—a very important feature for performance reasons.

All the information in `$params`, along with the `$object` node itself, will be passed to the `_sitenews_do_message()` function.

We will take a look at that function after we spend a little time looking more closely at defining and using a hook.

Defining a Hook

We have been examining hooks since the first chapter of this book. Now we are going to take an in-depth look at how a module can implement its own hook.

In this section, we will invoke a custom hook, implement that hook in other modules, and look at the mechanics of using hooks.

The goal of defining this hook is to make it possible for other modules to earmark content for inclusion in a site news message. This gives the module developers the ability to specify what content should be included in a report, and how it should appear.

We will start out by backtracking. Let's take another look at the hook invocation from the last section.

Invoking a Custom Hook

In the last section, we took a look at this line of code (called in `sitenews_send_action()`):

```
$content = module_invoke_all('sitenews');
```

The Drupal `module_invoke_all()` is one of the main hook functions. Its job is to call all the hook implementations for a specific hook. It searches all of the enabled modules looking for functions that match the correct pattern.

In our case, we pass the function the string `sitenews`. This tells `module_invoke_all()` to look for hooks of the form `<modulename>_sitenews()`, where `<modulename>` is replaced with the name of the module.

Naming hooks

In general, hook naming convention should follow module naming convention: A hook should have the name of the module in its name. There are two things to keep in mind. First, the hook name should be different enough from existing hooks that it is not mistaken for an implementation of another hook (check out `http://api.drupal.org/api/group/hooks/6` for a list of most of the hooks in the Drupal core). Second, a hook name should give an idea of what the hook implementation should do.

`hook_sitenews()` has no parameters. If it did, though, they would be passed in as follows:

```
module_invoke_all('sitenews', $param1, $param2, $param3);
```

All parameters after the hook name are passed to the hook implementations.

There are a few other useful hook functions, as well. The `module_hook()` function, which takes a module name and a hook name, returns TRUE if a module contains that hook, and false, otherwise.

Sometimes a function more specific than `module_invoke_all()` is needed. That's where `module_invoke()` comes in. It invokes the hook (if one exists) *only in the given module*. The `module_invoke()` function takes a module name and a hook name as parameters (and any additional parameters are passed on to hook implementations).

Finally, the function `module_implements()` takes a hook name, and returns a list of names of modules that implement the hook.

All these functions are defined in the `drupal/includes/module.inc` file, and the API documentation for that file covers all four functions: `http://api.drupal.org/api/file/includes/module.inc/6`.

So What Is a Hook?

It turns out that invoking a hook is as simple as running `module_invoke()` or
`module_invoke_all()`. So when it comes down to it, *what is a hook?*

A hook is really nothing more than a function that matches the pattern of a call
to the module functions we've just looked at. At bare minimum, all it takes to
define a hook in a module is a line like the one we used earlier—a line like
`module_invoke_all('myhook')` or `module_invoke('some_module',`
`'anotherhook', $param1, $param2)`.

Technically speaking, then, defining a new hook is trivial.

But there's a problem, and the problem is more social than technical. How will other
developers know about your hook? (For that matter, how will you later remember
your own hook?) After all, we can't expect a developer to read through the code of
our modules searching for calls to any of the four hook functions.

The solution to this problem—Convention.

Creating a hook_sitenews() Function

Defining a new hook took one line of code. But now we need to make it easy for
developers to use this hook.

There are a few ways to make your hook user-friendly.

The first is by including details about the hook in the documentation block of the
code that invokes the hook.

The second way is to create a hook function in your code. This function is not called
anywhere. Instead, it serves an instructional role.

 The Drupal API docs for hooks are compiled from a stand-alone file
(which is not included in the standard release) that documents all of the
core hooks. This is an alternative to including an unused function in a
module.

So to illustrate how our hook works, we might add a function to our module that
looks as follows:

```
/**
 * Use this hook to build content for a sitenews message.
 *
 * This should return an array of items:
 * <code>array('item_name' => $item)</code>
 * An item is an associative array with the following
```

```
 * fields set:
 *
 * - #weight: An integer from -10 to 10
 * - #content: Text content
 * - #title: A title for the text content
 *
 * Weight and content are required. If #title
 * is set, then it will be added as a title.
 *
 * @return
 * A content array.
 */
function hook_sitenews() {
  $content['report'] = array(
    '#weight' => 0,
    '#title' => t('Sample Title'),
    '#body' => t('Sample content')
  );
  $content['another report'] = array(
    '#weight' => 0,
    '#title' => t('Another Sample Title'),
    '#body' => t('More sample content')
  );
  return $content;
}
```

The main point of this hook function is instruction. It should never actually be called. (Neither `module_invoke()` nor `module_invoke_all()` will execute this function, since it does not follow the pattern of `<modulename>_<hookname>`.)

The documentation is intended to be more thorough to give developers a clear idea of what this function is for. The code is designed to give the developer an idea of how she or he might create an implementation.

So examining the above example, we can see that an implementation of `hook_sitenews()` is expected to return a data structure that looks something like a Forms API form.

It should return an associative array of items. According to the documentation, each item must have a weight (`#weight`) and a formatted body (`#content`). The `#title` field is optional.

As we saw in the last section, our `sitenews_send_action()` action function will execute these hooks, getting an array of content back. Later, we will see how these content items are sorted by weight, and then inserted into the body of the email message.

Now that we have looked at a way to document how a hook functions and what it should look like, we will move on. Let's implement this hook in a few modules that we have already created.

Implementing hook_sitenews() in Other Modules

Ready to start implementing our hook? Here, we will revisit some of our existing modules and retrofit them to make use of `hook_sitenews()`.

Let's begin with the module we created in Chapter 4. There, we created a random quotes feature, which was displayed as a JavaScript-enhanced block.

In the philquotes Module

Here, we will implement `hook_sitenews()` to return a random quote that will be included in our site news. We will need to edit `drupal/sites/all/modules/philquotes.module` to add this new hook implementation:

```
/**
 * Implements hook_sitenews() from sitenews module.
 */
function philquotes_sitenews() {
  $node = _philquotes_get_quote();
  $quote = $node->body
    ."\n-- ". $node->title; //<-- Quote origin
  $content['randomquote'] = array(
    '#weight' => 8,
    '#title' => t('Quote of the Day'),
    '#body' => strip_tags($quote),
  );
  return $content;
}
```

This function uses the `_philquotes_get_quote()` function that we created in Chapter 4. That function returns a random quotation node from the database.

Recall that we used the `title` field of our quote to store information about the quote's origin. The `body` field stores the text of the quote.

Once we have the quote `$node`, we do a little formatting so that the quote is structured as follows:

```
The only principle that does not inhibit progress is: anything goes.
-- P. Feyerabend, Against Method
```

Now we have the pieces we need to build the `$content` array that will be returned from the hook:

```
$content['randomquote'] = array(
  '#weight' => 8,
  '#title' => t('Quote of the Day'),
  '#body' => strip_tags($quote),
);
```

We set all the three fields. Since our quote is not particularly important, we assign it a heavy weight so that it will sink toward the bottom of the site news message. The title of our random quotes section will be **Quote of the Day**.

Finally, before we add the `$quote` to the body, we use the PHP `strip_tags()` function to remove any HTML tags.

In the biography Module

In the last chapter, we created a biography content type. Here, we will extend that module to implement the `hook_sitenews()` hook.

This implementation will return the three newest biographies from the database, formatted for inclusion in our site news email.

```
/**
 * Implements hook_sitenews() in sitenews module.
 */
function biography_sitenews() {
  $q = "SELECT nid, created FROM {node} "
    ."WHERE status=1 AND type='biography' "
    ."ORDER BY created DESC";
  $results = db_query_range($q, 0, 3);

  $new_bios = array();
  while ($row = db_fetch_object($results)) {
    $node = node_load($row->nid);
    $new_bios[] = theme('biography_sitenews', $node);
  }
  $content['biography'] = array(
    '#weight' => 0,
    '#title' => t('Recent Biographies'),
    '#body' => implode("\n", $new_bios),
  );
  return $content;
}
```

At the beginning of this function, we query the database for the node IDs of the three newest entries. For database portability and to incorporate paging functionality into Drupal, the database API includes the `db_query_range()` function. Generally, this should be used instead of the LIMIT SQL directive. (There are a couple of range-based functions in the Drupal database API. See `http://api.drupal.org/api/group/database/6` for a description of each one.)

> We don't do any checking to see if any of these biographies have been sent in past site news mailings. As a result, if less than three new biographies are created between mailings, the same biography or biographies may be sent again. A more sophisticated module might instead only select biographies out of the database whose creation date is newer than the last News Brief node.

After the query, this function loops through the results. For each node ID, it first loads the full biography node, and then passes this node on to a theming function. We will glance that that function in a moment.

Since `sitenews_send_action()` expects the value of `#content` to be ready for display, we use the theme engine here to prepare the content.

Once the content is all themed, the function creates the `$content` array, imploding the three biography entries into a single body of content (where each entry is separated by a blank line). The `$content` array is then returned.

In this module, the weight is lower (0). Biography content will be an important part of our site news, so we want it to float to the top.

Now let's take a look at the theme function to see how this content gets formatted before it is returned by the hook.

Theming Content before Returning It

Opposite, we called the `biography_sitenews` theme as follows:

```
theme('biography_sitenews', $node);
```

In order to provide this theme, we will have to do a little more retrofitting of the biography module. First, we will need to register this theme (along with the existing theme) in the biography module's `hook_theme()` implementation:

```
/**
 * implements hook_theme().
 */
function biography_theme() {
  return array(
```

```
        'biography_info' => array(
          'template' => 'biography_info',
          'arguments' => array(
            'dates' => NULL,
            'life' => NULL,
            'works' => NULL,
          ),
        ),
        // For Chapter 8
        'biography_sitenews' => array(
          'arguments' => array('node' => NULL),
        ),
      );
}
```

The highlighted code above is all we added—a registration indicating that this module provides a `biography_sitenews` theme.

Next, we create the theme function:

```
/**
 * Theme function for sitenews.
 */
function theme_biography_sitenews($node) {
  $options = array('absolute' => TRUE);
  $url = url('node/'. $node->nid, $options);
  $title = strip_tags($node->title);
  $body = strip_tags($node->teaser); // <-- Summary
  $text = implode("\n", array($title, $body, $url));
  $text .= "\n";
  return $text;
}
```

This simple theme function takes the `$node` object and turns it into three components: an absolute URL pointing to the Drupal content, a title, and a body. The body of a biography, as you may recall from Chapter 7, contains the biographical summary.

Title and body are stripped of tags, and the URL is constructed from the node ID. Then, all three are concatenated together into one text string and returned.

There is nothing fancy here. Formatting is minimal since our target client application is a mail program.

At this point, we've created a new hook and implemented it in two other modules. So when the `sitenews_send_action()` function executes `module_invoke_all('sitenews')`, these two new hook implementations we just created will be executed.

Let's return now to the `sitenews_send_action()` function to see how it makes use of the hook's results..

Completing the Action: Theming and Mailing

Returning to the `sitenews_send_action()` action we are defining in the `sitenews` module, let's continue with the line after the hook processing:

```
// Execute hook_sitenews()
$content = module_invoke_all('sitenews');
// Build params
$params = array(
  'node' => $object,
  'to' => implode(', ', $addresses),
  'subject' => $object->title,
  'context' => $context,
  'additional content' => $content,
);
$message = _sitenews_do_message($object, $params);
watchdog(
  'actions',
  'Site News "Send" action fired. Sending to !mail',
  array('!mail' => $params['to'])
);
```

Our call to `module_invoke_all('sitenews')` returns an array of content. Assuming that only the two hooks we created above were called, our returned array will contain an entry for `philquotes_sitenews()` and an entry for `biography_sitenews()`.

 Of course, for the hook to be executed, the module containing the hook must also be installed and enabled. In practical terms, both the `philquotes` module and the `biography` module would need to be enabled for us to get results from the hook invocations.

In `sitenews_send_action()` these results and other data are packed into the `$params` array, and then passed into the `_sitenews_do_message()` function, which we will see in just a moment.

Now we're getting toward the end of our action. The purpose of the `sitenews` action was to assemble a site news message (complete with the content of our news brief), format it, and then send it to all the users on our system.

So far, we have assembled the message and partially formatted it. The `_sitenews_do_message()` function will pull things together, invoking the themes to finish formatting, and then sending the mail message.

The function looks as follows:

```
/**
 * Internal function to prepare a message and pass it on
 * to the mailer.
 *
 * @param $node
 *    The news brief node.
 * @param $params
 *    An array of params.
 */
function _sitenews_do_message(&$node, $params) {
  $node = $params['node'];
  $content = $params['additional content'];

  // Theme the main node:
  $params['body'] = theme('sitenews_newsbrief', $node);

  // See common.inc (particularly element_sort() and
  // drupal_render())
  uasort($content, 'element_sort');

  // Render each block of content:
  foreach ($content as $item) {
    $params['body'] .= theme('sitenews_msgblock', $item);
  }

  // Send the mail:
  drupal_mail(
    'sitenews',
    'sendsitenews',
    $params['to'],
    language_default(),
    $params,
    variable_get('site_mail', NULL),
    TRUE
  );
}
```

This function is given the `$node` object (our newsbrief node) and the `$params` array, which contains several items set in `sitenews_send_action()`.

While the `hook_sitenews()` implementations have themed their content, the News Brief node's content still hasn't been themed. So we hand it off to the theme engine:

```
$params['body'] = theme('sitenews_newsbrief', $node);
```

In a moment, we will look at the theming function. The results of theming, though, are stored in the `$params` array. Let's continue with this function before looking at the theming.

Next, we have the array of content (`$content`) that was previously returned from `module_invoke_all('sitenews')`. But we want the content array to be sorted by weight, not by the order in which the module hooks were invoked. So we sort by weight:

```
uasort($content, 'element_sort');
```

The `uasort()` function is built into PHP. It takes an array to sort, and a callback comparator function. The function is responsible for comparing two items to determine which is first.

One of the reasons our hook used a data structure similar to the Forms API is so that we could take advantage of existing functions. The `element_sort()` function, a comparator defined in `drupal/includes/common.inc`, sorts based on `#weight` elements in an array. We can use that function and not have to write our own. So we pass in that function name as the second argument to the `uasort()` PHP function.

Once the array is sorted, we still have to do a little more theming. The modules have themed the content of each item, but we need to do some theming on the entire `$content` array, turning the link, title, and formatted body into one block of text. And as we go, we will add this to the `$params['body']` field, which already contains the formatted body of the news brief node.

```
foreach ($content as $item) {
    $params['body'] .= theme('sitenews_msgblock', $item);
}
```

The `sitenews_msgblock` theme is used to format each item returned from the `hook_sitenews()` implementations.

Now we have the body of our message. Already in the `$params` array (from `sitenews_send_action()`), we have a destination (`$params['to']`, which contains all of our users' email addresses) and a subject (`$params['subject']`).

Why send in bulk?

Why email the same message to all users at the same time? The answer is: performance. On a site with a thousand users, running this action for each user would be like executing 1001 page requests (remember, someone initiated the action). While Drupal can usually handle a load like that, it might take a little while. The user would be left waiting for a page load to complete.

For an even more scalable system, it would be preferable to send into batches, and perhaps even queue them in Drupal. By using Drupal's cron system, messages could be sent one batch at a time.

If personalization is important, this will require sending to one user at a time. It can be done by turning off some of the caching so that the filters do not cache their results, or implementing a waiting system that will keep the user who initiated the action appraised of the sending status. The result would be a module considerably more complex than the one presented here.

We are ready to mail the message.

```
drupal_mail(
   'sitenews',
   'sendsitenews',
   $params['to'],
   language_default(),
   $params,
   variable_get('site_mail', NULL),
   TRUE
);
```

This function is very similar to the one we created in Chapter 6. The first parameter is the module's name, and the second parameter is an identifier that will be passed to a `hook_mail()` implementation. We will look at the `sitenews_mail()` implementation in just a moment.

Next comes the `to` addresses, a comma-separated list of the email addresses of our users.

After that comes the language setting. It would be unduly burdensome on the system to try to translate the message to every user's language (which would require sending messages to each user one at a time). Instead, we simply call the `language_default()` function, which returns the site's default language.

Next comes the $params array, which we will make use of in sitenews_mail(), the mail hook implementation. The from address is set to the default site email address. And the TRUE flag at the end indicates that Drupal should mail this as soon as the mail hook completes execution.

By the end of _sitenews_do_message(), our message has been sent.

Before moving on to triggers, let's quickly look at the theme functions and the mail hook.

Theme Functions

The _sitenews_do_message() function called two themes. We now need to register and define these theme functions. Using hook_theme() to register the functions, we can create a hook implementation like this:

```
/**
 * Implements hook_theme().
 */
function sitenews_theme() {
  return array(
    'sitenews_msgblock' => array(
      'arguments' => array('block' => NULL),
    ),
    'sitenews_newsbrief' => array(
      'arguments' => array('node' => NULL),
    ),
  );
}
```

The theme_sitenews_msgblock() and theme_sitenews_newsbrief() functions are now registered; they just need defining.

First, theme_sitenews_newsbrief() takes the node and formats it for emailing:

```
/**
 * Theme to display a news brief in a
 * sitenews message block.
 *
 * @param $node
 *    The news brief node object.
 */
function theme_sitenews_newsbrief($node) {
  $format = sitenews_get_format('Tagless text');
  $text = strtoupper(check_markup($node->title, $format)) ."\n\n";
  $text .= check_markup($node->body, $format) ."\n\n";
  return $text;
}
```

This function transforms the $node content into a format suitable for mailing. The most interesting lines in this function are highlighted.

Our $node could contain HTML, XML, custom tags, and whatnot. All this is useful when displaying on the Web. But it is not good in a mail message. Also, when the content was created, some of the special placeholders we defined may have been used.

What we want to do to prepare this $node's content is to run it through the input format we defined at the beginning of this chapter.

To do this, we must first get the format ID of our input format (Tagless text) using the sitenews_get_format() utility function we created earlier in this chapter.

Once we have that ID, we can use the Drupal check_markup() function to make use of the input format. In the past, we've used check_markup(), but we've always accepted the default input format. However, this function allows us to specify (by format ID) which input format we want to use. So in order to use the Tagless text input format, with it's two filters, we need to call check_markup() like this: check_markup($node->title, $format). Using this format, the placeholders will be replaced and tags will be removed from the content.

The content this function returns will be ready for sending.

The last theme function takes the list of semi-formatted items returned from hook_sitenews() implementations and completes the formatting process.

```
/**
 * Theme for email messages.
 * @param $block
 *    A block with #title and #body set.
 */
function theme_sitenews_msgblock($block) {
  $msg = array();
  if (!empty($block['#title'])) {
    $title = strtoupper($block['#title']);
    for ($i = 0; $i < strlen($title); ++$i) {
      $underline .= '=';
    }
    $msg[] = $title;
    $msg[] = $underline;
  }
  $msg[] = $block['#body']  ."\n"; // <-- extra newline
  return implode("\n", $msg);
}
```

This last theme function takes each hook implementation's result and turns it into a separate section of the newsletter. It returns a single string with all of the items' formatted contents.

The hook_mail() Implementation

After the theming of content is done, the `_sitenews_do_message()` function sends a message to `drupal_mail()`. But that function in turn invokes `sitenews_mail()`, an implementation of `hook_mail()`.

We've handled most of the formatting already, and this hook implementation is nothing but boilerplate:

```
/**
 * Implementation of hook_mail().
 */
function sitenews_mail($key, &$message, $params) {
  switch ($key) {
    case 'sendsitenews':
      $message['to'] = $params['to'];
      $message['subject'] = $params['subject'];
      $message['body'] = $params['body'];
  }
}
```

After setting to, subject, and body fields, the message is automatically sent by the Drupal mail subsystem.

So if we were to send a message now, what would it look like? It would look something like the following screenshot:

THIS WEEK'S UPDATE

Dear Community Member,

Please enjoy your latest update from Site News.

RECENT BIOGRAPHIES
===================
Soren Kierkegaard
The Danish philosopher Soren Kierkegaard is best known for two things: his role as a forefather of existentialism, and for his radical take on Christian faith. By most interpretations, Kierkegaard was a fidiest, arguing that true faith needed no proof of God's existence. In fact, it was that radical expression of belief -- the leap of faith -- that empowered one to truly experience God's presence.
http://localhost/drupal/?q=node/21

Sextus Empiricus
The Hellenistic skeptic Sextus Empiricus is an important figure in philosophy not so much because of his own contributions. Instead, he is remembered as a compiler of arguments offered by the Pyrrhonian Skeptics. This group of skeptics held that happiness can be found in one's acknowledgment of ignorance. We can know nothing, they argued. So why vainly pursue either positive or negative dogma?
http://localhost/drupal/?q=node/20

Immanuel Kant
Immanuel Kant is considered by many to be the most important philosopher of the modern period. Inspired by Leibniz's rationalism, and challenged by Hume's empiricism, Kant undertook the project of developing a type of critical inquiry that could be used to evaluate reason, morality, and aesthetic sensibility.
http://localhost/drupal/?q=node/19

QUOTE OF THE DAY
================
Ontology recapitulates philology
-- W. V. Quine

========================
This message was sent from Philosopher Bios (http://localhost/drupal/). If you believe this message to be a case of abuse, please contact root@localhost.

In the preceding screenshot, we can see the title of the News Brief at the very top.

Underneath that is the content of the News Brief node. The original document looked like this:

```
{{salutation}},
Please enjoy your latest update from {{report name}}.
```

Its title was **This Week's Update**. But the call to `check_markup()` ran the placeholder replacement filter, replacing `{{salutation}}` and `{{report name}}`.

After that, the results of `biography_sitenews()` were converted into a list of entries, including links back to our site. Its low weight made this section appear before the quotes.

The random quote generated by `philquotes_sitenews()` appears at the bottom, formatted as its own section.

And what's that text at the bottom? It's the footer added by `philquotes_ mail_alter()`. We defined that in Chapter 6, where we talked about altering functions. With that there, we don't have to implement any sort of footer in our `sitenews` module.

Now we're done with the code. There's only one thing left to do. We need to wire this action up so that it will be automatically called when a certain event (namely, the publishing of a news brief node) occurs.

To do this, we will use the trigger module.

Adding a Trigger

The trigger module is included with the base distribution of Drupal. However, it is not enabled by default. It must be enabled in **Administer | Site building | Modules** before it can be used.

Triggers provide a way of linking Drupal events to actions. Much of this chapter has been devoted to creating a new action. Now it is time to take this action and link it to an event.

 In this chapter we create the trigger through the administration interface. In the next chapter we will create a trigger in code.

The first thing to do is go to **Administer | Site building | Triggers**. Under the **Content** tab there should be drop-down boxes for every event that can be triggered:

```
                                                              [more help...]
─Trigger: When either saving a new post or updating an existing post─────────
│ Choose an action                       ▼ │  Assign  │
─Trigger: After saving a new post────────────────────────────────────────────
│ Choose an action                       ▼ │  Assign  │
─Trigger: After saving an updated post───────────────────────────────────────
│ Choose an action                       ▼ │  Assign  │
─Trigger: After deleting a post──────────────────────────────────────────────
  No available actions for this trigger.
─Trigger: When content is viewed by an authenticated user────────────────────
  No available actions for this trigger.
```

For each available trigger, there is a drop-down list of actions that may be assigned to that trigger. If there are no actions for that trigger (as is the case with **After deleting a post**), then no drop-down list is displayed.

A trigger causes an action to be executed when an event occurs. The above screen is used to create a trigger. That is, it provides an interface for correlating an event with an action.

When we registered our action with `sitenews_action_info()`, we specified three different node-related events that our action can handle. Here's the snippet of code from that function:

```
$actions['sitenews_send_action'] = array(
    'type' => 'node',
    'description' => t('Send site news as email to all users.'),
    'configurable' => FALSE,
    'hooks' => array(
      'nodeapi' => array('insert', 'update', 'presave'),
    )
);
```

The **Content** tab of the screen shows all of the Node API hooks. We defined three— `insert`, `update`, and `presave`. These correspond to **After saving new post** (`insert`), **After saving an updated post** (`update`), and **When either saving a new post or updating an existing post** (`presave`). So we should expect to see our new action in each of these three drop-down boxes.

We could assign our action to any of these three events, but ideally we want the site news message to be sent any time a news brief node is published. And we want to check on this every time a new node is created or an existing post is updated. So we want to create a trigger for the `presave` event.

[more help...]

Trigger: When either saving a new post or updating an existing post

| Choose an action | ▼ | Assign |

Choose an action
node
   Publish post
   Unpublish post
   Make post sticky
   Make post unsticky
   Promote post to front page
   Remove post from front page
   Send site news as email to all users

Assign

Trigger: After deleting a post
No available actions for this trigger.

Trigger: When content is viewed by an authenticated user
No available actions for this trigger.

Now, every time a pre-save event occurs, `sitenews_send_action()` will be called. But it should only do something when the node type is `newsbrief`, and when the node is published. How is that done? Actually, we coded that part at the beginning of the `sitenews_send_action()` function:

```
/**
 * Action: Send an email message to all users.
 */
function sitenews_send_action(&$object, $context) {
  // If not a published sitenews, skip.
  if (!$object->status || $object->type != 'newsbrief') {
    return;
  }
}
```

With that taken care of, we are done. Now, any time a news brief is changed and marked published, it will be sent out to all of our users.

A hair trigger?

The trigger we have created here will invoke an action any time a News Brief is published. By default, editing a published module marks it as published and would result in sending off a new Site News mailing. There are other ways that we could have handled sending the message: scheduling a cron task, extending the administration interface to provide a message sending tool, and so on.

Summary

We have just finished the last module of the book, and it was a big one. In this chapter, we covered several important Drupal APIs and subsystems. Notably, we created filters, an input format, an action, and a new hook. We also revisited the mail subsystem and used themes to create email-friendly content.

Five modules and two themes—that's what we've created so far. To close the book, though, we are going to leave module development and look at another advanced programming feature of Drupal: Installation Profiles. We will create our own installer, which will install the Drupal core system and our theme and five modules.

9
An Installation Profile

In this last chapter, we will build an installation profile. We will take the base Drupal distribution, add the modules and theme we created here, and build a custom distribution of Drupal.

In this chapter, we will focus on the following topics:

- Setting up a custom distribution
- Creating an installation profile
- Selecting the modules to be installed
- Adding our custom content type from Chapter 4
- Configuring a trigger in the installer
- Adding additional steps to the installer
- Using the Forms API in an installer
- Specifying the default theme
- Building a final installation package

This lengthy list might make the task sound difficult. In fact, creating a custom installation profile is a straightforward process.

Introducing Installation Profiles

An **installation profile** is a special installer that includes prepackaged modules and themes, and can configure Drupal for a specific purpose. For example, it can install and configure custom modules and themes and even set system preferences—all from the installer. So the first time you log in after installation your environment is ready.

Building an installation profile is done on two levels:

- **The file system**: Starting from the base Drupal system, we will have to move some files around to get things configured for installation.
- **The .profile script**: Just putting the files in the right place isn't enough. We will need to build a special `.profile` script that will perform installation tasks.

We will perform both of these. In truth, though, the file system work is simple. Most of our time will be spent generating a `.profile`.

Why Use Installation Profiles?

"Sure, that sounds nice," one might say, "but why would someone need these?" Let's take a quick look at two scenarios that illustrate how a custom installation profile can be used. We'll start with the most obvious case.

Consider this scenario:

> *Philosopher Bios has become a popular website (remember, this is hypothetical). But requests have started pouring in for sister sites: Government Bios, Superhero Bios, Ancient Mesopotamian Bios... the public is clamoring for specialty biography sites.*

> *While we don't want to run all of these sites, we would be happy to help others get started. In the spirit of Open Source, we would like to release our system as a package. Sure, we could just release all of the modules individually and let others figure out how to put them together.*

> *But we could make life simpler by creating a single package that has it all.*

That's one scenario where an installation profile can solve a problem. Circumstances like this are the main reasons installation profiles were introduced. It is a powerful ability to be able to package customized distributions of Drupal.

Here's another that's worth considering:

> *Our Philosopher Bios site is drawing lots of traffic, and our ancient hardware is just not up to snuff. We need to move our entire site from an old server to some shiny new metal.*

> *But we don't want anything in the user interface to change. We want the same modules, the same theme, the same data, and the same layout.*

> *Migrating each piece is repetitious, boring, and just a plain old waste of time. Things would go a lot faster (and more smoothly) if we could just move the whole thing as one big package.*

This second case, too, can be addressed with installation profiles. While this isn't the primary purpose for which installation profiles were created, there are developers who use installation profiles as a migration tool. For an example, see `http://drupal.org/node/147720`. The SQL installation profile (`http://drupal.org/project/sql`) that is currently in development appears to be designed for such data migrations.

> **More than one way to skin a cat... or migrate Drupal**
>
> There are several different ways to migrate Drupal. Installation profiles provide one way—a way that might be particularly helpful in more complex cases. In many cases, simpler methods may be preferable. In the easiest case, simply copying the Drupal directory from one server to another and then dumping and loading the database may be sufficient. For an existing script to handle database dumping and loading on Linux systems, see this page: `http://drupal.org/node/59369`.

In this chapter, we will look at a case similar to the first case mentioned opposite. We will create a Philosopher Bios distribution of Drupal, complete with our five modules and our Descartes theme.

We'll go a little beyond just installing the modules. We will also configure some of the things that, during previous chapters, we did by hand.

- We will add the Quote content type from Chapter 4—his time through the Node API.
- We will programmatically create the trigger that we created by hand in the last chapter.
- We will give the user the opportunity to let us set the default theme to Descartes, instead of Garland.

These tasks will give us a chance to dive into some of the more esoteric features of installation profiles. But fear not. Installation profiles are not a black art. In fact, the profile (`drupal/profiles/default/default.profile`) that ships with Drupal has only five short functions, and much of the file (which is just over 150 lines long) is made up of comments.

However, first things first. We will begin with a pristine copy of Drupal and do a little copying.

Setting up a Distribution

Our first bit of work doesn't involve any coding. We need to set up the directories for our custom Drupal distribution.

Our goal is to create a distribution of Drupal that includes our modules and theme. We are not migrating a site.

Thus, we want to start out with a pristine copy of Drupal—one that has not yet been installed or configured. It's probably easiest to start with a fresh copy downloaded from Drupal.org. This ensures that we have the most recent set of security patches and so on.

Migrating tip: you've got it already!

If you are working on an installation for migration instead of one intended for new sites, there is no need to start from a pristine configuration. You will want to keep all the changes you have made (including, probably, the settings files and the contents of the `drupal/files/` directory.

Once we have a pristine copy of Drupal, we need to unpack it. To distinguish our distribution from the normal Drupal one, it is a good idea to rename the main directory. Borrowing from the module versioning convention, we will rename `drupal-6.2/` to `drupal-philbios-6.2-1.0/`. The first group of digits (`6.2`) is the Drupal version. The revision number (`1.0`) is the version number for our distribution.

Some installation profiles are released with versions like `6.x-1.x`. This is not particularly helpful. An installation profile is a specific version of Drupal. There is no such release as `6.x`, so this is not an accurate version identifier.

Inside `drupal-philbios-6.2-1.0/sites/all/`, we need to create the `modules/` and `themes/` directories. Even though we are making a custom distribution, it is still not a good idea to put our custom modules inside the `drupal-philbios-6.2-1.0/modules/` directory. It will lead to maintenance hassles, and it is too easy to overwrite your modules while upgrading Drupal.

Next, we need to copy all our modules and the Descartes theme into the `modules/` and `themes/` directories (respectively). The directory structure should look as follows:

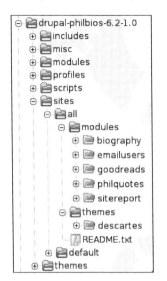

In the above screenshot, the modules and the theme we just added are shaded differently: `biography`, `emailusers`, `goodreads`, `philquotes`, and `sitenews` make up the modules, and the `descartes` theme is in the `themes/` folder.

Creating a Profile Directory

We have one more task to do before we change tracks and begin coding our installation profile.

In the above screenshot, there is folder named `profiles/`. This is where installation profiles belong. The default profile, which is responsible for performing a standard Drupal installation, is the only profile there.

We will add a new profile directory called `philosopherbios/`:

Profiles borrow their architecture from modules. Here, the `philosopherbios/` directory will serve as the holding place for files related to our installation profile.

Inside this directory, we need to create a `philosopherbios.profile` file. This will contain our installation profile script.

We're done with our file system work. Now we can begin writing the code for installation.

Programming Profiles

In some respects, installation profiles are similar to modules. Architecturally, for example, the directory layouts are similar. Just as Drupal expects a module folder to contain a `.module` file, a profile folder is expected to have a `.profile` file.

But there are some differences as well. Profiles don't have `.info` files. Profiles don't need to be installed or activated (simply being in the right directory is enough). Profiles aren't integrated into the help system, either. These are small differences. But there is one big difference that a developer should be aware of.

The profile performs a substantial part of Drupal's installation. For coding, this has a practical consequence. An installation profile runs before some pieces of the Drupal infrastructure have been activated.

Hence, the hook framework that we are used to is not available. Instead, a series of callbacks *similar* to the hook system is used.

The Forms API works, but has to be used with care. In other APIs such as menus, nodes, and actions, some functions can be used while others will not function properly. (The database API, in contrast, is fully functional.)

There is no list of functions that do or do not work in installation profiles. The best guide is to look in Drupal's installer. Many of the important utility libraries, like `include/common.inc`, are included and can be used safely. But with modules, some functions may work while others don't. It just depends upon what has been initialized before the installation profile executes.

Mostly, this doesn't have much of an effect on a well-constructed installation profile. Installation tasks tend to create and insert, and many such functions (regardless of API) work.

Sometimes installation tasks require writing a little extra auxiliary code. It may take a database query to accomplish what can usually be done with a function. For our installation-related tasks, though, we have all the tools we need.

Let's start on the profile.

The .profile Script

The Drupal installation system expects profiles to have certain features. These are implemented as functions that follow naming conventions like those of hooks. A function signature begins with the profile name.

For example, Drupal expects a function named `<profilename>_profile_details()` to exist, where `<profilename>` is replaced by the name of the profile. If this is not defined, the profile will not be available.

A `.profile` file should have the following functions:

- `<profilename>_profile_details()`: Provides basic information about the profile. (This is required for the profile to function.)
- `<profilename>_profile_modules()`: Lists the modules that should be installed with this profile.
- `<profilename>_profile_tasks()`: Handles the installation tasks.
- `<profilename>_profile_task_list()`: Provides a list of tasks that this profile will perform during an install.

While these four functions are used directly by the installer, a `.profile` file may contain other functions as well.

> **Using hooks_form_alter()**
>
> One hook, `hook_form_alter()`, can be used within the installer. With no module system in place, how is this possible? The installer has some extra logic to reproduce calling this hook without actually using the module system.

The Details Function

The beginning of our `philosopherbios.profile` script looks as follows:

```php
<?php
// $Id$
require_once('profiles/default/default.profile');
/**
```

```
 * Provide an installer for our specific set of
 * modules, content types, and so on.
 * @file
 */
/**
 * Provide details about this profile.
 */
function philosopherbios_profile_details() {
  return array(
    'name' => 'Philosopher Bios Profile',
    'description' => 'Use this profile to install the '
      .'modules and theme for Philosopher Bios.',
  );
}
```

One thing that should stand out is the use of a `require_once` directive at the very beginning of the file. Strictly speaking, this is not required. However, we can use a function or two from the default profile to perform parts of the basic Drupal installation. If we did not do this, we would have to replicate sections of that file, and then keep the code synchronized with each new release of Drupal.

The first function in this file is `philosopherbios_profile_details()`. The purpose of this function is to provide information that will help the user decide whether this profile is the right one. When installation begins, a user will be presented with a choice of profiles:

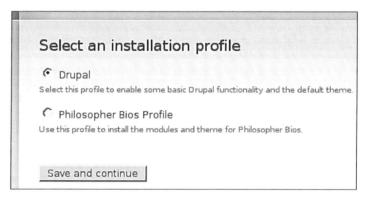

The array returned by `philosopherbios_profile_details()` is used to present our profile in this list. The `name` item becomes the profile title, and the `description` is used to provide some help text.

That is all that there is to this function.

The Modules List

Once an installation profile has been chosen, Drupal will step through a number of basic installation tasks, including language selection, system verification, and database configuration. Then it will begin installing the system.

Part of this task is module installation and configuration. It is the responsibility of the installation profile to specify what modules should be installed. We will accomplish this with `philosopherbios_profile_modules()`:

```
/**
 * List the modules that should be installed.
 */
function philosopherbios_profile_modules() {
  return array(
    // Drupal modules enabled by default (but not required):
    'color', 'comment', 'help', 'menu', 'taxonomy', 'dblog',
    // Other Drupal core modules  we need:
    'trigger',
    // Our modules:
    'biography', 'emailusers', 'goodreads', 'philquotes',
    'sitenews',
  );
}
```

As with the previous function, this function simply returns an array. To be specific, it returns an array of module names. Every module in this array will be installed and activated.

> **Where are the required core modules?**
>
> All the required modules—action, node, system and so on—are automatically installed. They are installed at an earlier stage of the installation process. *They should never be included in this list.*

I have broken the list above into three sections. Most Drupal installations will want to install these basic modules:

```
// Drupal modules enabled by default (but not required)
'color', 'comment', 'help', 'menu', 'taxonomy', 'dblog',
```

These modules—all part of the Drupal distribution—provide features that are used widely, and they are also all enabled in the default profile.

Next, we added the Trigger module. While this module is not enabled by the default Drupal installer, our installer enables it. Why? Because one of our modules, sitenews, lists it as a dependency.

Finally, there is the list of our modules:

```
// Our modules:
'biography', 'emailusers', 'goodreads', 'philquotes', 'sitenews',
```

Does order matter? When it comes to dependencies, it does. Modules are installed in the order they are listed. If Module A depends upon Module B, then make sure that Module B is installed first by putting it earlier in the list.

Once all the modules have been installed, the administrator will be prompted to do some configuring and create an account. All of this is handled by the installer, and is generally not changed by the installation profile.

After the configuration screen, control will be passed to our profile script again. This is where we will do the brunt of our work.

The Installation Task System

Most of Drupal's installation is done using a task system. In this system, Drupal proceeds through a series of steps (tasks). Each task is responsible for directing the installer to the next task, like a chain.

This is an important point: It is the responsibility of a task to redirect the installer to the next task. So a task can logically determine what the next task should be, based on its current state.

To get a detailed idea of how the task system works the best code to look at is install.php, located in the root Drupal directory. The install_tasks() function is particularly helpful for understanding tasks.

For example, Drupal performs the profile-install task, which is responsible for preparing for the installation of modules listed in philosopherbios_profile_modules(). Once this task is done, it directs the installer to the next task: profile-install-batch. This task does the actual installation of modules. A few more minor tasks are done before the configure task is run. This task displays the site configuration form to the administrator, which begins as follows:

Configure site

All necessary changes to *./sites/default* and *./sites/default/settings.php* have been made. They have been set to read-only for security.

To configure your website, please provide the following information.

Site information

Site name: *

Site e-mail address: *

The *From* address in automated e-mails sent during registration and new password requests, and other notifications. (Use an address ending in your site's domain to help prevent this e-mail being flagged as spam.)

Administrator account

Once this form is submitted, the `configure` task hands off control to the task we are interested in: `profile`.

The Profile Task

The **profile task** is the entry point for the installation profile. Most of the boilerplate installation work has been done. The database is configured, modules are installed, locales have been chosen, and even the basic site information (such as the site's name and the administrator's email address) has been stored in the database.

With the profile task, we will begin doing our own custom configuration.

A Basic Profile Task

When Drupal's installer hits the `profile` task (after running the `configure` task), it attempts to execute the `<profilename>_profile_tasks()` function, handing it two parameters: a reference to the task name (`&$task`), and the current URL for the installer (`$url`). The `$task` variable will always be initially set to `profile`.

If the installation profile needs no additional information from the user, it can do its installation and return without ever using either the $task or $url variables. In this case, we could have a philosopherbios_profile_task() structured something like as follows:

```
philosopherbios_profile_task(&$task, $url) {
  variable_set('my_variable', 'my_value');
}
```

In this example, the function does nothing more than adding a new variable to the database — perhaps for use by a module or something else.

There is one problem with the function above — a problem that might cause some confusion. The default Drupal installation profile uses default_profile_task() to create some content types (page and story), initialize defaults for nodes, and make a few tweaks for the theme system's display of node content.

If we don't include that functionality here, then we will miss a couple of expected types. What do we do?

One solution is to copy the code from default_profile_task() and paste it into our custom function. Besides being undrupalishly ugly, doing things this way can turn into a maintenance nightmare. Every time the Drupal code is updated, the profile maintainer will have to check the default profile and see if anything must be updated in the custom profile.

I suggest an alternative that, while also being slightly undrupalish, is easy to maintain and avoids gratuitous replication of code.

At the top of the profile file, we have the following line:

```
require_once('profiles/default/default.profile');
```

By importing the default profile, we can now use the default_profile_task() function defined in that file from within our code. Rewriting our original function to use Drupal's default_profile_task() function, we now have code that looks as follows:

```
philosopherbios_profile_task(&$task, $url) {
  default_profile_task();
  variable_set('my_variable', 'my_value');
}
```

Now we have set our own variables and let the default profile take care of default settings.

The placement of the call to `default_profile_task()` is important. Since it changes behavior of the node and theme systems, you may want to execute it first if you plan on either making changes to default node behavior or making use of the `page` and `story` content types.

Does this work with all `*_profile_task()` functions? Could I, for instance, use the profile task from another installation profile?

Only very carefully. The reason the earlier example works as it does is because the `default_profile_task()` is itself a simple task. Like the one we have created, it does not require additional interaction from the user. Or, to state it more concisely, *it performs only one task.*

But as we shall see shortly, profile tasks can be used to construct a complex multi-task series of events. In such a case, the results returned from the profile task may require additional processing by the installer—processing that we cannot easily provide or anticipate.

The bottom line? It is OK to use `default_profile_task()`. But using another profile task can cause unpredictable results. Know the code before using the profile task.

 Is it likely that the behavior of `default_profile_task()` might suddenly become more complex and break our code? Not for Drupal 6, and probably not for Drupal 7, either. Large changes would more likely make their way into `install.php`.

The profile task we have created is basic, and should give a very simple idea of what is expected by the installer. But it doesn't do much practical good.

Let's create a more sophisticated profile task—one that will actually do some good for our `phiosopherbios` installation profile.

A Complex Profile Task

Already all of our custom modules have been installed. But at various places throughout this book we have used the administration interface to configure these modules.

With our installation profile, though, we want to automate that process. Specifically, we want to do the following:

- Create the `quote` content type we defined in Chapter 4.
- Add a trigger to tie the `sitenews_send_action` action from Chapter 8 to the Node API's `presave` event.
- Give the user the option of setting the default theme to `descartes` instead of to `garland`.

This last step will require interaction from the user, so we will be taking advantage of the task system to design our own custom task.

As usual, we will start out by taking a glance at the function as a whole. Then we will cover the first two points. Implementing our own task is a little more complicated, and we'll cover that in more detail in a moment.

```
/**
 * Walk through final installation tasks
 */
function philosopherbios_profile_tasks(&$task, $url) {
  if ($task == 'profile') {
    // This is why we required default profile.
    default_profile_tasks(&$task, $url);

    // Quote content from chapter 4:
    $quote_type = array(
      'name' => st('Quote'), // <- st() is t() for installer
      'type' => 'quote',
      'description' => st('Quotations and witticisms'),
      'module' => 'node',
      'has_title' => TRUE,
      'title_label' => 'Origin',
      'body_label' => 'Text',
      'has_body' => TRUE,
      'custom' => FALSE,
      'modified' => TRUE,
      'locked' => FALSE,
      'is_new' => TRUE,
      'help' => '',
      'min_word_count' => 0,
    );
    node_type_save((object)$quote_type);

    // Pre-configure our trigger from ch. 8:
    // (see trigger.admin.inc)
    $aid = 'sitenews_send_action';
    $hook = 'nodeapi';
    $op = 'presave';
    $sql = 'INSERT INTO {trigger_assignments} '
      ."VALUES ('%s', '%s', '%s', 1)";
    db_query($sql, $hook, $op, $aid);

    // Rebuild the menu
    menu_rebuild();

    // Do the form:
```

```
    $task = 'philosopherbios_pick_theme';
    $form = drupal_get_form('philosopherbios_theme_form', $url);
    return $form;
  }
  // Because of this, we must create
  // the philosopherbios_profile_task_list() function
  if ($task == 'philosopherbios_pick_theme') {
    $form = drupal_get_form('philosopherbios_theme_form', $url);

    // See if the form was processed:
    if (variable_get('philosopherbios_theme', FALSE)) {
      variable_del('philosopherbios_theme');
      $task = 'profile-finished';
    }
    else {
      return $form; // try again.
    }
  }
}
```

This function handles two tasks: `profile` and `philosopherbios_pick_theme`. The first is responsible for creating the `quote` type and the new trigger. It is handled by the first `if` statement. That's what we will look at first.

If or switch?

When handling tasks, it is generally better to use `if` statements, rather than `switch` statements. Why? Because we want the ability for an early statement to change the value of `$task` and have other statements then act on that task. We can accomplish this most succinctly with multiple `if` statements.

Creating a Content Type

The first thing we do in the `if ($task == 'profile')` block is call the `default_profile_tasks()` function from the default profile. The reason for this was provided earlier.

Next, we define our `quote` node type:

```
// Quote content from chapter 4:
$quote_type = array(
  'name' => st('Quote'), // <- st() is t() for installer
  'type' => 'quote',
  'description' => st('Quotations and witticisms'),
  'module' => 'node',
  'has_title' => TRUE,
```

```
        'title_label' => 'Origin',
        'body_label' => 'Text',
        'has_body' => TRUE,
        'custom' => TRUE,
        'modified' => TRUE,
        'locked' => FALSE,
        'is_new' => TRUE,
        'help' => '',
        'min_word_count' => 0,
    );
    node_type_save((object)$quote_type);
```

Here we use yet another method for creating a new content type. Since we are not using a module, we cannot make use of hook_node_info() to do the creation for us.

Instead, we use a method that is generally reserved for content types created through user interaction. In fact, here we are using the same function to save the node type as the one that Drupal used when we created the quote content type through the administration interface in Chapter 4.

> **hook_node_info() vs. node_type_save()**
>
> How do you know which to use? Any time a module adds its own content type, hook_node_info() should be used. Only when the content type is not module specific should we need to use node_type_save().

Since we are using the low-level node_type_save() function, we need to define all the fields that will be stored in the database. Thus, our $quote_type array is a little longer than normal.

> If you would prefer not to worry about setting all of the defaults, you can break Drupal protocol and use the "private" node function _node_type_set_defaults(), passing it a sparser array. That function will assign default values to any attribute that is not present in the array.

In the above code, we use a new function: st(). This function provides the same behavior as the t() function. But during installation, the translation system may not be completely initialized. For that reason, the st() function should be used in place of t().

Rather than query user preferences to determine the language, st() uses information from the installer to set the language. It should not be used outside the installation context.

Once the array is correctly set up, we must cast it to an object before handing it over to `node_type_save()`.

```
node_type_save((object)$quote_type);
```

But that is all there is to creating a new content type in an installation profile.

Creating a Trigger

In Chapter 8, we created a trigger using the administration interface. For our installation profile, though, let's suppose that it is desirable to have this trigger configured upon installation.

The trigger API does not include a function for inserting a trigger. In fact, a trigger is essentially just a row in a database. So we will need to add our trigger by inserting a record into the database:

```
// Pre-configure our trigger from ch. 8:
// (see trigger.admin.inc)
$aid = 'sitenews_send_action';
$hook = 'nodeapi';
$op = 'presave';
$sql = 'INSERT INTO {trigger_assignments} '
  ."VALUES ('%s', '%s', '%s', 1)";
db_query($sql, $hook, $op, $aid);
// Rebuild the menu
menu_rebuild();
```

To insert an entry into the trigger table, we need four pieces of information:

- The Action ID (`aid`), which is the name of the callback function for the desired action. In our case, it is `sitenews_send_action`.

- The name of the hook to watch for events. In our case, we are looking for the `nodeapi` hook to be called. `trigger_nodeapi()` is the hook implementation that will watch for this event.

- The name of the operation to watch for. This is the operation that will be passed to `trigger_nodeapi()`. For us, it is the `presave` operation (or event) that we want to catch.

- The trigger's weight. If an event triggers more than one action, the trigger module returns the actions ordered by weight, and then the actions are called in order. We set it to `1`, the default.

In the preceding code, these four parameters are inserted into the `trigger_assignments` table. This is all that must be done to add a trigger.

At the end of the code, we rebuild the menus (`menu_rebuild()`), so that the changes we made that effect menu generation can be accounted for before the user first logs into the system.

Moving to the Next Task

Now we've created the content type and the trigger. Next, we want to get the user's input on whether or not `descartes` should be set as the default theme.

Doing this will require a few things: First, we will need to use a different task. Second, we will need to provide the user with a form for making the decision.

The end of the `profile` task is used to set up these two things:

```
// Do the form:
$task = 'philosopherbios_pick_theme';
$form = drupal_get_form('philosopherbios_theme_form', $url);
return $form;
```

The `$task` variable is set to `philosopherbios_pick_theme`. Then, a form callback is used to generate a form for display (which we will see later), and that form is returned. Sounds simple? Well, there's a little more.

The 'profile' Task is Special

If we did not change the `$task` from `profile` to `philosopherbios_pick theme`, if we left off just that line—what would happen?

What we would expect to happen is that the form would be displayed, and when it was submitted, `philosopherbios_profile_tasks()` would be called again with `$task` still set to `profile`.

In fact, this is the way that other tasks work, but not `profile`.

What actually happens is that the installer will go on to the final installation page *without ever showing the form.*

The installer watches the value of `$task`. It calls `philosopherbios_profile_tasks()` and then checks the value of `$task`.

- If the value of `$task` is unknown to the installer, the installer simply calls `philosopherbios_profile_tasks()` again, leaving the value of `$task` unchanged.
- If the value of task is `profile-finished`, then the installer stops using the profile and continues the installation process.

- If the value of $task is profile the installer assumes that the profile task was a simple one (like the one we looked at early in this chapter), and *considers the profile task finished*. Essentially, the installer treats profile-finished and profile the same in this regard.

So it is imperative that we set $task to something other than profile (or profile-finished) if we are going to do a multi-step process. Think of it as chaining together a series of tasks, where each step requires its own task.

By assigning $task the value philosopherbios_pick_theme, we define a new task. This means we need to register the new task.

Registering a New Task

Earlier, we set $task to philosopherbios_pick_theme. Now we need to let the Drupal installer know that we have added another task. This is done using philosopherbios_profile_task_list(), a callback that the installer will expect to find:

```
/**
 * List of custom tasks. This is a callback that
 * the installer expects.
 */
function philosopherbios_profile_task_list() {
  return array(
    'philosopherbios_pick_theme' => st('Choose Theme'),
  );
}
```

This function is simple. It returns an associative array with the task name as the key, and a user-friendly short description as the value.

Since the actual mechanics of the callback to philosopherbios_profile_tasks() do not make use of this task, what is the role of this function? Actually, it is mainly used to display progress information to the user:

In the preceding screenshot we can see how the information was used. This list is generated early in the installation process, and as the installer progresses through procedures and tasks, this display is updated to show progress.

With our task registered, we can shift focus again—this time to the form that will be presented to the user.

The Theme Selection Form

Once again, we will return to the Form API. This time, we will create a simple form to give users the choice between the Descartes theme we developed in Chapter 3 and Drupal's built-in Garland theme. The administrator's choice will determine which theme is used as the default. (Of course, this can still be changed later in **Administer | Site building | Themes**.)

The last lines of the first `if` statement of our `philosopherbios_profile_tasks()` function looked as follows:

```
// Do the form:
$task = 'philosopherbios_pick_theme';
$form = drupal_get_form('philosopherbios_theme_form', $url);
return $form;
```

The last two lines are what interest us now. We use the `drupal_get_form()` function to get the form that we will display to the user, and then we return that form. Since the task isn't `profile` or `profile-finished`, Drupal will display the form for the user to complete.

The first argument to `drupal_get_form()` is the name of the callback function that will create the form. All other arguments (in this case, only `$url`) are passed as parameters into the callback.

So now we need to create the `philosopherbios_theme_form()` function. By way of reminder, it is conventional for form-generating functions to end with `_form`. We will name ours `philosopherbios_theme_form()`.

Most of the Forms API works as expected, including the validation and submission callbacks. So if we need to perform some form validation, all we would need to do is define a function named `philosopherbios_theme_form_validate()`. To handle form submissions, we need only name a function `philosopherbios_theme_form_submit()`.

Here is the main form function:

```
/**
 * Form for selecting a theme.
 */
function philosopherbios_theme_form(&$form_state, $url) {
  drupal_set_title('Select a Theme');
  $form['text'] = array(
    '#value' =>
      st('Do you want to make Descartes your default theme?'),
    '#weight' => -1, // <- We want it on top!
  );
  $form['choose_theme'] = array(
    '#type' => 'radios',
    '#title' => st('Default Theme'),
    '#default_value' => 0,
    '#options' => array(0 => st('Descartes'), 1 => st('Garland')),
    '#description' => st('Set the default site theme.'),
    '#weight' => 0,
  );
  $form['submit'] = array(
    '#type' => 'submit',
    '#value' => st('Save and continue'),
    '#weight' => 10,
  );
  $form['#action'] = $url;
  $form['#redirect'] = FALSE;
  return $form;
}
```

We've seen a few functions like this in the previous chapters.

The first thing this form does is sets the title of the page with `drupal_set_title()`. Often, we can rely on other parts of the infrastructure to create a page title. But here in the installer, we will need to do so ourselves.

Next, we define the form, which is composed of the following:

- An introductory piece of text asking: **Do you want to make Descartes your default theme?**

- A pair of radio buttons (both are done with one `'#type' => 'radios'` entry) giving the user the choice between Descartes and Garland.

- A submit button labeled **Save and continue**.

At the end of the form are two additional properties:

```
$form['#action'] = $url;
$form['#redirect'] = FALSE;
```

The first tells the form where to go (like the `action` attribute in an HTML `<form>` tag). The second is normally used to tell Drupal where to redirect the user once the form is processed. But we don't want to redirect the user anywhere—we want them to finish the installation. So it must be set to `FALSE`.

When the form is rendered by `drupal_get_form()` and sent to the browser, it looks as follows:

What happens when a user presses the **Save and continue** button?

The form is submitted to the URL specified in `$url` (which happens to be the same URL used through most of the installer—the installer's state is not tied to the URL). This causes the code in `installer.php` to be re-evaluated again. That means it will check to find out what the current task is.

Returning to the philosopherbios_pick_theme Task

When the installer checks its state, it will find that the current task is still `philosopherbios_pick_theme`, and so it will call our `philosopherbios_profile_tasks()` function again, this time with `$task` set to `philosopherbios_pick_theme`.

Let's return to the profile tasks function and look at the second `if` statement:

```
/**
 * Walk through final installation tasks
 */
function philosopherbios_profile_tasks(&$task, $url) {
```

```
  if ($task == 'profile') {
    // ... Other stuff....

    // Do the form:
    $task = 'philosopherbios_pick_theme';
    $form = drupal_get_form('philosopherbios_theme_form', $url);
    return $form;
  }

  if ($task == 'philosopherbios_pick_theme') {
    $form = drupal_get_form('philosopherbios_theme_form', $url);

    // See if the form was processed:
    if (variable_get('philosopherbios_theme', false)) {
      variable_del('philosopherbios_theme');
      $task = 'profile-finished';
    }
    else {
      return $form; // try again.
    }
  }
}
```

Some of the code at which we looked earlier has been left out of this code snippet. The main code that we are interested in is highlighted. This is the conditional that will be executed when the $task variable is set to philosopherbios_pick_theme.

The first line retrieves the form. But this time, it will kick of the form submission handler. Before moving on, we need to look at that function.

The Submission Handler

When drupal_get_form() is called this time, it retrieves the cached form and hands it off to the submission handler. Following the Forms API callback procedure, our handler is called philosopherbios_theme_form_submit().

Here is the function:

```
/**
 * Form submission callback.
 */
function philosopherbios_theme_form_submit($form, &$form_state) {
  // Save our state:
  variable_set('philosopherbios_theme', TRUE);

  if ($form_state['values']['choose_theme'] == 0) {
    // Enable Descartes theme
```

```
        $sql = "UPDATE {system} SET status = 1 "
          ."WHERE type = 'theme' AND name = 'descartes'";
        db_query($sql);
        // Initialize theme system:
        system_theme_data();
        system_initialize_theme_blocks('descartes');
        // Set theme as default
        variable_set('theme_default', 'descartes');
      }
      // Otherwise, leave it at Garland.
    }
```

The first thing this submission handler does is store a variable in the database:

```
    variable_set('philosopherbios_theme', TRUE);
```

Here, we use the database to store a token that indicates our state. With this variable stored, we can later (from the profile tasks function) make sure that the form was actually submitted.

[Such state-related installer variables should always be removed from the database when the installation profile is complete. We will do this shortly.]

Once we have set this state token, we move on to the form.

We gave the user a choice of two themes. Glancing back at the form, the two themes were Descartes and Garland, each of which was given a specific index in an array:

```
    $form['choose_theme'] = array(
      '#type' => 'radios',
      '#title' => st('Default Theme'),
      '#default_value' => 0,
      '#options' => array(0 => st('Descartes'), 1 => st('Garland')),
      '#description' => st('Set the default site theme.'),
      '#weight' => 0,
    );
```

So when we get the form back, we will check to see whether the value of the radios was set to 0 (Descartes) or 1 (Garland).

Actually, to be more precise, we only care if it is 0. If the user chooses the Garland theme, which is already configured and set as the default, then we don't need to do anything. There is work if the user chooses to set Descartes as the default. Thus, we end up with a conditional like this:

```
if ($form_state['values']['choose_theme'] == 0) {
  // Enable Descartes theme
  $sql = "UPDATE {system} SET status = 1 "
    ."WHERE type = 'theme' and name = 'descartes'";
  db_query($sql);

  // Initialize theme system:
  system_theme_data();
  system_initialize_theme_blocks('descartes');

  // Set theme as default
  variable_set('theme_default','descartes');
}
```

If `$form_state['values']['choose_theme']` is 0, we have work to do. In fact, we have three specific tasks to perform:

- Enable the theme
- Initialize the theme
- Set it to be the default

First, we need to enable the theme named `descartes`. Since there is no convenient function that we can use for this, we do it with SQL:

```
$sql = "UPDATE {system} SET status = 1 "
  ."WHERE type = 'theme' AND name = 'descartes'";
db_query($sql);
```

Here we modify the {system} table. The system table is a big storage system for tracking theme and module settings. Fortunately, it is rarely the case that module code must directly manipulate this table. Here, however, we need to work on the table directly.

Basically, we need to change the status flag for the theme named descartes. If status is 0, a theme is disabled. We set it to 1 to enable the theme.

Now that the theme is enabled, we need to *initialize the theme*.

By default, a theme has no blocks set. But this isn't good. An administrator would not have immediate access to the main menu. Instead, they'd get a screen that looked something like the following screenshot:

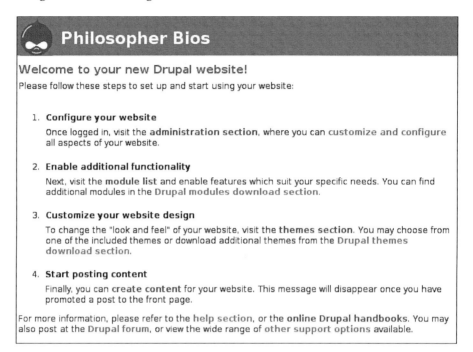

Notice the missing menu on the left side?

Usually, the theme selection system in the **Administer | Site building | Themes** page handles initializing a new theme and adding the default menu. We need to do that initialization here in the installer, though.

Drupal makes this work easier. It has a built-in method for setting up a theme the first time. But first we need to initialize the data for themes since the installer hasn't already done this step. So we make two function calls:

```
system_theme_data();
system_initialize_theme_blocks('descartes');
```

The first initializes the theme data (basically processing the theme .info files). The second function does the necessary theme initialization, including adding the standard menu to the left-hand column of blocks.

Two steps are done. The third step is to set descartes as the default theme.

Drupal determines which theme is default by using the `theme_default` variable stored in the main `variable` table. And as we saw earlier in this chapter and in the last chapter, the contents of the variable table can be manipulated with `variable_set()`, `variable_get()`, and `variable_del()`.

So setting `descartes` to the default is as easy as this:

```
variable_set('theme_default','descartes');
```

Now we have enabled and initialized the theme, and set it as default. When the user makes his or her way through the installer, the first screen he or she will see will look like the following screenshot:

But before we jump that far, we need to work a little on our installer. We need to return to the profile tasks function, `philosopherbios_profile_tasks()`, to finish up.

Finishing the Installation Profile

We're down to the last section of the `philosopherbios_profile_tasks()` section. We have looked at how the submission handler set the default theme as a result of the call to `drupal_get_form()` below. Let's continue looking at the `philosopherbios_profile_tasks()` function to see what happens after the form data has been processed:

```
if ($task == 'philosopherbios_pick_theme') {
    $form = drupal_get_form('philosopherbios_theme_form', $url);
    // See if the form was processed:
    if (variable_get('philosopherbios_theme', FALSE)) {
      variable_del('philosopherbios_theme');
      $task = 'profile-finished';
    } else {
      return $form; // try again.
    }
}
```

After the `drupal_get_form()` call, what we need to find out for sure is if the submission handler was really called. In other words, we want to make sure that the user really did progress through the theme-picking screen. We can tell by checking to see whether or not the variable `philosopherbios_theme` is set in the `variables` table.

Recall that we used `variable_set()` at the beginning of `philosopherbios_theme_ form_submit()`. So here we can tell whether the submission handler was run based on the presence of that variable.

If `variable_get('philosopherbios_theme', FALSE)` returns FALSE, then we know that the submit function was not run. The `else` block is executed, sending the form back to the user.

But if the call to `variable_get('philosopherbios_theme', FALSE)` returns TRUE, we know the submission handler was run. We just need to clean up and return control to the installer.

For our installation profile, cleaning up is pretty simple. We've only left one variable in the `variable` table. We delete it with `variable_del()`:

```
variable_del('philosopherbios_theme');
```

To return control to the installer, we need only inform it that the profile tasks are all finished. That is done by setting `$task` to `profile-finished` and allowing the function to return.

Taking a look back at the installer, the user chooses a theme and then clicks **Save and continue**.

The form is processed; the theme is enabled, initialized, and set as default; extra data is removed; and control is returned to the installer. From here, the install will proceed on to the final screen of the installation process:

That is all! If we were to go into the new site and look around, we would find all our content types (**Quote, Biography, News Brief**) available in **Create content**. The trigger would be activated for news brief publishing. The `philquotes` and `goodreads` blocks would be available for configuration on the **Administer | Site building | Blocks** page. Our user profiles will all have the option for administrators to send an email, as provided by the `emailusers` module.

Want to preconfigure your blocks?

With a little more work, the installation profile could add our `philquotes` and `goodreads` blocks to the default theme. This requires doing some low-level work on the blocks tables. A good place to start is in `modules/block/block.admin.inc`, specifically with the `block_admin_configure_submit()` function.

Now we have configured our custom distribution. All we need to do is package it.

Packaging the Distribution

We began with a fresh Drupal package. We added our modules and theme into the appropriate places, and then created an installation profile in the `profiles/` directory.

The last step is to take that set of files and build a package.

> **Remove your changes**
>
> If you used this distribution directory to test out the installation profile, make sure to get rid of any changes the installation might have made. Specifically, you will need to make sure that the `sites/default/settings.php` file is removed. (If you are using installation profiles to move your own site, you can keep the `settings.php` file if you'd like.)

Typically, Drupal is distributed as a tarred and gzipped file. If you have a UNIX-like environment, you can change directories to the location of the `drupal-philbios-6.2-1.0/` folder and create the distribution file as follows:

```
$ tar -zcvf drupal-philbios-6.2-1.0.tgz  drupal-philbios-6.2-1.0/
```

This will create the compressed archive file `drupal-philbios-6.2-1.0.tgz`.

That file can now be used just like the official Drupal releases. You won't even have to modify the installation instructions!

Summary

The focus of this chapter was building a custom Drupal distribution. To accomplish this, we began with a pristine Drupal archive, added our own modules and theme, and then wrote an installation profile to automate several tasks. Finally, we packed it all into a new archive file that can be used for installing a fresh copy of our distribution.

In the code we wrote, we focused on the callback functions used by the installer. But we also took a look at another way of adding content types, as well as the process of creating triggers from code. We used the Forms API to add an extra screen to our installer.

During the course of our book, we have looked at Drupal's architecture, created several modules and a theme, and now an installation module. We've looked at the major Drupal APIs and subsystems. We've implemented dozens of hooks, and used many key Drupal functions.

At this point, you should have the tools to develop sophisticated Drupal modules. Go forth and produce drupalish code.

Index

M

mail alter hook 171
Mail API, Drupal
  drupal_mail() function 165
  hook_link_alter() 172
  hook_mail(), implementing 167-171
  hook_mail_alter() 172
  hook_mail_alter(), implementing 173-175
  hook_menu_alter() 172
  hooks, altering 172
  mail, sending 165, 166
  mail footer, adding 173-175
  mail formatting, hook_mail() used 167-171
menus, Drupal 17, 18
module, biography
  about 181, 182
  biography.info file 183
  biography.install file 185
  biography_access(), implementing 203, 204
  biography_info.tpl.php 219-221
  biography_install() 185
  biography_schema(), implementing 187, 188
  biography_uninstall() 185
  hook_help(), implementing 183
  hook_node_info(), implementing 193-196
  module installation script 184
module, Drupal
  .info file, creating 24-26
  .module file, creating 26, 27
  copying 35
  default theme, overriding 112
  drupal_install_schema() function 185
  drupal_mail() function 165
  drupal_uninstall_schema() function 185
  foundations 97
  hook_block() function, implementing 29
  hook_help() function, implementing 54, 55
  hook_install() 184
  hook_mail() function 165
  hook_menu() function, implementing 146
  hook_schema() 185
  hook_uninstall() 185
  hook_user(), implementing 177, 178
  hook_watchdog() function 43, 86
  installing steps 34

  t() function 32
  theming 103, 104
module, drupal
  hook_node_info() 192
module, emailusers
  about 143
  callback function, defining 151, 153
  content, constructing 178-180
  drupal_mail_send() function 166
  emailusers.info file 144
  emailusers.module file 144, 145
  emailusers_compose() function 148-151
  hook_link_alter() 172
  hook_mail_alter() 172
  hook_mail_alter(), implementing 174, 175
  hook_menu() function, implementing 146
  hook_menu_alter() 172
  hook_user(), implementing 176-178
  mail() function 145
  mail configuration 145
  supported features 144
  user_load() function 152
module, goodreads sample
  Id directive, goodreads.info 24
  */ directive, goodreads.module 28
  /** directive, goodreads.module 27
  // Id directive, goodreads.module 27
  <?php directive, goodreads.module 27
  @file identifier, goodreads.module 28
  @see identifier, goodreads.module 28
  _goodreads_block_content() function 46-53
  core directive, goodreads.info 25
  description directive, goodreads.info 25
  goodreads.info, creating 24
  goodreads.module, creating 27
  goodreads_block() function 30, 31
  goodreads_block() function, configuring 39, 40
  hook_help() function, implementing 54, 55
  HTTP result, processing 45
  module content, displaying 38, 39
  name directive, goodreads.info 25
  php directive, goodreads.info 26
  t() function 32
  view operation 33
  watchdog() function 44, 45

Building Powerful and Robust Websites with Drupal 6

ISBN: 978-1-847192-97-4   Paperback: 330 pages

Build your own professional blog, forum, portal or community website with Drupal 6

1. Set up, configure, and deploy Drupal 6

2. Harness Drupal's world-class Content Management System

3. Design and implement your website's look and feel

4. Easily add exciting and powerful features

5. Promote, manage, and maintain your live website

Drupal 5 Themes

ISBN: 978-1-847191-82-3   Paperback: 250 pages

Create a new theme for your Drupal website with a clean layout and powerful CSS styling

1. Learn to create new Drupal 5 Themes

2. No experience of Drupal 5 theming required

3. Set up and configure themes

4. Understand Drupal 5's themeable functions

Please check **www.PacktPub.com** for information on our titles

Drupal

ISBN: 190-4811-80-9   Paperback: 268 pages

How to setup, configure and customise this powerful PHP/MySQL based Open Source CMS

1. Install, configure, administer, maintain and extend Drupal

2. Control access with users, roles and permissions

3. Structure your content using Drupal's powerful CMS features

4. Includes coverage of release 4.7

Learning jQuery

ISBN: 978-1-847192-50-9   Paperback: 380 pages

jQuery: Better Interaction Design and Web Development with Simple JavaScript Techniques

1. Create better, cross-platform JavaScript code

2. Detailed solutions to specific client-side problems